WHAT PEOPLE ARE SAYING ABOUT *7 V.I.R.T.U.E.S. OF EXCEPTIONAL LEADERS*

Amy Chambers' passion and commitment to improving the quality of leadership is evident in every word she's written. The V.I.R.T.U.E.S. she shares are game-changing and leadership-augmenting concepts. Yet, she doesn't stop there. Amy shares powerful practices to support readers in knowing how to implement the Virtues in their day-to-day work, to provide the difference-making leadership our world needs.

> – Amy L. Riley, Keynote Speaker, #1 International Best-Selling Author of *The Courage of a Leader: How To Inspire, Engage and Get Extraordinary Results*

"An eye opener for anyone building and leading a team. *The 7 V.I.R.T.U.E.S. of Exceptional Leaders* asks the right questions and gives the right answers for an introspective on leadership and how to motivate and keep a team. So glad I picked up this book heading into the New Year."

> – Maureen Ryan Blake, Maureen Ryan Blake Media Production

"Another leadership book" this is not! Amy Chambers has produced a tour de force of insight that any aspiring leader can implement immediately and garner results quickly. Highly readable and written in a conversational tone, the book is a delightful contribution to the leadership literature because it is not merely descriptive of what leadership is, but it is prescriptive on how aspiring leaders can lead effectively. Filled with realistic examples and brimming with encouragement, Chambers shows the reader how to leave behind your tired, old notions about leadership and shoot for the stars in bold new ways. A command performance. Bravo!

> – Ara Norwood, Publisher of Uncommon Sense

"Amy Chambers paints a compelling picture of 7 V.I.R.T.U.E.S. that underpin leadership character to shape the destiny of those they lead. The practical way the book flows is sure to guide transformation of individuals and teams alike."

> – Dr. Kasthuri Henry, PhD. CEO of Kas Henry Inc and Founder of Ennobled for Success Institute. www.kashenry.com

"Amy's successful leadership history, coupled with her curiosity to continuously learn more on the subject, have joined forces to create a compelling and useful guide that puts her experience into practical use. I found myself highlighting many lessons that I will fall back on as I face challenges in my leadership role. Not just another leadership book to read and put on the shelf, this tool will be a regular reference point as I continue my journey into the art of leading successful teams and organizations".

– Shannon Doiron, Chief Digital Officer, SkyOne Credit Union

"The perfect book for the modern leader in today's ever changing workplace environment. Amy provides compelling and authentic examples of real-world experiences that truly make this book highly relatable. It's a true illustration on how an effective leader can inspire the masses towards new ideas and innovations".

– Jeff Kern, Relationship Manager Membership Development, Arrowhead Credit Union

"This amazing book is truly inspirational and has changed my perspective on leadership. All of Amy's virtues, including Virtue 7: Showcase Swimming, has encouraged me to continue to demonstrate authenticity and to conduct myself in a veracious manner. Effective leadership is essential for a business to be successful and this book should be in the hands of every leader."

– Jesse Rivera, HR Manager, Hustler Casino

"I had the pleasure and honor to work with Amy for a few years and personally witness her leadership style. While reading her book I was smiling and reminiscing on the many moments I observed her putting these practices in place. She was able to make others feel valued and understood because she was always asking great questions and creating space for dialogue. Amy is a natural leader and a great communicator. I encourage you to read and apply what she is sharing in this book. You will grow tremendously as a leader."

– Katia Santos, Chief Administration Officer, SkyOne Credit Union

"Theoretical leadership books are everywhere. If you want a book that explains leadership AND gives you tools, this is the one. We have all been in meetings or worked with teams where one (or likely more than one) of Amy's messages were needed. Read this book and your meetings will be more effective."

– Donald Peaks, Chief Experience Officer
at SkyOne Federal Credit Union

7

V.I.R.T.U.E.S.

OF *exceptional*

LEADERS

BECOMING A LEGENDARY LEADER
WHO TRANSFORMS TEAMS

AMY CHAMBERS

7 V.I.R.T.U.E.S. of Exceptional Leaders

Becoming a Legendary Leader Who Transforms Teams

Amy Chambers

Little Pretzel Publishing

Published by Little Pretzel Publishing, Long Beach, CA

Editor: Karen Tucker, CommaQueenEditing.com

Cover and Interior design: Creative Publishing Partners, Creative Publishing Partners.com

Library of Congress Cataloging-in-Publication Data

Library of Congress Control Number: 2022923722

Amy Chambers

7 V.I.R.T.U.E.S. of Exceptional Leaders, Becoming a Legendary Leader Who Transforms Teams

ISBN: 979-8-9875178-0-2 (paperback) | 979-8-9875178-1-9 (ebook) | 979-8-9875178-2-6 (hardback)

BISAC Subject headings:
1. BUS071000 BUSINESS & ECONOMICS / Leadership 2. BUS030000 BUSINESS & ECONOMICS / Human Resources & Personnel Management

2023

DEDICATION

This book is dedicated to my uncle, Mark Chambers.

Thank you, Mark, for ALWAYS believing in me. I saw you ...

- *Pursue unconventional, risky ventures, even when it meant walking out on solid, stable jobs*
- *Stay close to numerous college friends for 40 years and make countless new friends along the way*
- *Exude positivity, enrich the lives of so many others, and write your own autobiography—all while dying of ALS*
- *Consistently make me uncomfortable with tough, candid conversations that transformed my life*
- *Encourage me to leave any lackluster job OR relationship; to know my worth, and never settle*
- *Give me advice no one else would, and continually urge me to follow my heart and my dreams.*

Mark, this book is for YOU.

I think of you often and continuously hope you're proud of who I've become today.

Your influence and fingerprint is everywhere in my life.

Thanks for showing me the way to an authentic, purposeful life full of meaningful connections and worthy pursuits.

I love you now, always have, and always will.

TABLE OF CONTENTS

FOREWORD

My first impression of Amy—when she was interviewing for a position in our organization in 2014—was that she asked almost as many questions as I asked her. She wasn't just looking for a workplace but an environment where she could make a difference. As I've been privileged to work with, mentor, and learn from Amy over the years, she's consistently prioritizing her passion for learning and growth, both for herself and to help those around her create success.

From my own experience in leadership over the past 40 years, I've found that individual success builds with the right combination of choices, effort, consistency, and humility. Amy excels at using each of these values as she developed her blueprint for exceptional leadership. I have had the opportunity to mentor and coach hundreds of leaders over the years; this has taught me that outstanding leadership begins with character, the foundation of who you are and who you are becoming. Amy has a strong foundation of character and integrity. She consistently lives up to her commitments, which is rare in today's leadership environment. Amy is an effective coach, mentor, and trainer focused on helping others develop and improve. All of which have provided the foundation for the 7 V.I.R.T.U.E.S.

This framework results from two decades of following her passion for learning and sharing that knowledge with others. The 7 V.I.R.T.U.E.S. is one of the most complete, straightforward, and actionable tools I have seen for developing foundational leadership skills. Amy has created a detailed roadmap for this development, complete with real-world examples. She takes you through the why, what, and how of becoming an effective leader, adding energy and enthusiasm to the journey.

– Joseph Whitaker, President & CEO, SkyOne Federal Credit Union

PROLOGUE

'll never forget the first moment I realized that leadership mattered.

I was 18 years old and working as a summer teller at the bank. It was my first real job, and the job was just that—a job. I was paid $8.50 an hour to balance a cash drawer and talk to people.

Both came easily to me, and I did my job well. But I have to admit, I had little awareness of what was going on in the company outside of my role—cashing checks, taking deposits, making change, and making conversation. Back then, my view of a job was simple: I showed up on time, waited on people, balanced the drawer, and left on time. Then, every two weeks, a few hundred bucks would land in my bank account. Awesome!

I'll never forget the morning that everything changed.

One day, the branch manager, Donna, told us a few senior executives would visit us later that week, before we opened the branch, so we'd all need to show up early. She instructed us that we'd all have breakfast together, meaning, Don't eat. And that was all.

Looking back now, I'm filled with so many questions that I didn't know to ask then: Why were they coming? What was the purpose of the visit? Was this routine? A punishment for poor results? A reward for good behavior? No clue. We were only told they were coming.

That morning would change my life. We all arrived at the branch ahead of schedule. The executives who were visiting us were late. We waited for them. Problem #1.

When they eventually arrived, they did bring breakfast—a bag of bagels, some cream cheese, and a gallon of orange juice—but Donna was so busy trying to impress them, these things were shoved aside. Everyone scrambled into their chairs, and the pressure to conform (even though I was hungry) was palpable. What wasn't present, however, was silverware, plates, or cups. So, nobody ate even though we'd been told we'd be eating together. Problem #2.

The executives made their introduction. They stated that they wanted to go through how we were doing on some key metrics and then they'd take questions. They also said they'd be staying a while and how excited they were to meet all of us.

I tried to stay engaged as the executives talked at a high level about these reports, citing various facts and figures. I had so many questions and wanted to learn. I scanned the room for similar reactions but found no visible mirroring of how I was feeling. Everyone smiled and nodded along approvingly. Time passed, and the meeting proceeded as a monologue, not a dialogue. Problem #3.

Suddenly, we were interrupted by a knock on the door. Sure enough, this meeting had run past our opening time, and now a customer was standing outside peering into the building, with his face cupped between his hands to block the glare of the early-morning summer sunshine. Problem #4.

"Oh, gosh, it's 9:02!" said the branch manager, still in her seat. I glanced at the clock, surprised by this. We had never opened late.

"Oh, yes! Of course, you should open," said one of the executives, standing. "We'll be around for a good while, and we definitely want to hear what's on your mind." And just like that, the meeting was over. No questions had ever been asked. Everyone scurried to replace chairs and get into our positions. For a few minutes, the scene was chaotic. Problem #5.

Donna ushered the executives into her office, where they closed the door to talk. Now, I have to admit, I can't say I was heartbroken by what had transpired so far. This was literally the first "work meeting" I'd ever gone to, so I hadn't had any idea of what to expect, nor had I spent any real time thinking about it. I was about to learn that was not the case for everyone.

Next to me that morning was Debbie. Debbie was older than me—perhaps 30. She'd been working at the bank as a full-time teller for years, and I couldn't help but notice how nervous she seemed. I hadn't connected all the dots yet, but Debbie was dressed nicer than usual. I noticed one of her regular blouses, but this day, she wore a shiny black blazer over it and was also wearing dress pants. As we worked, I also noticed that she anxiously and repeatedly smoothed down her hair and adjusted her outfit. It was out of character.

After the morning rush was handled, per usual, we had a brief lull around 9:30. "Everything okay?" I asked as I straightened my teller work.

Debbie somehow managed to train one eye on me while keeping her other eye deadlocked on the manager's office with the executives still inside.

"I'm just so nervous," she half whispered, half hissed at me. "Aren't you nervous?"

I felt dumbfounded—like I had during the first week of freshmen calculus before realizing college courses were going to be more difficult than high school ones. "Nervous about what?" I whispered back.

"Them!" She motioned with a slight tilt of her head. "This is my big chance," she added with another nervous brush of her hair.

Now I really felt stupid. "Big chance for what?" I asked, confused.

"My promotion!" she responded. This time it was 100% hiss. "Donna has been saying that today's visit is my chance to impress them, to show them what I'm made of, so maybe they'll make me a banker!"

My world got a little bigger in that moment, as this became my first-ever sighting of an engaged employee, connected to the bigger picture, wanting advancement and growth—and working hard for it.

Customers interrupted our conversation, and we both went back to our duties. Sometime around 10 A.M., the executives emerged from Donna's office and stood in the lobby chatting. I felt my heart beat faster, as I now knew this was the moment Debbie had been waiting for: As promised, the executives were about to come over, talk to us, and hear what was on our minds.

Then, in a blink of an eye, it happened. If I hadn't glanced up at exactly the right moment, I would've missed it! With a brief wave of their hands toward the teller and platform area, the executives headed for the door. Then they were gone, their dark suits becoming smaller in the parking lot with each passing moment. Problem #6.

Debbie was finishing up with a customer when this happened. Within seconds, she had locked her cash drawers and was heading toward the break room. For the first time in my career, I left my post without asking permission. I got up and followed her.

In the back room, I found Debbie already crying—actually, sobbing. This was the moment my world totally shifted. Through tears, Debbie explained to me that the suit she was wearing cost $300. She had gotten up ridiculously early that morning to curl and style her hair. She had taken home materials the night before (materials I didn't even know existed!) to practice some questions for the Q&A section that had been promised. Finally, Debbie shared that she had been working extremely hard as a teller for years, hoping she could ascend to the platform. Her performance was strong, but Donna felt that she needed the approval of these district managers to seal the deal. Problem #7: a powerless frontline management team.

I couldn't shake the scene of Debbie bawling her eyes out in the break room. She was committed to the overall company, committed to her immediate team and work group, but most importantly, she was committed to her own growth and development. That morning, it had all been overlooked. And nobody even knew anything about it. Those executives who had left without so much as a word to us likely had no idea who Debbie even was or what had happened that day. This moment stuck with me for years, and over time, I realized it was something of an atrocity.

That day, I didn't know what to say or what to do, but I did know TWO things:

1. Leadership matters.
2. If I ever got the chance to lead people—especially in the kind of roles these executives were in—I would see to it that this kind of thing would never happen on my watch. That people would feel ignored or invisible, unappreciated, and unvalued, or that a manager would feel like they needed my blessing or permission to make every decision. I made a vow that I would be a much different leader than what I had seen that morning.

Years passed, and it wasn't long before I graduated college and went into leadership myself. I soon realized that leadership is hard, grueling, taxing work. It's by no means as easy as it looks. During my darkest hours and toughest moments, I worked hard to connect with WHY I had chosen a life in leadership. It was because I had never lost sight of Debbie and that image of her crying in that back room instead of getting an opportunity to fulfill her great potential. On my leadership journey, I considered Debbie often and all the other people I had met along the way with similar stories. As I learned, tested, and experimented with various leadership concepts, I became somewhat obsessed with Debbie. Not just "actual" Debbie, but the idea of Debbie—all the people who are having lousy or even horrible experiences in the workplace. All the wasted talent and unheard voices. All the disengaged employees who simply show up and punch the clock instead of really leaning in. I became determined to figure it out: what behaviors, what practices, what principles really make a difference in leadership. It became my life's work, so that I could publish this book and help other leaders recognize what they need to do so there are no more "Debbies."

The framework I've devised is called V.I.R.T.U.E.S., and I've spent two decades crafting it. Through this book, you'll learn how important it is to set vision and have a view into the future that others can see. How critical it is to ask questions, engage your team, and stimulate conversation to foster trust and a real commitment. How integral consistent routines, structure, and discipline are to sustainable execution and results. How necessary terrific communication is. How paramount learning and understanding is—and how it needs to happen every day and is happening, even when leadership isn't around. How desperately people want to be encouraged and recognized. And finally, how essential it is that you lead by example and model all the other behaviors. I promise you that these 7 V.I.R.T.U.E.S. will change every-thing. I promise if you and the leaders around you practice these behaviors, you'll never have another Debbie again.

WHY I WROTE THIS BOOK

In the 17 years after graduating college, I worked at six different companies, held 16 positions, and had 18 different direct bosses. Data suggests this isn't uncommon and, if anything, is only becoming more common as millennials flood the workplace. One thing I was able to observe over these years was how common poor leadership is and how much of a difference exceptional leadership makes. Not just good leadership but exceptional leadership.

Of the 18 direct leaders I had in the last 17 years since college, I would only describe eight as "good." Of those eight, I would only describe four as "exceptional." That's only 22%. I feel tremendously fortunate. My observations suggest that most individuals are working with even lower numbers than that. Perhaps I was able to find exceptional leaders 22% of the time because I left roles and organizations where I wasn't getting exceptional leadership. Perhaps because I had become so obsessed with leadership, I sought out better leadership. Sadly, many people in this world who have a weak, poor, or bad boss won't choose to leave. In some cases, it will be due to fear—worrying they won't find another job with similar pay—or because change is hard. But in some cases, it will be because they don't know what exceptional leadership is. We don't always see it, so for many of us, it's hard to identify, and we're not even aware that our boss is failing us or how much more we deserve.

My research doesn't end with leaders I've reported to. Over the last two decades, I've watched hundreds of managers attempt to lead, and these statistics are congruent with what I see—less than 25% of leaders are truly exceptional. The ones who aren't have a huge cost on business. Their teams don't achieve outstanding results. Instead, they often get mediocre or poor results. Things take longer to accomplish or don't get accomplished at all, creating tremendous inefficiency and ineffectiveness. Trust doesn't exist, and most feel it can't be built, so silos and watercooler conversations gain momentum instead. Their teams have higher turnover, which causes increased recruiting, training, and hiring costs. And the reality is, folks aren't engaged around them. People are miserable, and everything is affected from people's health to their relationships at home. The problems are numerous, and the breakdowns occur at many different points.

For some, it's communication: the vision, objective, and goals aren't spelled out for the team, or just as bad, the team doesn't understand it or believe in it. Really poor leaders won't even know these things are happening. Some don't even realize they should be communicating a higher purpose for their team. Others have such poor awareness or poor relationships with their teams that they don't even know their team isn't on board.

For other leaders, there's a training, coaching, and development break-down or gap. Folks understand what's important—and may even want to deliver on it—but they're not equipped with the right tools or resources to do it, or they're not coached or developed to do it well. Again, leaders aren't often aware that this is happening. We don't know what we don't know, and some leaders depend on their teams to tell them what's missing or needed, but the team isn't competent enough to see it. Either they've never had coaching, tools, and resources before, or they've never gone to the intended destination before—which might be bigger, greater, or different than past destinations—so they're not aware of what they need to be successful.

For others, there's a clear vision and goal as well as tools and training, but there's no reward or recognition systems in place to keep people motivated or inspired. There's a reason teachers give out gold stars in kindergarten or awards for perfect attendance: people like feedback. They like to be noticed, recognized, and celebrated.

The list goes on, but as I settled into years of observation and analysis, what I realized was more than disappointing; it was downright concerning. Today, more people are disengaged at work than not, and not only does this wreak havoc on company and organizational success, but it wreaks havoc on these employees' lives. People are more stressed and overwhelmed, more obese and out of shape, and more distracted and detached than ever before. How are we going to solve the world's problems and build a better tomorrow for our children if we don't have the minds and hearts of our workforce actively engaged? We simply need to do better.

If you're like me, you've probably, at some point, had a great job. You've also probably had a not-so-great job. Or maybe even a terrible job. Think about the difference in your life during those times. When we have a great job and a boss we love, we come home excited, energized, and ready to take on our personal lives.

In those times, we've got something left over. We can invest in ourselves: we can journal, pursue hobbies, play with our kids, spend time with loved ones, exercise, and take care of our health. We can nourish the four major components or needs we have as humans (physical, mental, emotional, spiritual). This means we can still find time to exercise either on our own or by playing organized sports, find time to learn (doing a puzzle, reading a book, or attending a workshop), find time to invest in our relationships (help our children with their homework, devote time to our significant others), and then, finally, attend to our spirit (activities that make us feel whole like scrapbooking, art, music, poetry, or attending a play). We need these things. Without nourishing these key areas of our lives, we lack the ability to truly become wholehearted and happy people, capable of tremendous inner peace and joy.

These areas desperately need our time and attention, but they also require that we have energy to invest in them. When we aren't our best selves at work—getting to utilize our natural talents and gifts, those things we can do better and more easily than others—something dies inside of us. Oftentimes, when I ask people in these situations about their work life, their answers include the following:

- "I'm bored."
- "Another day, another dollar."
- "Oh, you know…it's just my job; it's not a career or anything."
- "It's what I'm doing right NOW…until I figure out what I REALLY want to do."
- "They say they want us to do XYZ right now, which is basically impossible."
- "They just don't get it."
- "I haven't had a one-on-one with my boss in forever. I don't know the last time we really talked."
- "I don't really know what I'm working on for my growth."
- "They always want us to do more with less."
- "One day closer to Friday! The weekend is almost here!"

If we're feeling this way 40 hours a week or more, how could we possibly have time to really engage and focus on the things that matter most to us outside of work? What do we have left over for the people we care about most in our personal life? What about the energy left over for that class or hour of cardio at the gym? Or what about that home improvement project we've been wanting to do or that gardening itch we've been meaning to scratch?

Sadly, our tendency when we feel overworked, undervalued, and not fully utilized or attached to an objective we care about is to come home drained and zapped of the energy we need for those things. It's no wonder we turn to the TV, our phones, or the internet to escape into someone else's life or a world that doesn't closely resemble our own. So, this problem with poor leadership and the disengagement it leads to isn't just about the cost it has on the organizations we work for. It's the cost it has on the rest of our lives and the world or society as a whole. This is why I wrote this book: to bring awareness to these issues that are critical for our workplaces and our society to address.

Now, if you've had a job you loved, think about that part of your life. How did you feel in those days, months, or years of your life? Fulfilled? Excited? Eager? Why was that? I'd argue that it most likely was because of the environment you worked in. You were in an environment where you were able to do your best, be your best. The reality is that LEADERS create the environments we work in. Highly engaged people I've interviewed often say the following things about their work:

- "I love my job. I love the people around me. I just love what I do!"
- "I'm really passionate about my career."
- "The time flies by. I don't even know where it goes!"
- "I got so busy, I forgot to take a lunch!"
- "My boss really cares about us—and shows it every day."
- "I'm able to be myself and be my best. My ideas count and matter. I count and matter."
- "I can't believe they pay me to do this!"
- "I get to do my best work here. It's a perfect fit for me."

People who make these kinds of statements leave work and go into the rest of their life in a very different way. They're energized, engaged, recharged, and ready to go. Have you ever seen the fuel light in your car come on, alerting you that you'll soon need gas? I have, all too many times. There's a sense of anxiety if you still have some distance to drive before you can pull over. It's not fun driving on an almost empty tank.

Our bodies, minds, and spirits are like gas tanks. Folks who have great leaders they love often love their jobs. Folks who love their jobs often leave work on a full tank of gas. They're able to zip along at any speed and head off to their next destination. Whether it be their yoga or spin class, their son's basketball game, or a book club with friends, they've got something left over, something left in the tank for the other areas of their life.

How people FEEL about their work and their jobs is largely determined by their leader.

When I watched Debbie cry because leadership was too incompetent to see her as a person—to acknowledge her and her feelings—something shifted in me. I realized that leaders are very powerful people. They literally have the ability to make other people cry. I'm a big believer in accountability and responsibility, and I believe we choose our own emotions; they're not given to us. Debbie chose to feel that way and cry. However, Debbie's reaction and response is understandable given the circumstances. Leaders have a certain power over other people, and that's because leaders set the ENVIRONMENT. They have the power to set people up in great landscapes or let them exist in ugly conditions—and the worst of leaders are so oblivious, they don't even know it.

As Spider-man is told, "With great power comes great responsibility." I can't think of anything more true. Leaders have a responsibility for the people in their charge. They have a responsibility to create safe environments where people can speak up, voice ideas, and share in the company success or struggle—and where people want to do that. Leaders have a responsibility to provide training, resources, tools, coaching, and development so people can grow, get better, and not only do their jobs more effectively, but also develop as better human beings. They have a responsibility to evaluate what's going on around them, to plan, do, check, and adjust, making a shift when things go off track.

Poor management often arises from folks who got into leadership wanting the power but not aware—or unaccepting—of the responsibility that comes with that power. Perhaps they were cultivated by other "bad" leaders who barked orders, gave direction, demanded results, and then washed their hands of the rest. That's unfortunate because that style of management is what's costing the organization time and money, and what's harming their people's personal lives.

As a human race, we are so diverse, so unique, that we have the ability with our tremendous capacity for learning and analysis to solve the world's problems. But to do that, we need to be ON. We need people to turn on their brains and be at their very best. When people are placed in poor, toxic cultures where their efforts go unnoticed and ignored, like Debbie, they shrivel up and withdraw. They become fearful of authority. They act timid and stuck. They question themselves and engage in self-doubt or negative self-talk. They lose that childlike spirit of innovation, imagination, and ideation that so many of us have when we are young. They start to wait to be told what to do rather than find the answers on their own. They fear change and stay static, developing what Carol Dweck (in her book, Mindset) calls a "fixed mindset" versus developing a "growth mindset." And so, while they can solve the world's problems (or maybe just their company's problems), they don't. Many of us don't even have the mental endurance or strength to cook or live healthy lifestyles when we go home. Instead, we've become a fast-food nation, looking forward to the weekend when we can finally "escape" before the "grind" starts up again.

What a lousy life! Many of us spend most of our waking hours at work. Shouldn't we demand and expect more out of our work? And more out of the leaders who guide us in that work? Shouldn't we demand greatness? I think so.

We need people at their best so they can do the things we can't. Whether you're in wealth management or a literature teacher, you're not the same person who can perform open-heart surgery or build an airplane. One thing we all have in common, wherever we are and whatever we do, is we have someone who leads us.

We deserve better leadership. There's a leadership crisis in the world. People, everywhere, are accepting and tolerating lousy bosses. In some cases, they don't know any better because they've never seen great leadership.

My partner, David, was working for a major airline, in an individual contributor role, when I met him. He has an incredible gift and talent for anything aviation related and is an incredibly gifted structural engineer with 25 years of experience being around planes, studying planes, and flying planes. He also had a keen interest in developing his knowledge and sharing it with others. When I asked him why he hadn't moved into leadership roles, where he could positively impact the lives of others, his answer was simple: "All our senior managers are stressed out. They look exhausted. They all rush around, work nights and weekends, and don't have a social life. I've never wanted that life for myself; it really doesn't look worth it."

I was absolutely dumbfounded. Leadership, for me, has been the most rewarding part of my career. I never felt like I "had" to invest in other people; I felt that I "got" to. There's such a difference. I had been gifted this tremendous opportunity to create environments where I could help other people begin their own journey of making themselves great. I communicated early and often, did a few things, put some guardrails in place, and then sat back and watched with glee as people would go off and become great. It worked—every time—and as it did, I developed a model for leadership: a system of beliefs of what leaders need to do to help unleash talent in others. What's stressful about that? There's no need to rush around or work long hours. When it comes together as it should, it hums perfectly, like a well-oiled machine.

As I reflected on David's comments, I felt a tremendous pain in the pit of my stomach. I realized that poor David had a distaste in his mouth about leadership, as a whole, because all he had experienced was poor leadership. David, someone who might have been a great candidate to lead others, now didn't even want to because he only knew of one way of leading—the wrong way. This is incredibly common.

Another close friend of mine, John, who works for a technology company, has described to me for years some of the most terrible leadership I've ever heard of. I've said many times, "Why don't you talk to someone about this? Your boss? His boss? HR?"

"Absolutely not," John has repeatedly told me. "HR just backs the bosses up. This is how things are done around here. You don't fight the system. I'd lose my job."

Really? I've thought. Lose your job for speaking up? For doing the right thing? For demanding more? For wanting better? How is that possible? I remember once talking to my boss about this topic, and he simply said, "You have to remember that they likely have a very different culture than we do. Where he works, that probably isn't acceptable."

How is that OK? I've thought to myself. How is that just or fair or right? And WHO is doing something about that?

Well, the simple answer is: YOU CAN.

I wrote this book because I wanted to voice my belief that there's a better way for leaders everywhere. I wanted to share the simple roadmap for great leadership that I created years ago and have been testing ever since.

Regardless of your role, you can start fighting for better leadership today. If you're like my friend John, and you're in an environment where you don't have great leadership, you can leave. You can start your own company or go elsewhere where you observe that there is great leadership. You can do what I did—explore the opportunities and culture at six companies until you find it. When you find it, you can hang on and never let go. You can push back on the leaders you see in the organizations you're in. You can recommend this book to them. You can help me continue a revolution that many others have already started—people like Liz Wiseman, author of Multipliers, or Simon Sinek, author of Start with Why, or Brendon Burchard, author of High Performance Habits, who also speaks about the 6 E's of Leadership. You can pass it along; you can join the crusade.

It's hard to fully explain my emotions when Debbie stood in front of me crying. I hadn't had any formalized training or teaching around leadership, but I felt something die inside me that day. I knew something was wrong. I felt angry—almost outraged—that she didn't have better leadership. I didn't know that moment would lead me to a life of leadership, but leadership has become more than a fascination of mine. As Conor McGregor so articulately pointed out, "to do anything to a high level, it has to be total obsession." Conor is right. I've spent years asking my teams what we were "obsessed" with. For many of the teams I've led, it's been the principles of servant leadership—caring, investing, coaching, development, training, teaching, evaluating, rewarding, recognizing, and then doing it all over again. What are you obsessed with?

If there's something in your life you really want, then it's going to require your full energy and effort. If you don't have great leadership around you helping create a great culture in your work life, then that's going to be hard to achieve. Your poor leader at work could be blocking you from achieving greatness. If you are that leader, it's imperative that you're obsessed with being a great leader. You took on a responsibility to do exactly that—to be great—when you took the job. No matter how bad the leaders were that brought you up, or came before you, you can change. You can adapt. You can lead in a new and wonderful way—where you commit each day to help others be great and unlock their potential—so we can turn this world into a better place. It's that important.

Before we begin, I want to add a word of caution for any senior executives who are reading this book. C-level executives will benefit most by ensuring the leaders and managers rolling up to them in their organizations practice the 7 V.I.R.T.U.E.S. of leadership outlined in this book. That's not to say that the 7 V.I.R.T.U.E.S. don't apply to senior executives and are only for middle or frontline managers. That's not it at all. However, the job of senior executives is more heavily centered around ensuring that they've got the right people working for them to carry that out. One of the biggest learnings I had in my role as a chief operating officer was that, all too often, we try to do the jobs of our people. At all levels, leaders are likely to get too involved in things their team should be doing. We don't empower others nearly enough. We often don't empower others enough because we don't trust others enough. This often happens because we don't have the right people, but we are too afraid to do something about it. We struggle to have tough conversations. We avoid being direct and truthful. We sugarcoat. We pick up the pieces for our teams. We tolerate mediocrity. None of that leads to success.

Some of the principles and practices in this book are heavily centered around coaching and training. Although two important things for any organization, they often are not the job of an executive. It's their job to ensure coaching and training is happening all around them. When executives step in to do these things for their senior folks, they strip away the ability, the power, and the desire for those who roll up to them to do it themselves. When it comes to routines, it's not often the job of the executive team to decide and define which routines work. It's important they, too, have a routine regimen, but that's going to look different than the routines their people have.

If you're a senior executive reading this, I strongly encourage you to make sure you've got the right people, then teach them this framework. You'll notice many aspects of the V.I.R.T.U.E.S. framework will also apply to yourself, but the biggest impact you'll see is by encouraging others to lead this way. So, if you have a corner office, I strongly hope you ensure these 7 V.I.R.T.U.E.S. are applied in every part of your organization.

A LEADER'S PLEDGE

Before you go any further, it's important you make a pledge with yourself. If you don't want to, or don't feel you can, you're not going to find a lot of value in this book. If your goal is to get something out of this book beside enjoyment, it's important that we agree on a few things. This book makes some key assumptions about being a leader, and leadership as a whole, that you must accept before you start. I hope you'll be able to say, "Well, sure, of course I can agree to/pledge to/promise that! Duh!" However, the sad truth is I've seen more leaders than I can count—some of them in senior or executive positions of leadership—who don't agree to the following things. This framework will only work for those who agree to the following:

First, you must pledge to remember that it's NO LONGER ABOUT YOU. For some, this might be obvious. But for many, it's not obvious at all. Many people in positions of leadership were promoted into those roles because they were really good at getting things done. In fact, they excelled at it, and most were recognized and rewarded for it. Then, they were given the ultimate recognition: they were promoted to manage and oversee others. Since getting things done often leads to promotion into management, it's not uncommon for leaders to have strong muscle memory, habits, and beliefs around getting things done and to want to continue doing that. But here's a glaring problem: True leadership is not about getting things done. It's about getting things done through other people. However, if you're in leadership, you no longer have any individual results. Your results are the results of your team. Your job is no longer about performing. Your job is about helping other people perform. So, you must pledge and promise, here and now, that you'll understand that everything in this book isn't about you. It's about the people who look to you for leadership.

The second part of this pledge dovetails with the first. If you're going to find value in this book and apply its principles, you must pledge to do the following:

1. To care about others
2. To want them to develop, grow, and get better

3. To recognize that it's your job to create an environment to help them become stronger
4. To understand that most everything you do affects others around you—and that's a big deal

If you're in a position of leadership but don't have an openness to these concepts, you are going to struggle. You, and your team, will always struggle to create consistent results. Leadership is not about being successful on your own or creating breakthrough results independently; it's about helping other people be successful as a team and helping them create breakthrough results together. A leader's job is to lay groundwork and create an environment where that can happen. It's important and taxing work, and it doesn't always come with a lot of credit, which is why the best leaders out there don't really need a lot of credit. Instead, they often find great fulfillment in watching their people do great things.

The people around you won't just develop better knowledge or skills on their own. They won't improve or grow without feedback, and some of that feedback needs to be tough, critical feedback. Some of it should be praise-based appreciation. Both kinds of feedback should be honest and candid. Your people aren't going to use the creative and innovative parts of their brains without knowing that it's okay to make mistakes, and even fail at times. They aren't going to develop fierce loyalty toward you unless they feel they can talk to you and confide in you. They aren't going to give it their all and put forth one thousand percent of their best selves if they don't feel valued as a human being—both at work and outside of work. They're not going to get excited and engaged about new projects if they don't know where things are heading. They aren't going to become resilient and adaptable to change if they don't see their leader showcasing the same behaviors expected out of them. Without all of these things, they aren't going to have those consistent, break-through results and stellar performance that everyone dreams about.

Guess whose job it is to make sure all that happens? You probably already know. It's your job. It's the job of the leader.

You're about to embark on a journey that will walk you through the 7 V.I.R.T.U.E.S. of truly exceptional leaders. This journey is a compilation of my journey over the last 21 years, both studying leadership and leading myself. It includes the good, the bad, and the ugly, but the ugliest I've seen, when it comes to leadership, is when leaders refuse to take the pledge I've outlined above. They might not say it outwardly, but at the end of the day, they don't really want to do the messy stuff to help people grow, get excited, get involved, get learning, get better, get going, and get it done. They either feel that the people in their charge should magically be better, they're too lazy or indifferent to address it, or perhaps worst, they're wholly unaware that their people are unhappy, burnt out, overworked, or —perhaps worse—underworked.

Most people go into leadership because they want to create change. They want to lead a team to do things better than before. Creating change for a team, a group, division, department, organization, or corporation—any entity—is tough work. Change cannot happen unless all, or a large majority, of the players of that entity change themselves. While some leaders think they can force others to change through brute force and authority, that's not typically how it works. True leadership happens when others change, not because they have to, but because they want to and choose to. Often, they want and choose to change because they've been influenced by someone they admire and respect, and they've been placed in an environment where change is not only possible, but it's attainable, makes sense, and is a truly exciting quest.

If nothing I've said so far scares you, and you're ready to join a leadership revolution where everyone around you gets smarter and does better; you create lasting, sustainable results; and you leave a legacy that will never be forgotten, then it's time to make the following pledge.

The Leader's Pledge is:

- I pledge to leave my ego at the door and develop humility, for I know my role as a leader is not about me and what I can do, but what I can help other people do.
- I pledge to focus primarily on the growth, development, happiness, and engagement of those around me, and I recognize that I play a big part in facilitating this.
- I pledge to work tirelessly to create an environment that allows others to do their best work.
- I pledge to ask for critical feedback and listen to differing viewpoints.
- I pledge to create a safe space for people to err and fail for the sake of learning.

- I pledge to recognize my results are no longer just mine, but rather, a compilation of everyone's hard work, knowledge, and skills—all of which, I can help shape.
- I pledge to believe that all of these things are a huge part of my job as the leader.
- I pledge to give credit away in good times and look in the mirror during tough times.
- I pledge to never cease or feel I've arrived in my own learning journey and my quest to become a better leader.

If you can't agree to all the things on this list, then this book is not for you.

If you can agree to some of the things on this list but aren't sure about others, don't worry. There was a time in my life that I was proud to be in leadership but also didn't practice everything on this list yet. You'll benefit greatly from the stories and examples found in this book, as they'll help you see why these principles are so important to great leadership.

If you can agree to most of the things on the list, then you're ready to light the world on fire with the V.I.R.T.U.E.S. framework, and I'm so excited you're here.

VIRTUE 1:
View To Your Vision

"Where there's no vision, people perish."
– Brendon Burchard[1]

How do you feel when you have something to look forward to? Maybe it's an upcoming trip, tickets for a sporting event, having a party or event at your home, or a night out with friends. Most of us feel good, excited. Our imagination runs wild with thoughts over what we might wear, the things we need to do before we go to that event, and what the event or function itself will be like.

What do *you* do when you have something to look forward to? Most of us plan for it. We change our behavior somehow. We might go out and buy something—sunscreen for the vacation, food and drink for the gathering at our house, or a new outfit for the night out with friends. We might print tickets for the sporting event or ensure we've gotten our other responsibilities done prior to the event. We might also do necessary things to set us up for success, such as calling a babysitter or handing off a project to someone else at work who will be covering for us.

Knowing what's coming down the road *changes* things because it changes us. It changes what we think, what we feel, and what we do. When we have information about something that is going to occur in the future, it affects what we do today.

This book will reinforce the idea that leadership is about getting other people to do things and helping other people to be great. It's about helping other people rise to their best and highest levels of contribution. It's about growing and developing talent. It's about helping everyone else around you think at a higher level and contribute at a higher level. Leadership is about winning over the hearts and minds of your people. It's about both the skill and the will. It's about helping people want to do more and be more. It's about helping them feel that fire in their bellies to show up and contribute at their best every day. It's about helping people feel engaged and eager to deliver for the organization they're in. But it's also about helping people be able to do that. It's about equipping people with the right tools and resources they need to be successful, and about helping people become more competent and capable to deliver and do well.

I've spent the last 21 years of my life studying leadership. I've observed literally hundreds of leaders do their thing, and there's no doubt in my mind that the biggest failings of leaders come down to an inability to do one (or both) of these two things: win the hearts and win the minds of their people. In some cases, leaders actually understand the concepts behind getting other people to want to do great things, but they don't equip their teams well enough to do those things. Then they never understand why their teams repeatedly come up short. In other cases, leaders focus on functional and technical skills and knowledge; they recruit and hire what should be the best talent with the right experiences, background, and credentials. But then they spend no time doing the things that continually reengage this talent. In most cases, leaders want to both motivate and empower their people, but they are somewhat clueless as to how to do it.

This book will advance in a progressive order. There's no doubt, in my mind, that leadership starts with vision. All great leaders and successful people who have ever accomplished anything had a vision of a future that was different than the present. They imagined a world that was better than their current reality, and once they established that vision, they worked hard to create it. They rallied their daily actions around it, and when times got tough, it was that vision that kept them going. If you haven't set a vision for your team, your team doesn't have any idea where it's heading; then sadly, you'll struggle incessantly to help define direction for your team.

Knowing what's coming tomorrow alters what we do today. How many times have we heard someone say, "If today was your last day alive, what would you do? How would you spend it?" If you knew, for sure, that your life were ending in exactly a month, you'd undoubtedly live very differently the next 30 days. You might quit your job, spend all your money on the nicest and most lavish things you can find, and do whatever activity you always wanted to do. Perhaps you'd give all your money away to your children or a charity. Perhaps you'd go apologize and reconnect to that long-lost friend. Why? Because you'd have radically shifted your perception about what the future holds for you, and having that information would change how you think and lead you to evaluate your priorities and what matters most. When armed with information for what tomorrow is expected to look like, we simply make different decisions today.

If we believe that leadership is, in fact, about helping people have both the will and the skill to win and winning over their hearts and minds so that people act differently, your people need to know where you're headed. The first Virtue of leadership is that you set up a compelling picture of what the future looks like, and you share it with your people so they can be excited about it too. Then, align their excitement levels and daily actions with whatever that vision is.

WHAT'S A VISION STATEMENT, ANYWAY?

The best companies in the world have vision statements. Companies like Disney, Apple, Amazon, Starbucks, Ritz-Carlton, and many more have a vision of what they stand for, where they're going, what success looks like, and how they're going to get there. Vision statements are hugely powerful for companies because they align people together with a common goal and shared purpose. A vision statement for what we're trying to accomplish helps bond people together.

Vision statements are often thought of as the "WHY" people do what they do. Vision statements answer the question of "WHY" the company exists. Vision statements are broad and give direction, and they are often aspirational in nature, meaning they can't ever be fully achieved, for example, improving or changing lives. A few examples:

Ikea: To create a better everyday life for the many people.

TED: To spread ideas.

Amazon: To be Earth's most customer-centric company, Earth's best employer, and Earth's safest place to work.

Nike: To bring inspiration and innovation to every athlete in the world.

Starbucks: To inspire and nurture the human spirit—one person, one cup and one neighborhood at a time.

When I read the vision or mission statements of these companies, I readily get chills. These are the reasons people want to work for companies: passion, alignment, shared beliefs. And it's what keeps them coming back to work.

I'll take this opportunity to note that not all companies identify or understand the proper differentiation between a vision statement, a mission statement, and core values. As we've just described, the vison statement of an organization or group is its WHY. It's what it aspires to BE. The mission statement, then, is the WHAT. It describes what the company or group actually DOES. Core values are the HOW. They describe the actual behaviors and actions that the company will take to accomplish the WHAT.

I'm not here to preach about what your vision, mission, and core values should be. I'm here to say that you should have them. When employees or members of an organization don't know what the vision, mission, and core values of its organization are—or they feel disconnected from them—you'll never see people march toward goals with the same clarity and purpose that you will when your folks DO know what they are, and, better yet, they ALIGN with those things. People want to know where the ship is headed. They want to get excited about it. They want a framework through which to grade their own behavior—something to believe in, to invest in, to stand for, and to fight for. And if your people are other leaders in the organization, this will give them something to talk about. Much of leadership is rallying the troops— getting them excited for the task at hand. How on earth can you rally the troops if you don't know what you're rallying them FOR?

If as you're reading this, you don't know what the vision or mission of your own company, group, or team is, that's a real problem. If you're in leadership, there's good news: you can DO something about that. Even if your overall organization doesn't have a clearly defined vision or mission, you can create one for and with your own individual team or workgroup. We'll talk in the next section about how to do that. If your organization does have a defined vision and mission, but you haven't spent any time with it, it's critical to do two things. First, spend time with it! Sit down and ask yourself if you're passionate and aligned with the vision and mission of your company. I'm here to tell you that if you're *not* passionate or in alignment with your organization's vision, you're going to struggle to feel fulfillment, joy, and inner peace while working there. Second, it's important that you talk to leadership about this vision. Maybe you work for an organization that has a vision and mission, but they're never discussed. It's up to you to ask for that. You can reach out and ask that more time is spent going through these things and finding ways to bring them to life. A vision and mission that is written on walls or papers around buildings but can't be repeated or stated by the employees who work there isn't any good. You might as well not have one. Vision and mission statements need to be discussed for them to be *alive*. They must be alive (or lived) for them to make any difference.

Now, it's time to explore what that looks like.

PRACTICE 1:
IT DOESN'T JUST BELONG IN YOUR DIARY. **TALK ABOUT IT**

Okay, so your company, division, department, group, or team has an established vision and mission, and you've told people what it is. You're golden, right?

I can't tell you how many times I've seen this be a key failing for leaders, teams, and companies. There's an established vision. It lives on the walls of various buildings; it might be posted in conference rooms, and it definitely gets discussed in new-hire orientation and appears on your company's website. In some organizations, the vision of the company is printed on mousepads, is the backdrop of computers, and even shows up on pens, mugs, and other company swag floating around. Yet nobody knows what it means because it's never discussed—or, at least, not *really*. Maybe it's only discussed a few times a year. And no one is held accountable to it.

That simply doesn't work.

If people aren't talking about the company's vision *often*—no, scratch that—constantly, then you don't have an effective vision. A company vision is not a "one-and-done" thing that you post up somewhere, talk about a few times a year, and then wait for everyone to rally around. The most foundational and basic job of a leader is to be the person who translates the vision to others on a daily basis. The most important and rudimentary thing any leader can do to drive success is make sure that their team knows what the vision is, understands it, and aligns themselves with it every single day. There shouldn't be a day that you're not thinking about how to drive your team to the vision you've set and ensure they're *also* thinking about how to drive themselves toward it.

One of the key failings for many of us—in business, in leadership, and in life— is that we want to believe that INTENSITY can make up for CONSISTENCY.

Many of us do this in many areas of our life. One is health and fitness. We'll eat poorly and won't exercise enough for a year then try to drop weight fast in the week or two before a big vacation. Post-vacation, any weight we lost prior all comes back. We might get to a goal weight before the cruise, but long-term health is never accomplished like this. College students "cram" for exams after not studying and keeping up with the class material all semester. They might pull out a passing grade on the final exam, but learning is always shortchanged. Leadership is also like this. You cannot fix a year of ignoring or failing to acknowledge something as important as your company vision by talking about it in one meeting each quarter. Just like health and learning are impacted in the previous examples, widespread adoption and efficiencies in execution are sacrificed for the leader who doesn't talk about vision consistently with his or her team.

Ensuring your team knows and understands the vision is not as easy as it sounds. Just because your team can memorize a vision statement and regurgitate the words doesn't mean much of anything except that your team has memorization skills. So what? Most students who cram before the final exam for that passing grade don't retain much of what they learned. The organizations you lead aren't like high school classrooms. If you're leading a team to deliver consistent, meaningful, and long-term results, then it's not good enough for people to know something once, or for a month, or even for a year. They need to feel deeply connected to it, driven by it, and motivated to DO something around it.

How do we show people that something is important to us? We talk about it. And how do we test for understanding? We ask about it. In addition to discussing your vision statements with those around you early and often, it's important you talk about them in the right way so that you can see true results. Since people learn from each other, it's important that you lead many of these discussions in a group setting, so people's view of the vision can be shaped, influenced, altered, and enhanced by others around them.

HERE'S HOW

So, you've humored me and you've set a vision and mission for your team. You've talked about what you want tomorrow to look like, and you've even set some goals for how you'll know when you've arrived. You're now willing to have some frequent conversations with your team about that vision and mission, but you don't know HOW. Here's a sample list of questions you can ask to get people as excited as you are about this dream or future that you're building together. However, what's even more important than the following list is the essence and intent behind them, which we'll discuss in a moment.

Potential conversation starters:

- Who can tell me what your company vision is? Thanks, Sarah. And today, if you don't mind sharing, tell us what does that vision mean to *you*?
- What did we do last week to specifically advance our company vision?
- What's one thing we can do this week to advance our company vision? That's a great idea, Paul. And how would that help us get to our goal of being... (insert company vision here)?
- What's a success story we have from the last few days or week regarding our vision? Who saw someone doing something awesome to help drive the vision?
- Why do we think this vision is so important?
- What happens if we don't achieve our company vision or advance it this year?
- What challenges have we been facing recently regarding acting on our vision? How can we overcome those?
- Who's got some ideas of new things we can do to achieve our vision that we haven't already talked about?
- What questions do you guys have about how we can bring our vision to life?

The basic plan is that you, as a leader, would facilitate dialogues like this on a weekly basis with your whole team. Seems repetitive? Yup, that's the point. It's supposed to be repetitive. Why? Because repetition works. Just ask my mother. Or any teacher, professor, or educator—which my mother was. She taught high school algebra and geometry for 36 years, and nobody can repeat themselves like she does. But guess what? She had some of the highest passing percentages and average scores for students taking New York State Regents exams in her peer group. Learning through repetition does work, and what you're really doing when you're having these conversations is checking for understanding and also ensuring that people find ways to self-solve their own questions, problems, and concerns.

When we talk about the same end goal with people repeatedly, we send people both subconscious and conscious messages that said end goal is highly important. It depends on the study, but tons of research say that in most companies, somewhere between 60% and 80% of people don't really know what the organization's most important goals or objectives are. Whatever success level you're at, can you imagine how much more successful you'd be if everyone knew the company's most important goals or objectives? Talking about these things in a group setting, with questions like the ones listed and with extensive dialogue, will not only help your team know what they are, but ponder and embrace them. If you go one step further and also talk about these things in one-on-one settings with your team members individually and privately, you'll not only lead a team who knows what these things are but actually executes on them with daily action. The results that come from a team that consistently acts on lead measures that drive them toward the same unified and shared goals are exponentially greater than the results from a team that doesn't.

Earlier, I stated that the specific list of questions isn't as important as the essence and intent behind the questions. Well, that's true. I want to draw your attention to a few key things from that list:

- *You ask for specific examples.* That's because without being able to recall specific times when things went well, cite specific challenges that stand in the way, or list specific actions that one plans to take, we rarely see actual progress. People are able to "fluff" their way through the dialogue. When you, as a leader, ask for specifics, people learn they can't do that anymore, and they start to think more critically about the questions at hand and perhaps also focus on it when you're not around, so if they get called on next time, they have something to say.

- *There is an opportunity to recognize success.* People love this. When you have a team that's working toward a vision or mission but you never take the time to acknowledge when things are going well toward that end, people can easily get discouraged. When you show your people that you want to hear actual, real-life stories about the vision and mission, you show your team that you truly mean it when you say they are supposed to be a way of life.

- *You invite others to discuss their challenges.* This may seem counterintuitive, but when you're wanting a team to change how they think about something or adopt new behaviors, there are going to be challenges. By allowing people to voice and share those challenges out loud, you give them emotional oxygen and psychological air. You normalize the challenges and also create a safe space for people to not only share what's going well but also what isn't going well. When you do this, you teach your team that they can come to you and talk about anything, which frees people up to admit if they're having struggles or problems (which they will). By talking about these things in a group setting, other people can offer suggestions of how they may have approached or overcome the same challenges, which allows the group to grow.

- *You ask for different perspectives.* This is key. When you're discussing a vision with a group, it's important that many people—and eventually, everyone—gets a say. This prevents you from running into the common trap of feeling like your team is fully engaged, but it's only because your three most talkative people keep answering for the group. By calling on volunteers and bringing people into the group who didn't share the previous time or haven't said much in the current meeting, you show your group that no one is exempt from participating and no one can "hide."

Know what your vision is. Share it with others. Talk about it every day. Use dialogue to ask questions to check and test for understanding. Ask for specifics. Talk about these things in one-on-one settings as well. Make sure your team is as excited as you are about those objectives. Encourage them to do this with others and when you're not around. If your team doesn't really know what the long-term goal is, what they're driving toward, or why they come to work every day, they can't feel passion and excitement about the future or pick the right actions today. They also can't connect themselves to the organization long-term. So double down on this, and often.

PRACTICE 2:
SIGN THE WALL (AND MEAN IT)

Several years ago, I was working as a district manager for a large commercial bank. One year, during the holiday season, every single employee, all 300,000 of us, got a letter from the CEO addressed to their home address.

It was unusual. We typically didn't get corporate communications at our home addresses and not from the CEO—at least, not like this. The letter wasn't the size of a regular letter in a business envelope, and it also wasn't the size of a hallmark card. It was oddly shaped, so it stood out against the rest of my mail that time of year when holiday cards from friends and family were rolling in daily.

When I read the letter, I also got the distinct sense that the CEO himself had written the letter. It just "sounded" like him—not one of his administrative assistants or a member of the Corporate Communications team or the executive team. The letter detailed our company's strategic plan and priorities for the upcoming year and reiterated, over and over, our vision for our customers and the difference we were trying to make in their lives. I have to admit that I got goosebumps when I read it.

A week later, as the year turned over, my boss told our team that he wanted everyone to bring their letter into our next district manager meeting. It was interesting that we all still had our letters. Not one person had thrown theirs out—a clue that other people had felt like the letter was special too.

We arrived at the meeting and our boss asked us to read the letter out loud. We all took turns, going around the table with each of us slowly reading a paragraph at a time. Then our boss engaged us in a discussion about what the letter meant to us and how we each interpreted our CEO's vision and message. Then, he asked us one of the more profound questions I've ever been asked by a boss: "Could you have written this letter?"

What he was asking was if each of us could have written this message on our own. It was a loaded question, brimming with multiple subquestions that took careful consideration. He was asking if we, too, knew the company strategy backward and forward—so well, in fact, that we could've described it as well as our CEO did. He was asking if we felt that same level of passion and commitment to the year ahead as our CEO did. He was asking if we wanted it as badly as our CEO did. If we were connected with the company's vision. If we could put it in our own words.

We all thought about it and went around and answered individually. All 10 of us agreed that yes, we, too, could've written the letter.

"Great," he said. "Then go do it. These are due back to me in a week."

So, off we went to write our own letters. I was very bought into the company's vision at the time, so my letter poured out of me. It flowed from my veins easily and naturally. I also love to write. I eagerly looked forward to my boss's feedback. There was no doubt, in my mind, that when he asked us to write these letters and turn them into him, he was looking to understand and validate his perceptions for how well each of us understood the strategy and vision for the company as a whole—understanding that was a huge litmus test or predictor of their success (although certainly not the only thing that matters).

The experience was a fantastic one. A few weeks later, we met again, and we shared the letters with one another, getting to hear the different ways in which we worded the company strategy. Everyone had done a solid job, and it seemed there was a good deal of understanding of where we were headed, why, and what needed to be done. This wasn't unexpected since we were all in district manager roles, each overseeing at least 200 people and most of us overseeing 15 different banking centers. Then our boss leveled us with another question: "Could your direct reports write these letters?"

Same as the last time, we all went around and answered. This time, the room was a little more hesitant and quiet. I was intrigued by that. Our direct reports were all branch managers. Many of them were strong leaders and did a good job at hiring and managing talent, running their branch, managing their audits, hitting their service and sales goals, and coaching and developing people. But their skill sets were probably more varied than ours, and some of them weren't as well connected to the true vision of the company as we were. At the time, I believed that my team was nothing but awesome (I mean, how could they not be? They reported to me!). Obviously, this was naive on my part; every team has opportunities to learn and grow, and it's often the ones that think they don't that have the biggest blind spots. Nonetheless, it's what I believed at the time, but I wanted to validate this theory for myself, so I dove into assigning the same activity to them that our boss had assigned to us.

It was the tail end of January when I asked my direct reports to bring in their letters, so many of their letters were tattered, had stains on them, or had been ripped open so impulsively that there were tears across the letter. Still other managers had either lost the letter or thrown the letter out and had photocopied one from a colleague to be prepared for the meeting.

When we went around the room and read the letter, some understanding and fervor for what the company was trying to do had been lost in just going down one level of the organization from my role to theirs. When my 15 branch managers turned in their written letters, the difference was even more apparent. Not everyone's a great writer, but I wasn't reviewing the letters for perfect grammar and shiny delivery; I was reading for general content and understanding. It was clear that I had a wide range of people on my team: some who understood where we were headed nearly as well as the CEO himself; some who had written just as strong, if not stronger, of a letter as I had; a few who seemed completely lost and unable to articulate what our company was trying to accomplish. I also had everything in between.

This experience was a huge wake-up call for me. I look back now and laugh at myself for being so confident that my team would pass this test with such flying colors. This experience taught me the value of really digging into things when you're feeling confident, checking for termites, or lifting up the hood and inspecting underneath. Whatever metaphor we want to use, the bottom line is that we're often too confident in our own people. It's why the exploratory questions in the previous section are so important—they will expose your team's understanding, awareness, knowledge, passion, confusion, acceptance, or disagreement. It's a great example of why you must engage in true dialogue—not monologue—with your people on these topics.

I can't tell you the number of times someone has told me, "Oh, don't worry, I don't have any problems with that," only to find a whole heap of problems once they really dig in. Having my team write these letters and being disappointed in many of the results showed me that activities like this—"show me, teach it back to me, then do it in front of me"—make all the difference in the world. The most important thing to remember is your WHY when it comes to these kinds of activities. It's not to call people out, make them feel weak, criticize where they're at, or put someone on notice, corrective action, or discipline. It's so you can really understand where people are at, so you can then help those people get stronger and rise to the level of others.

Writing the letter itself proved to be helpful. When we went back a second time to discuss what we had each written, the weaker folks on my team were able to learn from the stronger players. Since they had all written a letter, they were able to engage in a great dialogue and push back on one another's statements and what they meant. It was obvious that thinking advanced, and those who thought they nailed it (but didn't at all) became visibly more self-aware of that. When the activity was over, I asked them the same question that I'd been asked by my boss: "Could your whole team write these letters?"

They weren't as confident as the district managers had been, but my region agreed to do it. Every branch manager went back and asked their entire staff to write the letter.

One branch of mine took this task especially seriously, and not only did the branch manager lead the branch to write the letters, but they cleared out a whole wall in their break room to put the letters up. That branch had 28 employees, including their business partners (who didn't report to the manager and also didn't roll up to me), and everyone participated (which is a great example of how things work when there are strong bonds, solid relationships, no silos, teamwork, and group thinking: It doesn't matter who your boss is. If you're asked to do something, or you observe someone you respect doing something, you're more than happy to be part of it. It's not about being required to, it's about wanting to.) From the tellers to the personal bankers, assistant manager, mortgage guy, and investments guy, everyone wrote the letter at this branch. Then, they began conducting their morning huddles in the break room by the wall where all the letters were pasted up.

The branch really got into it. They had purchased supplies to make the letter-writing fun. Some people had used colorful markers and stickers to decorate their letters, and each person's letter was mounted on a different kind of construction paper, so the wall also ended up being a display of each person's personality. Of course, the same gaps between the strongest person and the weakest (in terms of understanding) still existed. But that was okay. I knew that simply doing the activity would increase everyone's understanding from whatever point it had been at before, which is always a win. A secondary win was that the team was clearly bonding over the letters.

Then, without any additional instruction or prodding from me, the branch took it one step further. They worked together to take the best and their favorite sentences or words out of one another's letters and compile them into one letter that described the CEO's vision. They put an overarching statement of their understanding of what it all meant up on the wall, above their letters, and then they all signed the wall next to that letter.

They signed the wall because they said they wanted to be in agreement of what this vision meant every day for them at this branch. By signing the wall, they were all agreeing to carry out the vision in all the ways they said they would in their letters. Their signatures on the wall were a commitment to live the vision every day. I was more than impressed with the initiative this team took; I was blown away.

A few months later, I was visiting the branch and observed their morning huddle. One of the employees made a negative comment about his results that month and about how challenging it had been for him to be successful. He ultimately said something that wasn't aligned with the vision on the wall.

It was encouraging to see that his comment was immediately addressed. Comments like this often aren't addressed in the moment or even after the moment. They're also not often addressed in public (and sometimes they shouldn't be). But this team felt such trust with one another that they regularly addressed things out in the open.

What blew me away most was that it wasn't a leader who addressed him but a peer. The colleague spoke up and said, "Hey, you can't do that. You can't say that. That doesn't go with our vision." I was shocked by this display of peer-to-peer accountability, but his last statement stopped the show for me. "YOU SIGNED THE WALL."

Perhaps even more awe-inspiring was the reaction of the gentleman who made the original remark. He immediately acknowledged that he woke up on the wrong side of the bed that morning and a personal struggle was affecting his mood. He admitted that his comment wasn't in alignment with one of the core values around thinking positive, being resourceful, and finding solutions—and apologized. His peer flashed a warm smile and heartfelt nod of forgiveness, and the group moved on. I stood there, frozen. This group had self-solved a morale issue, and management hadn't uttered a word. By the way, when people tell me that you can't get entry-level employees who aren't college educated or compensated with big salaries to buy into this kind of stuff, I think to myself, "The hell you can't." My biggest data point in thinking that comes from this moment.

This branch of mine went on to put up the best results in my district that year, and some of the best in the greater area. They blew out most of their goals at nearly 200%, and I'd never seen employees so happy to be working somewhere before. The bottom line? They signed the wall. They spent a lot of time working to understanding what the organization's vision and mission were. They also figured out how what they each personally did every day connected to the greater vision of the company. They agreed to carrying it out, and they held each other accountable for doing so. Those were the accepted and agreed to rules of the game at that branch.

Once you've explained the vision to your team and they've explained it back to you, the next step is to ensure people really understand it. Asking people to put it in their own words, talk about what it means to them, and give daily examples of how they're living it will go a long way in showing people that you're serious about it. It shows your team that the vision isn't a fleeting thought or disappearing anytime soon like some other company initiatives do. But after you've done those things, it's so important that you ask people to COMMIT to it. Whether you have them sign a wall or dip their finger in blood to show commitment is totally up to you. But ultimately, you have to ensure that your folks feel the vision is not a negotiable. People must know if they signed up to work for the organization, they signed up to drive the organization's vision. If they're not ready, willing, and able to do it, they can't work for the organization. It's your job as the leader to set that expectation and help your people get there.

You may not do what this branch did and write on a wall with pen. Signing the wall can be figurative. Signing the wall is asking folks to acknowledge, in their own words, what the vision of your company or the team means to them. It's asking them to publicly support it and talk about it. It's asking them to commit to it and do something about it. It's asking them to live it. Do these things in private, as one-on-ones, but also do these things in large groups so that real team traction and momentum can grow. When a group shares a collective and powerful vision for their future, something magical happens. So, don't be shy in asking others to socialize their vision for the vision together, as a team. When there's joint accountability—where everyone looks to each other to participate and engage—that's when you'll see your team come alive and take off.

PRACTICE 3:
EVERYONE'S SIGNED THE WALL. **NOW, ENFORCE IT**

We've talked about how important it is for a team to know where they're going, what they're fighting for, and why. It's equally critical for them to understand how they're going to get there and by when. It's important for roles and responsibilities to be set up and for them to know who does what. If you've done everything we've talked about so far, you're off to the races.

But sometimes, it's not enough. Whenever a team is on a path toward success or greatness and working hard to pursue something, especially over a long period of time, it often gets tough. Challenges come up, unexpected bumps in the road surface, issues emerge, and sometimes it becomes hard to even work together. People have differences in opinion, and since building relationships can sometimes be tricky, it's not uncommon for teams to reach points where individual team members start to question the dream, the goal, or the quest as a whole. One of your roles as a leader is to set clear expectations for what will be tolerated and what won't. While great leaders always allow for dissent and differences of opinion, one area where they do not allow for dissent or differences of opinion is around the vision itself. Great leaders know that everyone must be aligned with the overarching vision, mission, and strategy. Those who aren't have to go because they cause too much harm to the group if they stay.

I'll never forget the first time I heard Cy Wakeman speak. If you don't know her, she's phenomenal. In 2018, she was the keynote speaker at my company's all-employee annual event. She delivered an outstanding presentation, and so many points stood out to me, but perhaps the biggest one was her "no third option" concept. Cy's belief is that truly successful leaders who lead truly successful teams only allow their people one of two options: you're either in, and you're fully in, or you're out—fully out.

Here's my view: Option 1 is that you're super excited about the company's strategy, you're on board, and you figure out how to spend every day embracing it. Option 2 is that you don't feel that way, and you're out. You're not on board with the company's strategy, vision, mission, or core values. You disagree with it or aren't prepared to execute on it, so, you leave. You figure out a way to exit the company as quickly as you reasonably can and go elsewhere.

Or leadership makes the decision for you if you won't make it yourself. But you don't stay and continue to work at an organization where you don't align with the organization's values. Note: Option 2 doesn't make you a bad person. It doesn't make you wrong and the company right. Nor does it make the company wrong and you right. It simply means that you have a difference of opinion over what the organization should be doing, or you, for whatever reason, can't fully support it at the time. That's more than okay, but you must exit.

That's it. There is no third option. But you know what? I've seen multiple employees—and worse, the leaders and companies they work for—tolerate a third option far too often. People do make a third option, and sometimes, their boss or leadership team even knows about it and allows it. In fact, at some organizations, leadership itself is engaging in a third option!

What does this look like? Well, the third option usually goes something like this: it's the employee who complains about the strategy or the direction in private circles around the watercooler or in the lunchroom but has no real plans to leave. They whine about the recent "changes in policy," moan about their lousy boss, roll their eyes and shake their heads (visibly or not) at the new initiatives with no real plan to embrace it. They talk about the past and the "way things were" and throw up roadblocks at every new attempt to change or accomplish something in the "new" way.

Does this sound familiar? Do you know someone like this? My guess is that you do because these individuals are at almost every organization. They're neither fully in nor fully out.

They've got one foot out the door, or they should, but instead of going peacefully, they keep coming to work every day and whining. They'll talk about how unfair things are or make a snide comment over management's recent decisions. They'll mutter about how their suggestions weren't taken and talk smack on the leadership or the organization as a whole. Then they'll stay, sort of do their job—or at least keep up the appearances of doing their job—and collect a paycheck.

Why would anyone do this? I'll tell you why. It's way easier to sit in the stands and critique then to be in the ring duking it out. While this excerpt from Theodore Roosevelt's famous "Citizenship in a Republic" speech from 1910 is long, it speaks to how we should think about and handle critics, who are pursuing the third option in organizations:

It is not the critic who counts; not the man who points out how the strong man stumbles or where the doer of deeds could have done them better. The credit belongs to the man who is actually in the arena, whose face is marred by dust and sweat and blood; who strives valiantly; who errs, who comes short again and again, because there is no effort without error and shortcoming; but who does actually strive to do the deeds; who knows great enthusiasms, the great devotions; who spends himself in a worthy cause; who at the best knows in the end the triumph of high achievement, and who at the worst, if he fails, at least fails while daring greatly, so that his place shall never be with those cold and timid souls who neither know victory nor defeat.

I've always loved this quote, and throughout my life, I've learned there is nothing more true. It's remarkably easy to play Monday-morning quarterback and harshly grade the flawed performances from our favorite football stars in Sunday's NFL game. It's equally as easy to do in regard to leadership's decisions at companies who are headed in new directions—or, heck, any direction at all. It's much easier to be on the sidelines, watching the game from afar, making comments about the wrong play, the wrong pass, the wrong pursuit. The reality is that almost everything in life, and definitely those pursuits worth doing, are harder done than said. Critics love to criticize, but their opinions shouldn't count for much.

And yet, this is a major problem at most workplaces. These people's opinions do count. Why? Leadership is either unaware that it's happening or tolerates it. Leaders often tolerate it because they are either too afraid to address it head-on—using principles from two of my favorite books, The Speed of Trust by Stephen M. R. Covey and Crucial Conversations by Kerry Patterson et al.—or they don't know how to address it. In some cases, leaders choose not to address it because they see merit in either the technical/functional skills of the person or see value in some of that person's results. Perhaps it's your best salesperson who closes the most each month, but you wonder about their questionable ethics. Or perhaps it's the "Negative Nancy" or "Debbie Downer" on your team who resists you at every weekly IT meeting but has superior and unmatched application support skills that nobody else possesses and would be extremely difficult to replace.

It doesn't matter the reason, but often, these critics are allowed to persist. Not only that, but in many cases, they persist loudly. They'll recruit others to join their gossip squad. As a former peer, Shannon Doiron, used to say, "They are disengaged and actively recruiting." So, much to Teddy Roosevelt's dismay, the critic does count...unless leadership handles it.

Here's the bottom line: You're in leadership and share in the vision of your company. You've worked with your team to explain what that is, engaged your team in dialogue, checked for understanding, and allowed your team to cite specific examples and challenges in achieving it. You're recognized top performers and helped others gain a clear picture of what success looks like. You've done what it takes to get others excited about it, share in it, and see how they, too, play a role in it. Now, it's time to enforce it. By no means can you ever allow anyone to not be on board with the vision or the mission. It will derail your entire team.

"You either condemn or condone." – Donald Peaks, Chief Experience Officer

We'll talk about this quote again, but this is the first place you'll see this concept. Donnie Peaks, one of my favorite bosses, taught me this valuable lesson many years ago. You either condemn or condone, but you do not do anything in between. If you're ignoring something, especially behavior of one of your direct reports, you are condoning. You send the message to others that whatever they're doing or saying is okay, even if not verbally. When you ignore poor behavior (either because you're not aware of it or because you're too lazy or afraid to do something about it), you silently signal that it's okay for others to do that behavior as well. And presto, you've created a space for critics who want to pursue a "third option" to live. And not only to live, but to fester.

When you allow people to exercise this "third option," you're telling your entire team that it doesn't really matter if they're in or they're out. You're telling your team that it's okay to be half-in, half-committed on the bus, without really being on the bus. That's not even leadership. How can any team move forward if the entire team isn't moving forward? When certain people are holding the team back, derailing culture, fighting against agreed-upon norms, the team will never be able to make progress.

This is not a case of "Let's wait and see" or "Let's hope they figure it out" or "Maybe it'll work itself out." When you observe and determine that you have people who are not 100% with you and the company vision, those people have to go immediately. Well, not quite immediately. It's the job of leadership to directly ask them: "How do you plan to get excited about these initiatives? How do you plan to get on board? What are you going to do to get fully invested in what we're doing here?"

Ultimately, if there's no good answer, and you determine your employee doesn't plan on doing any such thing, then you can't let them stay. I don't care how long they've been with the organization or how good they are at processing transactions, closing deals, solving equations, driving forklifts, or sending astronauts to the moon. It shouldn't matter that they perform the best open-heart surgery you've ever seen. If you make your organization's vision or mission a non-negotiable, then them not being on board is just as serious as them doing something immoral, unethical, or illegal. If you lead a team of nurses at a hospital and someone intentionally harmed a patient, they'd be gone, right? If you lead a team of tellers at a bank and someone stole money out of the vault or cash drawer, they'd be gone, right? If you work just about anywhere and someone sexually harassed another employee or a customer, they'd be gone, right? Well, willful assaults on the company vision or mission are about as serious once an employee has been made to understand that's how you feel.

"First it's you. Then it's them. Then it's you." – Donnie Peaks

No one can live up to expectations they don't know you have. People cannot be expected to act a certain way if you haven't made it clear to them that they ought to act a certain way. If you haven't told your team your expectations that everyone gets on board with the vision and the mission, then it's your fault if your employees don't. I'm writing this book because my belief is, sadly, that many companies have lousy or lackluster leadership. So, the reality is that if you're new to an organization or a team, the people you're now leading are probably coming off some level of poor leadership in the past.

Maybe it wasn't the leader that directly preceded you, but likely sometime before that person, they have experienced bad leadership. Experiences lead to beliefs, and beliefs lead to actions; so, if in the past, it was acceptable to not really get on board with the vision, but instead, go through the motions or fake it, then recognize it's going to take some time and work on your part to help people understand it's a new day and there's a new sheriff in town.

I believe that many companies widely fail in terms of leadership development. We're in the middle of a legitimate leadership crisis that spans most industries and sectors, and most countries too. If you don't bother to tell your folks how you feel about something and what your expectations are, you can't expect them to delight you by magically doing the right thing or even knowing what that is. In other words, it's your fault.

If you've done all that—setting clear expectations and communicating them—and your people then act out and test you once—but especially more than once—well, that's on them. In other words, it's their fault.

But what if you don't do anything about that, and you let those things go? Well, then it's back on you. You've condoned the behavior, and you better believe your folks are learning that not being on board with the vision is totally okay, and they will do it again and again. Also, addressing offhand remarks or lack of engagement too briefly and in a half-hearted way is another form of condoning. If you make a comment in front of the group who is going "below the line" by saying something like, "Okay, now, let's not think that way," but do nothing else, your people may stop doing it in front of you, but they'll absolutely do it behind your back. One of the key jobs of leadership is to know and understand what people are saying when you're not around. You don't need to spy on them, install bugs in their offices, or be lurking in the bushes late at night to overhear what they say to their spouse about you and the vision. In fact, doing so violates the trust that's so important to build with teams, especially teams comprised of the right people. If you build trust and adopt the practices described in this book, you'll be able to tell who's with you and who's not. It's partly why asking the questions laid out before is of such critical importance—so you can determine who's with you. But once you know your cast of characters, you have to enforce your vision above all else. If you identify that there's someone who isn't on board with the vision, that must be addressed in a major way. If you don't, your whole team will fall apart.

One of the most jaw-droppingly horrific instances of this I heard came from my boyfriend, David, while he was working for one of his past employers. The company had established some core values for the organization—behaviors it expected its employees to align with, even though these were rarely discussed. At my prodding, David encouraged his team at work to start talking about the behaviors more often. The group agreed to periodically use some of its regular meeting time to discuss examples of how the company was practicing the behaviors and/or use the behaviors in a sentence. One of these behaviors was "Positivity," and during one of the first meetings where the group had agreed to discuss the behaviors, one of the employees in the meeting said, "Well, what I can say is that this company positively sucks!" I was disappointed to hear that someone would make a statement like this (although, sadly, it's probably fairly common), but what disappointed me more was that the entire group all laughed at the comment. Obviously, this team had never "signed the wall" together.

"Well, what did your boss say?" I asked David, eager to hear how management handled the outburst.

I was horrified to hear that, not only did the leader not address the outburst, but he reacted with an awkward chuckle. The leader had neglected to get the team excited about the company's vision, failed to firmly establish that there was "no third option," and then neglected to enforce that by holding the team accountable to practice what they said they'd preach. To top it off, he had even joined in on the banter and bad-mouthing the organization. I was shocked and appalled by the lack of leadership. In the few years David worked in this group, I never heard about the group accomplishing anything of much value, and in the end, the leader ended up resigning, as did some of the group.

I promise you: you won't get anywhere without a vision of the future that people can rally around and get excited about. But you also won't get anywhere if you don't share the vision, talk about the vision, and enforce the vision. Can you imagine how successful NASA would've been in 1969 if only half the team had been committed to the one main goal of putting a man on the moon? It wouldn't have happened. If you don't get everyone on board with the vision, the few people who are disengaged are likely to recruit followers, and you'll spend a disproportionate amount of time negotiating for your team to get on board and never get anything that matters done.

This is one of the key differences between a true leader and a supervisor, or someone who's simply in charge of other people on the corporate directory. Leaders don't exist to manage payroll and approve vacation time. We don't put leaders in place to make sure buildings don't burn down (unless, perhaps, they're the chief of a fire department) and that everything remains status quo. We put leaders in place to set things on fire (unless they're the chief of a fire department). We put leaders in place to enhance things—to make waves, create ripples, initiate change, improve upon what was there before, and to light things up. The first and most important role of a leader is to ensure that the team is marching in a unified direction and is excited about the task at hand.

VIRTUE 2:
Involve Others

"I think the most important leadership lesson in the world
is that people support what they create."
– Brendon Burchard[1]

reshman year of college was one of the academically hardest and most confusing years of my life. In high school, I had graduated in the top 3% of my competitive senior class. I took several AP classes and breezed through most of them without putting forth *that* much effort. My high school GPA was a 97%, and I graduated eighth in my class of 262 while also being involved heavily in sports, student government, National Honor Society, community service, the church, and other clubs and various leadership positions. I had an active social life and did it all without blinking an eye.

Freshman year of college, I was running a C+ average and felt I had no time for extracurricular activities. (Perhaps I had gotten the idea that C+ was something smart people strive for, since I kept seeing C+ on the cover of my engineering friends' textbooks!) Jokes aside, this was hardly anything to write home about. Fortunately, I didn't have to! The university wrote home for me. During spring semester, right before the break, the notice that I was on academic probation in calculus—carrying a D and at risk of failing the class—was sent to my parents' house, and after their mail was delivered that day, my parents called my dorm room so quickly I hardly had any time to think of an explanation. When they threatened to drive out to Notre Dame, to escort me home for spring break so I could spend the week studying in peace and quiet, I agreed that I'd find my way home on my own. I spent spring break of my freshman year studying. It wasn't even close to what I had imagined when so many people had promised me that "college will be the best time of your entire life."

Sophomore year started out differently. Unlike freshman year, when I was only able to take general requirements for my biology major, like biology, chemistry, and calculus, I took some electives like political science and philosophy. When grades came out at the end of first semester, a trend was emerging: Cs and Bs in biology, chemistry, and calculus and As in political science and philosophy.

"That's it!" I instantly declared. "What I'm good at must have changed!"

I marched down to Notre Dame's Office of Administration, switched to a double major in political science and philosophy, and off I went.

I never really paused to ask more questions like, What happened here? Why had I done so well in math and science during all of high school—at one of New York state's most competitive schools—and yet, I couldn't hack those same disciplines in college? Was college really *that* much harder? Had my natural abilities to learn and absorb information really shrunk or changed that much?

I realized years later that I had made a decision to leave something I loved (biology, math, and science) for something I didn't care for as much but felt I was good at (political science and philosophy). It also wasn't until years later that I realized how our strong desire to do what's comfortable, familiar, and safe can stunt our growth. When we're afraid of struggle, challenge, mistakes, and failure—and choose to run away from these things—we rarely discover our true selves, and we also rarely grow and evolve into who we're really supposed to be. So, in part, my decision was somewhat unfortunate. I ran away from tougher class material and low grades and swiftly decided that because I hadn't figured it out *yet*, I wasn't going to figure it out and needed to make a change.

It also wasn't until years later that I identified a key piece of the puzzle that, sadly, I never bothered to turn over as I made these decisions. It was the class size. The biology, chemistry, and calculus classes I had taken freshman year easily had 100 to 300 students in them. We sat crunched together in huge lecture halls while our professors would show slides that were only truly visible to the first 10 rows.

In high school—and my sophomore-year college electives—I was one of 20 to 30 people. These classes were heavily based on student participation and group discussion. I was able to raise my hand, test my understanding, ask questions, and clarify expectations. I could enter ideas or thoughts into the discussion then be validated or corrected.

I also got feedback: "Yes, that's right, Amy. You're on the right track," or "No, Amy, that's not quite it; let's explain this again." Other students did the same, and so not only did we learn from the professor, but we learned from *each other*. Learning was a social, involved process. It wasn't so much that I had become more talented overnight in my new coursework versus the previous ones; it was that I was in a different *environment*. I felt valued, appreciated, and acknowledged, and I got to take an active role in my own learning. I could speak. I could contribute, ask, and write. I could take notes because I could see the blackboards or whiteboards, and thereby, I could see myself in the learning process. It made all the difference.

Not only was I learning more in these classes, but I was also having more *fun*. I was involved. I mattered. And I wanted more.

Leadership is a lot like this. When we lecture our people—telling them what to do, when to do it, and how to do it—rather than *involving* them in conversation around what *they* think we should do, when it should be done, and how they'd like to do it, we rob people of *their* learning journey and strip from them an experience they can never get back. Leadership isn't a democracy, and leaders won't arrive at every decision by giving all their people ballots and then tallying the votes. However, when people feel like they have a voice, and you regularly invite them into the conversation, something beautiful happens. When you involve others in things—information sharing, group discussion, planning for the future, goal-setting processes, their own development—your team will automatically feel more engaged, excited, energized, eager, and empowered. And people who feel these things are often more successful than those who don't. This virtue is all about involving others in any way you can, and it's one of my favorite of the 7 V.I.R.T.U.E.S.

PRACTICE 1:
MAKE THE PLAN WITH THEM, NOT FOR THEM

There are multiple ways to involve people in organizations and at work, but one of the most important and transformative is to involve people in their own growth and development. If we're serious about doing this, it means that both the leader and the understudy will need to get more involved in their coaching. This section is all about coaching. It serves as precursor to the much deeper look we'll take on coaching in both Virtue 3 on routines and Virtue 5, which delves more into how understanding and learning works.

Throughout my career, I've spent thousands of hours watching managers coach their employees. For years, this was my favorite thing to do. In my banking career, I spent years as a district manager and regional director, and I would visit branches and observe managers coach their tellers, bankers, and partners on how to provide better customer service, sell more, or just be *better*.

There's no doubt that *individualized* coaching and development planning with people make the biggest difference in employee engagement, production, and results. Situations where people get feedback in groups can be helpful and are a good supplement for individualized coaching, but it should not serve as a substitute for it. Team meetings, huddles, and cooldowns are places where coaching and feedback are often provided, and these are beneficial too. Group dialogue—like I had in my college classrooms once I left the sciences and moved to the arts—is really valuable. But without private office hours with professors to supplement it or one-on-one sessions with peers, it doesn't mean much. People need, want, and literally crave feedback, and they want to be involved in that process.

The biggest thing you can do as a leader is to engage your people in their own development. Whatever your plan for your people or the outcomes you desire to see from them, the best thing you can do to ensure those things happen is to *involve* them in the plan itself. When we debrief something that we saw someone do (or try to do), such as sell to a client, it's important that we, as leaders, take specific notes and then share those with the employee. I use the word "notes" intentionally. Years ago, at a leadership training focused on coaching and giving feedback, I learned one of the most valuable lessons in that class: "quotes equal notes." The workshop was designed to help provide more specific and useful feedback to others. After that experience, I learned the value in writing down almost everything that you see and hear going on when you watch someone whom you plan to coach. I can't tell you how often we try to coach people without having these "quotes" or "notes," and our feedback often comes through either as an attack or too vague. The reason for both is often that we're paraphrasing what we think we heard or what we remember, which has already become filtered through our own paradigms or lenses. Don't make this mistake. Take *notes*, which can often be verbatim *quotes* of what you heard. This will allow you to be straightforward and specific when you provide your understudy with feedback.

In addition to being able to share exactly what you saw and heard when you coach, it's also important to get *their* sense of how they feel they did, what *they* might change, and what *they* feel they're working on. Then, when it comes time to "make the action plan"—something every coaching session should include—you've made it more likely that the person you're coaching will *want* to help make the plan. They'll be more excited to commit to the calls to action that you agree, together, to set.

Since it's going to be *their* plan that *they* execute, it's really important that they play a huge part in making it. If the plan for success is that the employee will start calling 25 clients a day and asking, "Do you have a few minutes for me to ask you about your financial goals?", it's going to be *them* doing it, not you. So why would you make the plan without their input?

So often, I've observed as managers rattle off a list of things they want an employee to do while the employee just nods in a chair nearby. Sometimes, the employee doesn't even nod! Sometimes the employee doesn't even take notes! It's blown my mind how many times I've seen a manager continue to talk anyway. When this happens, the leader conducting the meeting has no idea if the employee has come along with them, agrees with them, or understands what's being said any more than the professors lecturing in those college auditoriums my freshman year did. There's no temperature check. As a side note, every now and again, I'll go to a meeting on a complex topic where a lot of information is being disseminated. It's great to see a speaker stop and poll their audience—sometimes electronically—to make sure they're still engaged, grasping the information, or gaining new knowledge. It serves as a bit of reset: The audience is reminded that they're supposed to be engaged and learning, and the voting buttons ask for their input and attention. It's a great way for the speaker or coach to ensure that too many people aren't lost and to make course corrections if needed.

In coaching sessions, one-on-ones, group meetings, and presentations, leaders must slow down and ask questions. We must create *dialogues*, not monologues. When coaching employees on things we specifically observed, great leaders ask questions such as:

- So, how do you think that went?
- Why?
- What do you think you did well?
- If you could go back in time, what might you do differently?
- How do you think this could go better?
- What would you focus more on next time?
- Tell me more about that.
- Why do you think that?
- What would be the benefit of that?
- Why would that help you?
- What would that accomplish?
- What would that look like?
- Why do you say that?
- Why are you feeling that way?

- What would you like to work on going forward?
- What can you commit to?
- When will you do that by?

When we don't ask these kinds of questions, we miss a critical part of the process of developing and coaching someone. Great leaders don't coach and develop people all by themselves. Rather, they facilitate a process where, over time, people learn to develop and coach *themselves*. Aren't the best employees at work self-driven? Aren't the best students self-motivated?

Whether we're coaching little league or a direct report at the office, things go better when the person we're coaching *wants* to improve, *wants* to learn, *wants* to grow, and is actively involved in creating that process on their own. The most successful people are involved in their own development. Throughout my career, I would often feel confused when we'd sit down with someone to debrief them on their performance, and the leaders did all the talking. I would think to myself, *Don't we trust this person? I sure hope so because we're a bank. They have keys and combinations that give them access to some of the money.*

It sometimes felt that we trusted them to manage their cash drawer, but we didn't trust them to manage their own performance. A simple question like "How do you think you're doing?" inspires people to self-assess their own performance. And once they do that—regularly and consistently—it's often shocking how many more of their answers they can produce. Follow-up statements and questions such as, "I see. Yes, I noticed that too. What do you think you can do about that?" leads to even more remarkable answers from people. If you want people to step up, become more involved, ask better questions, be more driven, assess their own performance, and find their own solutions, then you have to create a landscape that fosters that kind of thinking. But you can't do it sporadically or periodically. You have to do it consistently and regularly, where they learn to count on it and expect it. The hard truth is this: If you want your people to change, *you* must change. If you want your people to get better, *you* must get better as their boss.

The beauty of this course of action is that we also get to see where people are at mentally. Let's say you've been asking your employees to fix, correct, change, improve, or enhance the current results. You ask them for suggestions. They come back with a "great idea" to deface the building, destroy company property, or cheat, lie, and steal. It's not ideal, but at least you know you have a problem with alignment. You know that something has gone wrong with the first virtue of setting vision and giving other people a view to it. Your next step would be to work from there. All too often, however, it seems that managers give up on asking people what they think because they tried it once and were disappointed by the answers.

I've heard it all. Things such as:

- She doesn't really know what to do about this problem or issue.
- If he knew what to do, he'd do it.
- She needs me to tell her what to do and how to do it.
- That's why I'm the manager/leader—I have the experience.
- I've already been down this road. I have it figured out.
- That's why they put me in management—so I can dispense my knowledge on these things.
- They're not ready for that kind of responsibility.
- Something could go wrong if I left it in his hands.
- We don't have time for this.
- I can do it faster. It's just easier if I do it.

Recognize anything on this list? I sure do. Not only have I heard these things from leaders who reported to me, but I've said these things before! I said them much more often some 15 years ago when I was new in leadership, but even once I had years of experience, I'd sometimes fall into old patterns of thinking and subconsciously say something like this about a particular person or situation. By the way, you don't have to say these things out loud to think them. And you don't have to consciously think them to subconsciously think them. So, whether you've said them out loud or whether you've wanted to think these things, most of us have these thoughts at a subconscious level at some point.

The **keys to success at doing better** than this are the following:

1. Understand (and accept) that these statements are harmful and why.
2. Recognize these behaviors in yourself. Again, they might be thought or said subconsciously.
3. Replace these behaviors with something else. Put a new behavior there.

This might be hard to hear, but nothing on this list is spoken by a true leader. That can feel quite counterintuitive because—here's the rub—there's going to be times that everything on this list is *true*. You probably *have* been there before, and you probably *do* have it figured out. Along with the others on the list, you probably did really great when you were in that role. In fact, it might even be what got you promoted into leadership in the first place!

But guess what? You're not in that role any longer. Leaders who say or think these things are right—because they're in management, they probably do know better and can do it faster! But management isn't about *doing* things; it's about helping *other people* do things. You're there to transition your skills to someone else. Telling people what to do and how to solve a problem never effectively *transitions* skills to other people. Asking questions, helping other people self-discover, letting them come up with their own answers, and then slightly redirecting them when they're off track—now that's what *does* help people build skills. So, while all the statements on this list might be true, it doesn't mean that saying them—either to yourself or out loud—is the right thing to do. If you really want to be a leader, this is when you're going to have to rise above what's easiest or fastest or what has felt right in the past. You're going to have to resist that temptation to give into old habits and give away the answers. Instead, you're going to have to *involve* others in a learning process—their own.

WHY DON'T WE DO IT?

Time and impatience are probably the two biggest reasons. We don't like people's first attempts at the process, so we give up on people—and usually early. It takes more time to do things this way. I've heard some of the worst answers to questions like, "So, what do you think you can do about this next time?" I made the joke earlier about an employee suggesting they could deface the building or trash property because I've heard answers that are almost that surprising and inappropriate. I once watched a teller (we'll call her Maria) seriously tell her manager that she thought the girls at the branch could wear bikinis outside the bank and wash cars on Saturdays while their customers went inside the branch and had a financial review.

After that incident, the manager turned to me in horror and said privately, "I am SO sorry. See, this is exactly why I don't ask them questions like that."

"Questions like what?" I asked.

"ANY question where they have to self-discover," the manager sheepishly replied.

"Don't be sorry," I said. "I'm not. The fact she was able to answer like that was because you did a great job of asking an open-ended question. She felt safe enough to give you an idea, and she's understanding that you want to find ways to attract new customers, get them inside, and grow the business. The only thing I'm sorry about is that you seem to think you did the wrong thing. Keep asking her and help redirect her answers back on course. Share with her that we're not going to start washing cars in bikinis and talk about the 'WHY' with her too. Let's remind her that she should show up this Saturday in her professional work attire. Let's also get her second thought, her next idea. But don't stop asking for her input. Her answers will get better over time."

I also was able to reassure this manager that when I had been in her shoes—soliciting ideas on how to generate more traffic, more conversations, and thus, more growth in our branch—I had come across similar surprising ideas. An example: The tellers at one of the first branches I managed had felt so involved, trusted, and empowered that they actually executed an idea without my permission. They had taped signs on our exterior ATMs saying that the ATMs were broken and customers had to come inside for service! It only took a few hours of heightened foot traffic in the branch and me overhearing a few complaints about an "out-of-order ATM" before I did some digging and found out what had happened. Initially, I was livid. But instead of blowing up and losing my cool, I found the strength to calm down so I could have a rational conversation with my all-too-proactive (and perhaps mildly unethical) team members that thought deceiving our customers to get them inside was a good idea. As we talked, I recognized the creativity, innovation, and desire to win that sat at the center of this lousy idea. I also recognized the lack of judgment and that perhaps this team was not ready for quite as much trust and empowerment as I had extended.

That manager followed this process, and a year later, I came back and watched this manager coach Maria again. This time, the manager asked her the same question about how we could drum up more business. This time, her answers included things like taping a penny to the receipts at the teller line and stamping "A penny for your thoughts?" next to the number to call to take a survey on our service. Another thought was taping a dollar bill on the tellers' name tags with a little sign that read, "This $1 is yours if I don't tell you about our free financial review."

These were some of the more innovative ideas I had heard from a teller (a far cry from bikinis and false signage), and as the manager continued to coach Maria this way, she grew tremendously. Another year later, Maria had been promoted to a personal banker and became one of the most successful salespeople in my region. How? We involved her in the process of self-reflection and thought, and we didn't give up on her because of one dopey answer. If anything, that first answer showed us where we were with her and how we needed to invest more time, ask her more questions, and involve her in her journey of growth and development. This was simply a case of Donnie Peaks' motto of "First it's us, then it's them, then it's us." We hadn't surpassed the first "us" yet.

If you don't do this as a leader (ask questions and involve your people), you'll write a lot of action plans that will never have great execution because Brendon Burchard is right: people support what they create, and they don't support what they don't create—at least, not as much. If you don't ask for people to help you write their own action plan, they won't be as invested in it. One common trick I've seen great leaders do is to have the employee who is being coached hold their own pen; they literally write the plan themself. I'm ambivalent on this. Holding the pen absolutely creates a sense of ownership and empowerment, but quite honestly, employees who speak the plan out loud as you write or type it up can have the same impact. What's most important is that you've designed the plan with their input and involvement.

Many times, I've seen call center managers listen to calls and come to the coaching session with an action plan on the coaching form already filled out. Why even bring the employee into the meeting or meet with them at all? What are they there for? They can read, right? If you're going to do it that way, you might as well just hand them your coaching form and action plan that you've designed for them as you walk by their desk.

Involve your people in their coaching. Have them assess their own performance. Have them create their own action plans. Make the plan *with* them, not *for* them. You'll be surprised how much more often and effectively plans get executed. Never write another action plan again—unless it's for yourself.

It does take more time to coach people this way. But what you gain is so valuable. You save time in the long run by not having to repeat yourself, rewrite plans, and talk about the same things. Have you ever had this experience? You create an action plan for someone but they don't execute on it? So then, you write a new one—or God forbid, you write the *same* one? Oftentimes, this is because you didn't have your employee's full buy-in from the beginning.

INVOLVING OTHERS WITH REGARD TO COACHING AND DEVELOPMENT

We all know that the definition of insanity is doing the same things over and over but expecting different results. I can't tell you the number of leaders I've seen over the last 20 years who act insane every day. They coach their people by *telling* them, *ordering* them, and *mandating* things for them. Sometimes, leaders will do this in group settings, not even in one-on-ones. (Group accountability can be *one* form of accountability, but when it's the *only* form of accountability, it often isn't effective.)

Sadly, when leaders don't make the time to meet with people privately and individually, their people's unique and individual traits, strengths, weaknesses, opportunities, fears, personalities, talents, skills, and abilities never come out. Too many leaders are trying to lead their teams—teams comprised of individuals—and don't have the foggiest idea *who* their individual people are. Don't make this mistake. Get to know your people. Ask them questions about what they like, what makes them tick, what they're passionate about, what they want to do or accomplish in the next few months, year, or many years. Then build plans around them and around those things—*with* them, *for* them, and *about* them.

If you're in a situation where you're hoping someone will somehow "perform" on their own without guidance and mentorship from you—because "I told them how important this was!" or "We talked about it!"—check yourself. Did you *really* talk about it? Was it *really* a discussion, a true dialogue? Or was it more of a monologue with you setting and clarifying expectations and them mainly nodding or smiling? Perhaps at the end, you even got some agreement like, "Okay," "Yes," or "Sure."

A word of caution here: "Okay," "Yes," and "Sure" are some of the more dangerous words we can hear when we're creating action plans *with* someone. These words don't really mean much except that someone is *saying* they're going to do something. For some people, saying, "Okay, I'll do that" often means, "Okay, I'll *try* to do that" or "Okay, I *plan* to do that." Some employees really *want* to do what you'd like. Few employees show up to work thinking, *Okay, I'm going to try to do a really BAD job today. Yeah, that'll be fun.* Most people want to win and be successful—and feel like they're impacting positive change in the world and doing meaningful work, especially when that work aligns well with their natural talents and gifts, which we all have. You'll never *really* know how your people are feeling about the action plan you created with them unless you ask questions and extract the thoughts, feelings, worries, and plans around or behind the "Okay," "Yes," and "Sure."

The other big lesson I've observed from watching people coach is that action plans need to be consistent until they're accomplished. Too many leaders try to teach their people calculus before testing to ensure that their people know how to do algebra or geometry. Coaching and development in the workplace aren't dissimilar to how we learn as we're growing up as children and young adults in school. Things build on each other.

In my field of work, there's a list of about 100 things that make for great salespeople and providers of exceptional member experience. And there's a stepwise progression to them, in terms of level of difficulty. As an example, we might say that strong service providers and sales employees potentially do some or all of the following:

- Smile and happily greet their customer with a warm welcome into the business
- Make eye contact, stand, and shake hands (if in person)
- Obtain that person's name and then use it
- Build rapport on a personal level with conversation about interests, hobbies, and plans
- Ask open-ended questions about customer needs and wants
- Ask permission to ask more questions, to dig deeper, to see if the member has needs or wants that they're not expressing or aren't even aware of
- Paraphrase or repeat things back to the customer to make sure both parties are on the same page

- Make recommendations and use benefit statements to help the customer see or find value in the proposed solution
- Gain commitment from the customer to proceed or move forward
- Overcome objections and concerns, if there are any (and often, there are)
- Own the outcome and fulfill on the agreed-upon next steps
- Set expectations for the future and what will happen next (delivery of a product, a follow-up call, an approval coming via an automated system or email, etc.)
- Hand the person a business card
- Thank the person for their business
- If the experience has been a good one, perhaps ask for a referral from the person's network
- Do wrap-up work after the customer leaves (storing information or notes about the interaction in a CRM system or tool, setting reminders for anything else that needs to be done, etc.)

These are the list of things a leader in sales might want to work on with a direct report. The most common pitfalls I've seen happen are:

- Leaders won't pick the right entry point for the person they're coaching. They won't pick basic foundational things (algebra) first, but instead skip straight to the more complex things (calculus). Impact: We give our understudy too much, and they simply can't handle it because they don't have skills they need first.
- Leaders won't be specific in how they discuss the things on the list. They're vague or generic in their language. Impact: Our understudy has no idea what to change or do differently, and no results happen.
- Leaders won't ask enough questions to check for understanding and commitment. Impact: Our understudy may not agree with the plan, or perhaps doesn't have a chance to air their concerns or worries about the plan. They'll instead walk away with no intention to do it.
- Leaders aren't consistent enough in their coaching. They'll either set a plan on one of these topics and not follow up on it, or they'll create multiple new plans in rapid succession on different topics without ever really resolving the focus from the first plan. Impact:

Our understudy is either too confused to change or doesn't invest time or effort into the plan because they know it's likely to change anyway.

I've seen situations where a salesperson is put on an action plan around asking more open-ended questions. The leader will observe that their employee is an order taker and does whatever the customer asks without probing for more information to see if there's other opportunities. Or perhaps, the questions are personal ones. You've observed an interaction and heard the customer say, "I just got back from vacation with my two kids and family; it was great timing because I'm starting a new job next week," to which your employee says, "Uh-huh, that's great. Hope you had fun. Okay, so about that new checking account…"

You coach your employee on responding to clues and cues. You're specific in what you've observed, you've asked questions of your employee to gauge their engagement, and you've decided that this is exactly the right area of focus for an action plan that isn't too easy (algebra) or too difficult (calculus). It's exactly the right plan for this particular employee. Together, you agree that going forward, your employee would respond to this kind of information by saying something like: "Oh wow! That sounds awesome! Tell me more about that. What are your kids' ages? Where did you go? What's the new job?"

You and your employee agree on exactly what's going to happen next— what questions the employee will ask and what it will *look* and/or *sound* like. As a side note, all great action plans clearly explain what the changed behavior will either *look* or *sound* like. I can't tell you the number of nonspecific, vague plans I've seen over the years that never got executed on because *no one*, sometimes including both the manager and the employee, could tell me what on earth was *really* supposed to happen, and everyone had different interpretations of what it all meant. We'll talk in greater detail about this in a bit.

What happens next is very important. Your involvement in the plan, as well as the plan itself, needs to be *consistent*. When you give someone feedback on a Tuesday in July and then don't come back to check in on it until a Thursday in October, you can bet your bottom dollar that no progress, or very little, will have been made. People need, want, and crave feedback to do better. Most people like reinforcement and can deal with positive *and* negative forms of reinforcement. They want to know what they're doing well (or not).

This is huge misconception in our world today. A lot of leaders fear giving tough, constructive, critical feedback to their people, so they avoid it. The reality is, people do want to get better, and when we involve our teams in their own action plan creation, when we show up to coach and develop them every week, when we genuinely care about their success, and when we have an open and honest relationship with them, our people will welcome our tough feedback too. This is assuming they like the job they're doing and the role they're in. And if they don't, what a great way for you *both* to find out—through consistent and frequent dialogue and rigorous debate.

The frequency I've seen work best in most environments for coaching, development, and following up on previously set action items is *weekly*. This works well for frontline employees to C-level executives, but it's especially important for entry-level and mid-level employees. If you come back once a week—52 times a year—and simply check in on your previous action plans, you'll easily double the likelihood that those plans are going to be understood and acted upon. So often, coaching and development discussions and action plans aren't ever executed because no one ever comes back and expresses interest and care in the action plan of the employee or their development in doing it. Often, the employee then will think, *Well, if my manager or boss doesn't care, then why should I?* or, *We haven't talked about that in weeks—I guess it must not be that important.*

One of the things I've learned throughout watching coaching in progress is this:

THAT which gets talked about or gets measured gets done.

If you want to show your people that something is really important to their success as an employee, your success as their leader, the success of the team, or the success of the organization, go back weekly and talk about it. Again and again.

Now the other half, which is as important as you showing up consistently for coaching sessions, is consistency in the action plans themselves. Think about the person I described who was put on an action plan to ask more open-ended questions and respond to cues and clues. What would happen if, the next week, you chucked the plan on open-ended questions and instead wrote a new one that focused on using the customer's name? Or demonstrating empathy? Maybe you'd do this because the situation you watched happened to be with a customer whose name was difficult to pronounce, so that time, he didn't execute on that well. Or because the interaction happened to be with a customer who had just lost her father, and your employee didn't know how to respond to that.

As tempting as it may be to coach to whatever situation is arising at that moment—and change your action plans accordingly and often—I can assure you this one thing: If you don't keep an action plan CONSISTENT, until the employee masters the skill you placed on the original action plan, progress with that initial plan will not happen. Nothing will ever really get done.

In my many years as a regional manager in financial services, I used to visit branch managers who had made action plans for their personal financial advisors and bankers. I was consistent with my visits and also consistent with their action plans, so we got to a point where there were action plans and documented coaching conversations for every employee in my entire territory. These plans were organized in binders or folders, and I would show up at their offices to visit and go through the plans. On paper, everything looked great, and I was proud of my leadership team for taking my feedback on coaching and developing others so seriously.

Then, I got smarter and added a new step to my inspection process. I began going around and asking the employees, "So, what are you working on?" after just having read their plans. It was amazing to me how few employees even *knew* what they were working on and couldn't speak it back to me. The question I always had for the manager was, "If they don't know what they're working on, how likely do you think it is that they'll be able to improve it?" Not very likely, right?! Most of us don't lose weight, get a promotion, fix our relationships, or achieve financial goals without trying. And it's hard to try to do something if you don't know what you're supposed to be trying to do.

Remember this conversation from Alice and Wonderland?

Alice: Would you tell me, please, which way I ought to go from here?

The Cheshire Cat: That depends a good deal on where you want to get to.

Alice: I don't much care where.

The Cheshire Cat: Then it doesn't much matter which way you go.

Putting someone on multiple different action plans, giving them too many different and changing focuses in a short period of time, makes it darn near impossible to get results. When this happens, your people won't be clear on the direction you're wanting them to go. And, for the person with no direction, it doesn't really matter what they do.

As I dug into the problem of people not knowing what they were working on, one key issue showed up repeatedly: the plans kept *changing*. I remember being on so many field visits where, over an eight-week period, someone's "weekly action plan" would look like the following:

- Week 1: Ask more open-ended questions—two personal and two financial—in every conversation you have.
- Week 2: Use the customer's name at least three times in every interaction you have.
- Week 3: Demonstrate empathy better. When customers share sad or tough things about their lives, say something like, "Oh gosh, that's terrible. I'm so sorry. How are you doing?"
- Week 4: Skipped. No coaching completed.
- Week 5: Overcome conflict. When a customer acts dismissive of your recommendation, get them to talk about why they're not interested or what's holding them back.
- Week 6: Always ask the customer for a referral from a friend or family member, and give out extra business cards, especially if the customer is happy with you!
- Week 7: Skipped. No coaching completed.
- Week 8: Ask more open-ended questions. Find out why the customer came in and what their plans are for the rest of the year and respond to cues and clues.

No wonder people who had been coached this way couldn't tell me what they were working on! I wouldn't have known either. Employees who are coached this way are left with nothing but confusion.

The reason this happens is that the coach or manager would go off to coach without looking at the previous plan. They would grab a notebook, blank sheet of paper, or perhaps a blank coaching form and head straight into observing a situation. Then after the observation, they'd respond to that particular situation and start there, as opposed to starting with the *previous action plan.* For those of you who are familiar with Stephen R. Covey's work *The 7 Habits of Highly Effective People*, this smacks of Habit 2: "Begin with the End in Mind." When you know in advance what your "end in mind" is, creating an action plan for how to get there becomes simpler. When you've already seen, in your mind, what an ideal employee looks like (what they would say and what they would do) and you've described this to your employee (and talked it through *with* them), then you don't need to change your action plan based on the situation or the interaction of just that day.

When you sit down to coach, develop, or observe someone, it's best to start where you previously left off. You can go into the observation, coaching, or one-on-one with that person's previous action plan already in mind. You, as the leader, know what was on the previous plan, and that's exactly what you're looking for that day.

As the leader, your part in the conversation might go something like this:

> Brad, today I'm going to watch you make calls to clients so I can help you get better at that skill, just like we talked about last week. Do you remember what we said we were working on last week?
>
> That's right, asking more open-ended questions! What are some examples we talked about last week that you've been practicing?
>
> Okay, that sounds great. So, as I watch you today, that's what I'll be looking for.

One of the benefits of this approach is that you show Brad that you are reliable, predictable, consistent, and that *you* also do what you say. You show your employees that if they agree to working on something, you will be back. You'll be back to help them with it, to cheer them on, and to acknowledge their growth and progress. You won't forget about them or their plan. When we don't coach our employees consistently and don't keep their plans consistent, our employees learn a different lesson instead: It doesn't really matter if they say, "Yes, I'll work on that," because you might not remember they said it, you won't be back to check on it, and you'll move onto something else even if you *do* come back.

This consistency ensures that your team members know you expect consistent progress on the same plans, showing them that not only do you expect them to be involved in their development, but you want to be involved too. When high expectations for consistent follow-through are set, your employees will want to be more involved too, and they'll know they need to be. Without consistency, like in the previous eight-week example, people find it harder to be as involved or excited because they can't mentally keep up with what's going on. As human beings, we crave a certain amount of structure and familiarity.

Society often teaches us that "easier is better." Even as children, we are taught to seek out the path of least resistance. Hard is bad. It takes a strong person with what Carol Dweck calls a "growth mindset" to recognize the value in doing hard, challenging things. So, most of us feel that if we have a boss who isn't going to make a big deal out of something, and we can stay in the group, collecting a paycheck, we will. If we can persist without having to do something new or different, we will. We think, *Why am I going to bust my tail working hard to change something that I'm never going to get credit for or isn't going to be followed up on anyway?* Hard to argue with that.

When we jump around and never "close things out" with others *before* we skip onto the next hurdle or objective, nothing ever gets done. Similarly, if we only see someone do something *once*, we never know if it's going to "stick." When we pull people off action plans too soon, our employees can often regress because they didn't get enough consistent practice to make the new skill a *habit*. If the leader turns their attention to something else, the employee will certainly turn their attention too. I always say, "Make sure it becomes part of their DNA before you move on."

Remember: your people helped write the action plans they're on. They made those plans *with* you and now *own* those plans. When we come back consistently to check in on progress and the plan stays consistent until it's improved before moving onto the next skill, we help people establish a foundation and then build on it. It's not dissimilar to how bricks are layered on each other as a wall is built. People love working on something consistently that matters and seeing your commitment to help them progress. They respond to it, so don't miss your opportunity to help people develop new skills and long-term routines that will stay with them for the rest of their lives.

It's hard. But I promise you, it'll be worth it. It'll put an end to you having to go back and coach on the same things over and over without different results. Insanity isn't fun.

PRACTICE 2:
VOW TO NEVER RUN ANOTHER MEETING

Have you ever sat in a "bad" meeting? I have. I don't know anyone who hasn't. Although there's a variety of reasons that some meetings stink, some of the most common are:

- The leader/facilitator/person running the meeting drones on...and on...and on.
- There's no real dialogue or opportunity to voice your opinion, disagree, argue, or say much of anything.
- You're not terribly interested in the topics or don't see how it's relevant for you and your work.
- There's no clear or set agenda, so no one is sure what the meeting is about.
- There are no takeaways or calls to action at the end, so it feels like nothing was accomplished.
- The meeting runs over its specified time frame, then everyone starts watching the clock impatiently.

I can't tell you how many years I spent "running" meetings before I realized how ineffective they were. I wanted to think my meetings were typically more effective than most: I would bring partners and guest speakers to break up the day; I'd always have a section on recognition and reward so people felt valued or appreciated; I'd often assign one to two speaking parts to other meeting participants ahead of time so it wasn't just me talking. But sadly, my meetings often *did* run over their established time frames, we'd constantly get off track, and I would struggle to corral the group back into the discussion I wanted to have.

When it comes to Virtue 2, it's vitally important that we *involve* people in most everything, but definitely in meetings. If I could offer you one piece of advice on how you run meetings, it's this: Don't. Don't *run* your meeting.

If you want to consider yourself a facilitator for a meeting, good. Then, stick to that. Let's talk about what this looks like.

GIVE YOUR MEETING AWAY, STARTING WITH THE KICKOFF

Since we know things work best when people are involved, you can start by focusing on that. First, give much of your meeting away. One of the most effective things I've ever seen teams do—and it becomes especially effective when it's done *consistently* over *time*—is to kick off your meetings with a "leadership thought." I call it this because, for years now, most of my meetings have been with other leaders, but if the meeting is with a group of salespeople or customer service representatives, you can all it a "sales thought" or a "customer service thought." Heck, calling it a "weekly growth share," a "motivational moment," or "this week's spotlight" works too. This "moment" could be a YouTube video, a quote, an excerpt from a book, or even an object that someone brought in as Show and Tell. But importantly, you don't open your meeting—someone else does it, at least part of the time. Perhaps you put together a schedule—you do it 50% of the time, and the members of your team do it the other 50% of the time.

This might sound scary, especially if people weren't given the opportunity to do this before. You're probably thinking, *But I'M the leader. They need to hear from me. Meetings should start with me sharing my focus, my priorities, my views, and my vision on where we need to go.* Trust me, there will be time for that. But empowering your team to share with you in setting the tone for the meeting will work wonders at helping them understand and embrace what you're trying to accomplish. If you're empowering your people in even these basic ways, there's one thing I can assure you of: they're probably a lot more capable than you're giving them credit for.

Let's say you get over your fear and try this. You then might cringe at how weak the first one is compared to the message *you* could've delivered. But it doesn't matter. Our role as leaders is to help *others* get better, not to hear ourselves talk. People can't get better at something unless they're actively practicing it, right? Think about something you practice a lot, whether a sport, an instrument, or working with your hands. No matter what you practice, the truth is, it works. Want to get better at something? Then *do that thing.* Practice it. Over and over. Once you do, you'll find that you get better at it. So, if you want your employees to deliver better "motivational moments" or "leadership thoughts," they'll need to do it. So, don't give up if the first one stinks.

When you give the motivational moment to a meeting participant and then demand discussion and debate on whatever they shared, something happens. Not only does the person who is leading the discussion and starting the meeting feel empowered, the whole group feels empowered. They know that you trust them enough to *lead themselves*. That's huge. When people are given that, they get far more interested in what's going on, pay better attention, take better notes, and are more inspired to *do* something about it afterward. What does all of that lead to? Better results.

NEXT, GIVE AWAY THE AGENDA

I also encourage you to give away several components of the meeting's agenda for others to lead and facilitate.

Call people in advance and say, "I'd like us to talk about last quarter's results. Would you mind leading the discussion on that?" Everyone has unique talents and abilities. In any midsize group, there's usually a financial or numbers guru, an extraverted communicator, a creative innovator, an operationally minded genius, an artsy person, etc. When you give people topics to present on and discuss that *they* are passionate about, their natural strengths and greatness will emerge, and that's a great thing. I've sat in thousands of meetings during the last two decades—most work-related but plenty in an academic setting or with a volunteer or community board. A constant phenomenon I've observed is that:

> *People are often more interested in learning from*
> *their PEERS than they are from their BOSS.*

Or they're at least equally as interested. When a group of people listens to their boss, it's easy for them to say, "Okay, but you're not really *in* my role. You don't face what I face. You simply don't *get* it." And if a group is feeling this way, no matter how much they might respect their boss, they're also likely to somewhat disregard or forget the feedback or instruction after the meeting. When we allow a group of peers to spend much of a meeting sharing their own successes, best practices, and real-world struggles and challenges with one another, that sends a different message. You're showing your people that you believe in them and trust them to figure it out. You help them recognize how to self-solve their own problems and not lean on you as much. You empower them. They get stronger together, building each other up. They perk up and get more interested. And frankly, you show them that you don't think you're the smartest person in the room.

"You might be the smartest person in the room. But you're not smarter THAN the room." – Donnie Peaks

Besides, even if you *are* the smartest person in the room, having other people feel that way will only stifle their intelligence. The best decisions often come out of truly interdependent teams. As smart as each of us are, none of us are all-knowing or all-doing. We all have strengths and weaknesses, and the beauty of teams is that each person brings something different to the table, even if it's just a different way of looking at something. When we work together in groups, with space for all to be heard and given a chance to express ourselves, we often come to much smarter and better solutions. You also continually raise the bar for what people's thinking and intelligence looks like—how each can contribute. People get even smarter and more capable as you do this because you're forcing them to practice. Giving away your agenda items in advance and having multiple people lead a different section of the meeting means they have to prepare. It means that you, the leader, aren't the only one preparing and thinking about the meeting in advance. Other people are pulling information, doing research, gathering thoughts from others, and finding solutions. It's no wonder that leaders who operate this way have more engaged and capable teams.

THE 4 DS: DEMAND DISCUSSION, DIALOGUE, AND DEBATE

All great meetings have dialogue. Honest, straightforward, candid dialogue. If we're going to involve people in their work and expect incredible results, then they have to be involved in their meetings. This means they need to have the space to speak up, the desire to speak up, and the ability to speak up.

"They're just a quiet group," some managers have told me. "Silence is golden!" is another popular cliché I've heard when managers pause to get feedback and no one speaks up or asks a question. No, silence is NOT golden. Silence is scary.

When you've got a group of people in a meeting that's either 10 minutes or 10 hours and no one speaks up, that's a problem. Oftentimes, the problem stems from a culture that's been created by the leader. Everyone has tacitly agreed to accept the established culture, live with it, and not question it. This is no bueno, and if you've got a team where this is happening, you *can* do something about it—today.

Group dialogue starts with the leader and their ability to demand such dialogue. Initially, it's leaders that create the expectation for it and show their groups repeatedly that they *want* such dialogue. Here, what you DO is far more important than what you SAY. I've seen countless leaders say things in meetings like, "I really want your feedback here" or "I have a completely open-door policy," but then their actions show the team immediately and continually that nothing could be further from the truth. When we *really* want our people to speak up, we *show* our people that, day after day, by what we *do* to support it.

The best facilitators can show the group that they want their opinions by doing some of the things we've already talked about: inviting one of their direct reports to kick off the meeting; giving away other agenda items, asking people in advance to prepare to share with the group on a topic. But those aren't enough. The leader has to show the group that they expect to discuss some of the items on the agenda. Great leaders who demand great dialogue will often say things like:

- What does everyone think of what Jane just shared?
- What are some other thoughts on that? Who sees that differently?
- Eric, what are your thoughts on this topic?
- Do we think this is the right course of action? Why?
- What do you guys think we can do about this?
- What are some steps we can take next?
- What are we going to do with the information we just heard today?

Let's talk more about how you'll *actually* do this. Great leaders do four things really well to create discussion, dialogue, and debate.

SILENCE ISN'T GOLDEN. GET PEOPLE TALKING.

First, leaders ask open-ended questions of the group to get people talking. They don't fear silence. They don't reword questions or double- and triple-stack questions when no one responds right away. They sit and wait until the group answers. Over time (again, *consistency!*), groups learn that the leader is not playing around.

They learn that their leader is going to *demand* discussion before moving on, even if the leader has to wait all day. At some point, unless you have terribly disagreeable employees who are *trying* to get fired, your employees *will* speak up. People want to contribute, to add value, to share their thoughts. It doesn't matter if they're salespeople, students in a class-room, IT engineers, or accounting brains. Everyone has opinions and a voice, and once it becomes the cultural norm to speak up and share, they will. You have to set the tone in the beginning and stick to it.

All too often, I've seen leaders ask a question of a group and then panic if more than a few seconds go by and no one answers. They jump in to save the team. They'll say, "What I mean by that is…" or "Okay, let me ask it this way…" Your team probably doesn't need you to do that. It's likely that they're reflecting on what you said and going through an internal thought process. Or it's because you haven't done this much before so they're caught off guard and not entirely sure if you want only positive information or if they can share their challenges, worries, and doubts too. Sit and wait. Allow for some silence. Over time, the answers will come more quickly because you will have *taught* people that they can count on you facilitating meetings in this way.

CREATE A SAFE AND SECURE ENVIRONMENT FOR SHARING.

Second, strong leaders create safe and secure environments for people to speak up. Great leaders know how hard it can be for people to disagree with others in a group setting, and they work tirelessly to remove the natural, subconscious, and innate discomfort so many of us have with speaking up. Most people have numerous fears when it comes to publicly speaking and sharing within a group. They fear being judged by the leader or the group. They fear being wrong and thought foolish or stupid. They fear not being able to express themselves well. The list goes on.

Great leaders work hard to show people continually that, while some answers or kinds of thinking are better than others, it's okay for people to be themselves and express the truth about wherever they're at. That's how growth and learning take place. Mistakes happen. It's okay to tell on yourself.

It's okay to show weakness. It's okay to say, "I have no idea," "I'm not sure," "I must've forgotten that—can you remind me what that is?" or "No, I haven't done that yet."

Poor leaders make big deals of these moments. They publicly criticize, reprimand, or chastise employees who make mistakes, say incorrect things, or show poor, low-level thinking. Decent leaders don't make big deals out of these moments; they sort of ignore them and move on. And while that's better, it's not much better. For the learning and the message of true safety and security to stick, really strong leaders *do* make big deals out of these moments, but they become big, *positive* moments. Great leaders will publicly use moments where a person made a mistake or said something silly to help the group know that these are okay. The best leaders I've seen will say things like:

- Sarah, thank you so much for having the courage to say you don't know the answer. I bet you're not the only one. Let's talk about this then. Who can help Sarah with this?
- Tom, I really appreciate the bravery it took to share this mistake with the group. Because you've been so honest about what happened, we've all been able to learn something today. I thank you so much for that. I hope we can all be as confident as Tom, in the future, to share.
- Sandra, I bet you're not the only one who fell behind on that task. Let's talk about what got in the way. What are the actual challenges you guys are facing with this? How can we solve these?

When leaders publicly reward the courage and bravery it takes to admit fault and weakness, others over time develop the confidence to do the same thing. The relationship between the team members and the leader develops too. When someone is considering admitting a mistake or weakness, it becomes less about them feeling fear, guilt, or shame than about the kind of *environment* the leader has created for the group as a whole. It's an environment where everyone can learn from one another and be themselves. Group meetings become more like family dinners, where each person is free to express themselves, without edits or reform. The more some people in the group start to do that and go unscathed—or are even verbally praised or rewarded for it—the more the rest of the group will follow suit.

The most wonderful aspect of this approach is that, once there's an understanding that this is part of the group's culture, it doesn't take so much involvement from the leader. In fact, after a while, it takes hardly any involvement from the leader because the group members hold each other accountable for it. The leader simply has to maintain its momentum. The group continually becomes more engaged because they're able to tackle the truly tough issues, the things that are undiscussable in other groups, the things that are *really* on their minds. Stephen Covey has called this the equivalent of "psychological air" for people, and I've literally seen people breathe deep sighs of reliefs after they get big things off their chest and realize they aren't going to be shunned or punished for it. People often feel a great sense of gratitude that they have a place where their *real* problems are shared, hammered out, and the solutions found together—as a team.

People won't speak up unless they feel safe. It's hard to admit or draw attention to the parts of ourselves that aren't so pretty. Thinking about social media and the message of today's marketing and advertising, it's often this: You're supposed to be perfect. How you look and come across matters.

What if you could turn this notion on its head? Instead of the "highlight blog" that many people run on their Facebook or Instagram pages, your meetings could be a "blooper reel," where people can come as they are, put their real selves and issues on the table, and get real help from others who have already walked a mile in their shoes and have the experience and wisdom to advise one another. Now, who wouldn't want to come to a meeting like that? This can be your team. But *you* have to create the space for it and then not shy away from it when it happens.

Why is this so hard? Sometimes you'll hear things you don't like. You'll find out that project you thought was almost done is barely getting started. You'll learn that some of your people are more incompetent than you realized and will need more help from you to develop competence, which, of course, will take some of your time. You'll find out that people whom you thought had great relationships with each other and talked regularly in a healthy way can barely stand each other or being in the same room. You'll find out that the results aren't as good as you think, or perhaps, the activities and behaviors that were supposed to lead to those results aren't as good as you thought. You'll find out there's issues in your business that you didn't know about.

So what? You can handle that, can't you? The biggest things we have to fear in our businesses and our teams are the things we *don't* know about. Wouldn't you rather know? I had an old boss who used to call this "checking under the hood" or "checking for termites." He'd point that while your car might still be running fine, or you don't need to tent the house just yet, it's important to check into things that are unseen to the general eye—things that can only be seen upon much closer inspection but could cause you far more problems in the future.

Discovering or hearing about the real issues from your team in meetings is tough, but if you want to be a great leader, it has to be done. The worst thing you can do is revert to your former, subconscious, and emotionally charged self and say something like, "Wait, what? I can't believe this! I thought we were done with that. How did we get so behind on this? I need to know what on earth we're going to do now!"

Although difficult and requiring a lot of patience, staying calm no matter what you're told and telling people how thankful you are that they feel comfortable to speak truthfully to their peers and you—showing them that's what you *really* value—will help you grow your business dramatically.

If you haven't been doing this, don't fear. Just start. It often starts with *you* being honest too, admitting your own character defects and faults. Try something like this: "Guys, I've been thinking. I don't feel we have enough dialogue in here, and that's my fault. I haven't done a good job of creating it. I want to show you guys it's okay to speak your mind. I'm going to make some changes, starting today. I really want to hear what's not going well, what's going wrong, what you're struggling with."

It's important to note that you may have to start small. If you've had a company culture or team dynamic that runs counter to this, you'll find that change doesn't happen overnight. If people have felt unable or even oppressed to speak up in the past, they won't be able to trust that you mean it when you say it's now encouraged to suddenly get real. People have had experiences with you that have led to some closely held beliefs. It's not common for people to change, even though it's very common for people to promise it. So, telling your team that you plan to change won't do much good right away. But if you start to *show* them that you are changing, you'll be shocked at how quickly progress will happen and then continue. So go ahead—make some amends, make some statements, and then back them up with action. Don't get discouraged when your group doesn't become talkative and freely gush about their opinions overnight. Stay the course, and it will turn, like a cruise ship slowly backing out of a port and beginning to turn the ship to sail away.

I'd like to share a tool that's paid off huge dividends for me: the power of reinforcing things that happened in a group setting *after* the fact. It's one thing to say to someone in a group meeting, "I'm really happy you had the courage to say that." But if you go around after the meeting and touch base with people *again*, you'll build credibility far quicker. When you connect with someone on a one-on-one basis a few hours or days after a meeting—whether through an email, text, or call, or even in person—and reiterate what you said before, the statement becomes infinitely more powerful.

Finding someone later and saying something like, "Hey, I really meant what I said in there—you did great today. I was so proud of you for speaking up. I'm trying to get the group to understand that it's okay to admit mistakes they made or things they're a bit ashamed of. You helped me with that today, and I hope you continue to do that," works wonders.

I call this the "rule of two." When you really want to hit a message home with someone, make sure you say it at least two times, in two different ways or two different settings. When I tell people something in a group setting and then tell them again individually—where they have the chance to respond to me without anyone else watching—the message always sinks in deeper, and hearing it a second time shows them how much I really meant it.

GET MULTIPLE VIEWPOINTS.

Third, when creating (rather, *demanding*) the dialogue, discussion, and debate, great leaders always get multiple viewpoints. Far too many leaders set up the perfect environment for dialogue and put a question out to the group—strong, open-ended questions at the heart of what's really on people's minds—and when they get the first answer, they're so excited, they STOP THERE.

Maybe they love the answer. Maybe from their perspective, it's even the RIGHT answer. Maybe they're in a rush. Maybe they don't understand the importance of gathering multiple points of view. For whatever reason, they stop after that first answer and never seek out additional viewpoints, including any *conflicting* viewpoints. I can't say enough how important it is to intentionally gather conflicting viewpoints. In a group of people, it's nearly impossible that everyone will see things the same way. Part of creating the safe environment and helping people *want* to contribute more is showing them it's not only *okay* to disagree and have an alternative point of view, but it's *encouraged*.

So often, this doesn't happen. One person will answer or contribute, and the leader will respond to that person. After that, the case is considered closed, and discussion moves on. Exceptional leaders don't do this. Instead, they'll smile or nod, and maybe acknowledge that first answer by saying, "That's great, Mark, thank you for sharing!" But then they'll say something like:

- What are some other viewpoints?
- What are other people doing?
- Anyone doing something differently than this?
- Who sees that differently?
- What are other thoughts on this?

Leaders who do this are showing the group that there's more than one way to skin a cat (my apologies to all you cat lovers). Let's rephrase that. With almost anything in life, there's multiple ways of thinking, more than one approach that works, and more than solution. When leaders ask for multiple viewpoints on every issue, question, or discussion topic, they show their group that they care about *everyone's* opinions, and they also acknowledge diversity of thought and those unique characteristics that make us all different.

When leaders show their teams that they're interested in multiple perspectives, then no one gets disappointed or engages in any kind of negative self-talk when they hear the first answer if it's different than theirs. They don't have to shrink in their chair and think, *Oh, I guess that's the right answer. Mine was different. I'll keep quiet.*

When people know they have a leader who consistently wants multiple viewpoints, people stay engaged in the conversation because they know there will be a chance to share *their* answer. To do this requires much self-awareness, discipline, and intent. It's easy to hear something you like and roll with it instead of looking for more contributions, including ones you *don't* like or that may make you uncomfortable.

The beauty of encouraging multiple people to contribute is that things people say are heard and interpreted differently by different people. We all have an ego, and you may think that, as the leader, you're always going to say the right thing to influence your people, to spark that light bulb turning on in others' brains. Don't fool yourself. At times, your team will learn more from hearing each other reason and talk out loud than they will from *you*.

Remember this quote? "You might be the smartest person in the room, but you're not smarter *than* the room." This is the key reason for gathering multiple viewpoints. The collective intelligence of the group is going to outweigh any one person's intelligence—including you, the leader. So set up questions and debates where multiple people get a say, and people are jumping over one another to get into the discussion, finishing each other's sentences. If you've done this right, you'll notice that people won't always chime in to supportively say, "That's exactly what I was thinking!" But they'll feel free to express their true thoughts and feelings, which can stir minds, hearts, and hands because people will have new breakthroughs while listening to others in the group.

By doing this, you'll also show your team that you're humble. You'll show that you don't believe you have all the answers or that one superstar or top performer has all the answers either. Instead, you'll show the group that you care about everyone's thoughts and feedback, and you can be influenced too. Humble people, who are open to new ideas and willing to listen, get more engagement, interest, support, and loyalty than those who are not humble, open, and willing to listen.

LEADERS SPEAK LAST.

Fourth, leaders who are strong at demanding discussion, dialogue, and debate almost always withhold their own comments to the end. Ever see a leader rattle off their opinion about something controversial and then say to the group, "That's how I see it, but I really want your feedback too"? What happens? The group tends to agree with the leader.

We're taught as children to respect authority. Something about having "Manager" or "Leader" in your title commands the respect and deference of other people, at least to one's face (sometimes what's said or felt behind their back is a different story altogether).

That's nice and all, but the best leaders are aware that this happens, and instead of marching around with pride because of it, they develop an even greater sense of humility. They know that others are going to defer to them and tell them whatever they *think* the leader wants to hear. They know how dangerous and risky this is, so they take dedicated and consistent steps to try to avoid this reaction in people. They don't assume it's someone else's problem, saying things like, "Well, I can't control other people. If other people act that way about me, that's on them, not me." They recognize that Isaac Newton was onto something with his famous third law of motion:

For every action, there is an equal and opposite reaction.

They recognize that if they act too proud, too arrogant, too domineering, too unapproachable, they'll get the opposite reaction in others. Others will shrink down, go quiet, and become unsure of themselves. These actions don't create more respect, admiration, and loyalty; they tend to create the opposite effects. Leaders who are differential to others, include others, and demand the 4 Ds will also get the opposite reaction—a team more confident in their own abilities and willing to take chances in speaking up and ideating.

Speaking last helps with this. When you stop giving your team all the answers and instead create dialogues dependent on *everyone's* contributions, something happens. When no one's voice outweighs another's, including your own, something happens. Teams are able to think for *themselves*. When team members haven't been influenced or persuaded yet by the leader, they are free to voice whatever opinions they have on hand. They also don't feel as bad, when they find out later, that their viewpoints didn't match your own, especially if you consistently and publicly point out how great a thing it is that members of the group see it differently and how those differences of opinion make the whole group stronger.

If you always speak first, you'll get quicker consensus, more agreement, and less opposition, but is that really what you want? The price you'll pay for that is huge. You'll miss key opportunities to learn what people really think, and even worse, you'll miss the opportunity to create an environment where people explore, experiment with, and uncover what they really do think. Without doing this, it's entirely possible and even likely that the real problems, issues, and also the real solutions are locked away in people's heads, unable to get out because they weren't given the invitation (or chance) to noodle on it.

People like to know the "why" behind things, so it helps dramatically to give it to them. You can say, "I have some thoughts on this, but it's really important for me to hear from you all first. I'd really like to know what you're thinking about this."

As you prepare to speak last, remember rule #3: Get multiple viewpoints. Don't just get one and then chime in to agree or disagree with it. When you do that often, you'll never get a second or third opinion. Gather multiple viewpoints and *then* share your ideas. Sometimes, as leader, you'll make an executive decision to override the group and do what you think is best. Be sure to make it clear to the group that you still valued their opinions and contributions that influenced your decision—even if they don't agree with it. But also have times when you allow yourself to be influenced and persuaded by their thoughts, showing them that they can win too. Over time, everyone will realize you're all on the same team, and so *their* individual win, *your* individual win, and the *group* win all become the same.

PRACTICE 3:
GET YOUR PARTNERS TO THE POTLUCK

When I was a district manager at a large commercial bank, I once worked for an area executive, Lynn Lu, who had this mantra: "Your partners should be at every potluck." Potlucks, at least where I worked at that time, were a rare thing, but the quote and the concept stuck with me.

No matter what business you're in, you probably have business partners who support you. In branch banking, the branch has many relationships with folks who visit the branch and sell services and products to customers when a need arises, like a residential mortgage partner, a commercial real estate partner, and a wealth management partner. The branches work to refer to these business partners often.

What Lynn Lu was saying was, if you do something at your branch, why wouldn't you invite your partners? You want them to take good care of your customers. You want them to close the deals you send them. You want them to refer back to you. And if you want to be more successful at referring to them, you need their help too. Who knows more about their products and services then they do? So, if you want to be highly successful, then you should want them to help train your people on what they do. That's a lot of wants and needs.

This means they should be engaged in your huddles, meetings, and even some of your coaching sessions so *you* can learn too. If your partners are willing to teach some of your people, it's probably important that you, as a leader, show up to some of that too. That way, you can learn what your people have been taught by the partner so you can reinforce it after they're gone.

This concept will surface more when we discuss Virtue 5, which is all about understanding and learning. For now, I'll say that it's shocking how many leaders send their people to training but never sit in on the training class themselves or seek out information about the training. If you don't make a point to get more involved *yourself* on what your people are learning when they're away, you can bet that whatever "training" you sent your people to will become almost worthless. Again, people drive what their boss or manager makes important, so if the training topics are never discussed, covered, followed up on, or measured again, it's unlikely anyone will execute on it after the training is over.

If you want to build better relationships with other departments, groups, verticals, units, or teams, invite these groups to do things with you. Invite them to your meetings, huddles, coaching sessions. Have them shadow you. Shadow them. Send thank-you emails for the great things they do. See if you can get invited to something *they're* doing. And for gosh sakes, if you have a team lunch or potluck, invite them.

Relationships are like flowers. They need sunlight and water—as well as time—to thrive. When left unattended, they don't get the nourishment they need to survive. The old adage is "out of sight, out of mind." So, if you want to be remembered, get in front of people. If you have business partners that you want your employees to remember, get those people in front of one another. Relationships don't get built out of thin air.

Think about a friend you haven't seen in a long time. Let's say this friend used to call you often, asking you to do something. For a long time, you were busy or didn't feel like going out and doing what they were offering. So, you declined their invitations, saying you'd rather hang out another time. This happens a few more times. What eventually happens? Your friend stops calling you to hang out. We show people how much care we have for them by how much *time* we're willing to invest with them. When we never reach out to book time on someone's calendar to get to know them better or see what's going on in their world, we can't possibly expect to have a great relationship.

In so many organizations, business lines and units don't have great relationships with one another. Retail doesn't like the product promotions that Marketing is pushing. Accounting is too demanding in asking for reports to be filed by deadline. IT isn't moving fast enough to get major upgrades done. So-and-so "just doesn't understand" the way another group works. These feelings and statements ultimately surface because people haven't involved others enough in their day-to-day activities to learn from one another and see what their colleagues that perform different job functions are up against. Silos and walls that are invisible to the eye (but all too well felt) go up around us, and it becomes tougher to get things done in timely manners. When groups have to work together, it can be almost excruciating. This leads to everything from a generally mild sense of irritation or bitterness to outright hostility or watercooler conversations where everyone gathers to complain about each other. Ouch.

Have a "potluck" (either literally or figuratively) and make sure to invite your partners. Don't do things without offering invites to the people you care about most. Identify the key influencers and teams who affect your team's success, and make sure those people are interacting with your team frequently. Show them the value of that. Mandate it at first, if you have to, but don't leave it to chance. People will, again, take the easy road until they find value in going the road less traveled.

I'll also note that if you're in a business with customers, clients, shareholders, stakeholders, or members, this concept works with them too. I've worked at institutions that would have regularly scheduled and frequent "Voice of the Customer" sessions, where we'd send invitations to clients and have them come in to engage with us in a general discussion about how things are going. Not all customers sung our praises. We'd often pick a mix of those we knew were satisfied and those who weren't, and we'd bring them together with a goal of soliciting their valuable feedback—whether it be a pat on the back or the brutal kick in the pants we needed. I personally took more ideas and thoughts away from our clients who weren't happy; figuring out how to better run a business that pleased them became an obsession for me. It takes a strong (but, again, humble) leader to invite clients to your "potluck" that you know aren't thrilled with you. Do it anyway. You might learn the most from them. But if nothing else, you've shown them that you care about them and want to involve them in your crusade for the truth of what's going on in your business.

PRACTICE 4:
KNOW THAT ANYONE CAN PLAY—AND LET THEM

Have you ever been conducting business with a company and dealing with an employee who, at some point, tells you that what you're wanting help with is beyond their abilities? It sounds something like this:

- Oh, I can't do that. I'm *just* a teller.
- I'm not allowed to reverse that fee. You'd have to get a manager for that.
- I don't know the answer to that.
- I'm not sure. I'm *just* a cashier. They don't tell us that kind of stuff.
- It's policy.
- I'm not sure why, but that's just how it is.
- I don't have the authority to do that.

How frustrating are these kinds of answers? What I see all too often in corporate America is that employers don't trust, empower, or enable their people nearly enough. People are often underutilized and being played at levels far beneath their capabilities. This practice is about course-correcting that trend and recognizing how important it is for leaders to give their people opportunities to learn new things, step up, and contribute more.

I want to be clear that not everyone can be cross-trained in every function your business has. It's just not feasible, nor is it effective or necessary. Successful businesses aren't successful because every employee can do everything, but rather, because every employee can do *their* job really well—and wants to. They have both the skill *and* the will. I can't even imagine trying to learn the IT side of a company's business. I can barely change the input on the television so I can switch from cable to play a DVD. (Yes, I still have a DVD player, and yes, I still use it.) This might be a mild exaggeration, but what isn't an exaggeration is that my brain isn't wired for certain kinds of work. I wasn't genetically blessed with technological genius, but it's also something I have little desire to learn; it doesn't align with my innate talents and learned skills. I'm not passionate about IT in the same ways I am about building relationships with people, communication, and leadership.

We're not all designed to do everything in the world. I'm sure you can easily think of someone you know—whether friend, family member, or colleague—who would be absolutely terrible at your job. You can also identify someone whose job *you* would be terrible at. It's why "it takes a village."

Now, there's a difference between healthy defining of roles and responsibilities and simply cutting people off at the knees because "they don't have experience" or "they haven't done that *yet*." One of the biggest mistakes I see leaders make is that they allow the defined roles and responsibilities of employees to be so rigid that when people show great promise and tremendous potential, they don't even bother to recognize it, much less nourish that talent begging to get out. That's when people leave the organization.

About a year after I graduated college, I had the opportunity to work at a bank branch outside of Baltimore, and that experience profoundly shaped my understanding of leadership and, in turn, my whole *life*. At the time, I was in a Management Development Program, and I worked at this branch for one short year, fulfilling my stint as a personal banker before moving into "management," where I would become an assistant manager and then a branch manager at other branches. As an individual contributor, I grew by leaps and bounds, learning more about leadership in that year alone than I would learn from my leaders in the two years that followed—when I had moved into leadership and managerial roles.

How did this happen? How could I learn more about leadership during the year I wasn't *in* leadership than in the following two years when I was?

The reason was simple: I worked for a great leader, Trish, who recognized that leadership was about *involving* everyone, not just fellow leaders. She realized that she was not the only person who could lead. Anyone could lead. And so, everyone did.

As time progressed, I began to show some good execution on the sales side. I was able to talk to clients about their CD money and get them excited to meet with a financial advisor. I was able to talk to customers who had equity in their homes about options they had to establish lines of credit for home renovations. I was able to talk to people knee-deep in debt about consolidation products that could lower their monthly payments. We had a teller named Angie who was really interested in learning more about these things too and was eager to move over to the sales side as soon as she could. However, she didn't have any experience. Remember Debbie? Who so badly wanted that promotion? Angie was just like Debbie.

I haven't seen Angie in over 15 years, but I remember her like it was yesterday. She was from Trinidad, and her English wasn't the greatest, but she was reliable as heck—always punctual, dressed professionally, and trying her hardest. Her effort was the top thing that stood out to me. One day, in a regular one-on-one with our branch manager, I shared that I thought Angie had promise. Perhaps I was encouraging her to spend more time with this teller or coach her more.

Instead, Trish smiled at me and said, "You know, I have an idea. Why don't you mentor and coach her? You're looking to learn more about leadership, and soon, you'll be in leadership, so this will be great for you. Plus, I've noticed she's really taken a liking to you. Why don't you take two hours a week away from your day job and mentor her? Then, on a monthly basis, we'll all sit down, and you two can share with me everything she's learning, everything you're learning, and how it's going. Deal?"

At this point in my career, it was one of the most empowering things I'd ever been asked to do at work. Before I was in leadership, I had been given permission to lead. A small piece of someone else's development had been entrusted to my care. You could look at the leader who had this conversation with me and say, "She's just trying to give something *she* should be doing—developing *her* team—to you." But she *was* developing her team. The proposed activity meant that two of us got to grow, not just Angie. And Trish got to focus her energy and attention on things where *she* was most needed. For the next several months, I coached Angie, and it was one of the most rewarding experiences I ever had. Even though I wasn't formally a leader yet, my boss had asked me to lead someone. Because of the trust extended to me, I felt more confident, respected, valued, and appreciated. At the same time, I felt challenged too. I was getting to make an impact in an area that mattered to me. It was a perfect fit and what Stephen Covey would call a win-win in his book, *The 7 Habits of Highly Effective People.*[2]

We also had a financial advisor, John, at the branch who was always invited to the potlucks. (And that branch did have potlucks from time to time!) Trish also empowered John, another individual contributor, to lead.

John supported other branches, and Trish wasn't even his boss, but John still chose to make ample time for us, even though he wasn't an official member of our team. But that didn't matter. In both John's eyes and our eyes, he *was* a member of the team. John wasn't interested in formalized boundaries, titles, or roles listed in a corporate directory, so it didn't matter that he was "only" a supporting partner to us. He didn't feel that way, and neither did we, so none of us acted that way. Herein lies the beauty of self-fulfilling prophecies: We make them true because we believe that they are (or will be) true, and then we act in accordance with those beliefs.

John would frequently visit our center and speak to us in our morning huddles or afternoon sales meetings. He also took it upon himself to coach and develop me. He wasn't charged or entrusted with my development, but he chose to do it because he *wanted* to do it and because he sought the same "win-win" outcomes that Trish did. John knew that not only would *both* he and I benefit from me knowing more about what he did in the wealth management world, but he also knew that our customers would benefit too, and in turn, the organization would benefit. So, John created more than a "win-win" but rather a "win-win-win-win." I was only 22, but this was a beautiful thing to see showcased.

Other financial advisors at this company, when asked to help train or coach the personal bankers in their branches, would often say, "Well, that's not my job," to which I would wonder, "Well, whose job *is* it, then? You're the most qualified. You're the subject matter expert. You're a partner to this branch, and the dedicated financial advisor of this branch. You want referrals from the branch, right? So, if you're not willing to take this on, who will?" The answer was invariably one of two things: it was either the job of the branch managers or the job of the training department.

But guess what branch I was happiest and most productive at? Guess what branch others were happiest and most productive at? Guess what branch got the best results? Guess what branch had the least amount of turnover and attrition? Yep, it was this one. Referrals to John were through the roof at that branch, and when I talked with our customers about what John did, I was able to do so with more proficiency, confidence, and knowledge than my counterparts who worked in environments where this partnership and involvement with everyone was not happening. I didn't sound like the unempowered, unknowledgeable, entry-level employee I described at the beginning of this section, and that's because I was in an environment where *everyone* could play and did.

At the end of the day, when we involve everyone in the training, learning, coaching, and development of people, *everyone* wins. Employees should *want* to be involved in bettering each other because they have a long-term approach and vision and know that their return on investment—of time spent coaching and advising others—isn't lost forever, but instead is critical in helping develop a better future state for everyone. During my year at this branch, I learned as much about sales and leadership from John as I did from Trish. And Angie learned as much from me as she did from management.

Here's the key to coaching, development, and leadership: *anyone* can play. Peers at the same level can learn from each other. Employees can learn from business departments in other divisions. Employees who are senior to one another but not in a direct reporting relationship can learn from each other. It often takes the leader's permission—and sometimes even the leader's urging—to make this happen, but once set in motion, it's hard to stop the fantastic momentum this creates. What happens is something magical: it doesn't all ride on the leader's shoulders. When leaders make the mistake of thinking they're the *only* person who can teach anything or has valuable wisdom or insight, then that team's development is limited to one person—the leader. It should be no surprise that teams that utilize multiple people's knowledge and wisdom outperform teams that only leverage the knowledge of one.

Seems obvious enough. So, why would anyone do this? Why wouldn't we, as leaders, want others to help us in the education, development, and knowledge-sharing process? Usually, the answer is ego. Our egos are very powerful. Our egos can often lead us down incorrect paths; sometimes those paths are riddled in fear. We fear that others around us will be stronger than us, more powerful, better liked, or more respected. We want to hoard knowledge because we think that it's only *us*, the leader, who should or can develop and grow a team. That's just nonsense, and it's what I call a "scarcity mindset." A scarcity mindset is the belief that there's only so much to go around—like the amount of apple pie in a pan. If I give a piece away to someone else, then there's less for me. An "abundance mindset," however, is the belief that there's more than enough to go around, and that everyone can win and be successful.

Sometimes it's our scarcity mindset that leads us not to want to involve other people at all—in projects, on committees, in training, in big decisions. We sometimes fool ourselves into thinking that if we share our people with others, there will somehow be less for us. That's just not true. When we involve people—regardless of their role—in learning and development, and do it often, we all win.

Don't make the mistake of saying out loud or thinking that someone can't do something *just because*. The excuses we make of why someone can't do something might include things like:

- They're too new in that role (or too new to the company). It's too soon.
- They're too young. They need more experience.
- They don't have enough seniority. Others have been here longer who should get that, do that, have that (*even if these others are not as qualified*).
- They're just a [teller, entry-level employee, cashier, novice]. They aren't in a position yet where this is part of their job.
- They don't have formalized training in that. They should go take a class or get a certificate. Then they would be eligible to make a presentation on this.
- They haven't done it before.

Sadly, these arguments are for those who are *afraid* of possibilities. I've seen the most inexperienced people, who were newest in a role, had no formal training, and were fresh out of high school or college, come up with the best ideas, make the best decisions, and be the most ideal candidates for all sorts of things.

John didn't have formalized leadership training when he helped develop and coach me to be better on the phones, better at connecting with clients, and a better human being. Trish, our manager, simply believed in him and his ability to do that. She had seen how capable and consistent he was, which was the only test he had to pass. She leveraged and utilized him. In turn, he loved it, I loved it, and we all learned together. Similarly, I wasn't in any kind of leadership role, nor had I been given much formal training, when Trish let me take Angie under my wing. But Trish knew that giving people stretch assignments and opportunities they had not been given *yet* would be how they would *learn*. Maybe we weren't perfect at it the first time. Most likely, we *weren't*. That's where practice and experience come in so handy. Great leaders know that mistakes and blunders, especially in the beginning of an experiment, are to be expected—and that's *okay*. That's more than okay; that's what life is all about. It's our challenges, our tough moments, our mistakes that help us learn, grow, and evolve. What employee or person doesn't really want to do that?

One of the most interesting things that happened when Trish let John lead me and let me lead Angie was that she essentially created additional leaders in her branch. In so doing, she duplicated herself, increasing her capabilities to do other things through creation of more time, which she won because she had entrusted some of the leadership to others. She hadn't been granted any additional leadership headcount on paper, but in practice, she had done exactly that.

As mentioned, this branch was very successful. When we were at large-scale events, people would come up and ask Trish what was leading to her success and how she was able to "get it all done." She always gave all the credit away, citing how engaged and supportive of a team she had surrounding her, which made it possible. I would watch others nod and smile and say they understood, but I could tell that they were unsatisfied with her answer. Perhaps many of them thought, *But I'm trying to do that TOO. I have huddles. I have meetings. I involve other people. They just don't respond. Or they're not capable of doing it MY way (which is, of course, the RIGHT way).*

Trish would often invite others to observe our team (another form of *involving others*) or offer to go visit them, but oftentimes, these offers would get turned down. Many people felt they didn't have *time* to go learn, and perhaps, they were also either too prideful or too afraid to open themselves to blind spots they were missing in their own business.

Sadly, what they could have come to understand is that what Trish was doing was *much* different than what they were doing. She was truly empowering people to not act alongside her, or even act as *her*, but rather, to act as *themselves*—with nothing but their desire and passion to guide them. She trusted us to figure it out, and she set great parameters for ensuring we would; so, we did. At her branch, there wasn't just *one* leader or manager; *many* of us felt like leaders or managers, even when it came to leading and managing ourselves.

If others had come to visit us, they would have seen many examples of this in motion. Trish created ample opportunities for us to get involved with the business. Every morning huddle and afternoon meeting was littered with spots where Trish gave away her meeting. For a long time, I owned "Product Knowledge," and at each monthly meeting, we'd carve out 20 minutes for me to do an activity to teach the branch about our services and products. Trish allowed me the runway to do this any way I wanted. Some months I would make a trivia game to play. Other months, we'd pull questions and answers out of a hat. I came alive in those moments, and even though I was only 22, I felt empowered—like I had a real spot in running the show. Trish also had a great habit of never answering questions but rather posing them. Each time any of us came to her with an exception, override, or reversal request for a customer, she'd ask, "What have you looked at so far? What do you think we should do? Why?" I learned quickly to come with my research and homework already done, having pulled everything from the account history to the number of previous refunds someone had been given. I learned how to think for myself and come with my own recommendations. As I did this, conversations with Trish changed naturally. Instead of me asking for her thoughts or permission, I'd say something like the following:

"Mr. Jones is wanting a waiver on some fees. He was assessed 10 insufficient funds fees over the last four days. He was on vacation with his wife, out of the country, and this was simply an oversight. This has never happened before, and there's no notes on the system. He's been a customer of ours for 32 years. He had money in savings to cover these fees, but that account wasn't linked as overdraft protection to his primary checking. I've done that now, so this shouldn't happen again. He's willing to take accountability, so he's only asking for half of them back, but due to our great relationship, I think we should do more than that. I'm thinking we either do eight of them, or even refund them all."

I only learned how to research all of these factors because of the questions Trish patiently asked me the first few times I came to her. Each time I came back, I got smarter and more prepared, returning with more information until eventually I came with recommendations around what I would do if I were the manager. As Trish saw my reasoning skills strengthen, she would often listen and say, "That sounds reasonable enough. Based on what you're sharing, I think this is a good decision on your part." At some point, she cut me loose entirely and told me that I no longer needed to come to her unless I felt I should. I had been granted the permission to do free refunds and exceptions on my own—not only up to a certain dollar amount, not only for the good clients. Trish had empowered me to use my best judgment—judgment she had vetted through involving me in the decision-making processes until I had become strong enough to make decisions on my own.

This happened in 2005, but 10 years, four companies, and eight roles later, I was shown one of the best YouTube videos on these topics. As discussed earlier, I've spent years making it a point to "give the meeting away," and during one such meeting, a direct report of mine was tasked with kicking it off by doing his own leadership thought. He brought a video he found online called "MindSpring Presents: Greatness" by David Marquet.[3] The video has more than 2 million views and is a replica of the principles I'm advocating for here. I strongly suggest you watch it. According to Wikipedia:

L. David Marquet [mar-'kay] is a retired United States Navy captain and the bestselling author of *Turn the Ship Around* and *Leadership is Language*. He was the commander of the submarine *USS Santa Fe*. He turned the submarine from the worst in the fleet to the most successful by using a "leader-leader" model of leadership. He became captain of the submarine in 1999 and, since his retirement, the submarine has continued to win awards.[4]

When I saw the video that first time, I couldn't take notes fast enough. What Marquet describes is identical to the style of leadership I've seen work best, and it has everything to do with this book.

In the times I've been most successful in my roles, I've involved the most people. I was 29 when I was given my first district manager role at a bank. I oversaw 15 bank branches and about 250 people. Some of my peers would give me grief at how maniacal I was about knowing every single person's name in my territory, including every teller. Others would laugh at my plans to ensure that the tellers were on coaching and development plans to shadow the bankers or make presentations at the morning huddles or monthly meetings. I always felt horrified when someone would comment, "Oh, you don't need to involve her in *that*. She can't do *that*. She's just a *teller*." What these peers failed to understand was that *anyone* and everyone could and should play. After all, I started at the bank as a teller too, and many senior executives who ended up in chief roles also did. We never know who the future CEO is going to be, but whoever they are, they probably got there by working in environments where their bosses believed in them, trusted them, gave them increasing responsibilities over time, and created opportunities where they could learn new things. Not "later," not "in a year," not "when they're ready," but now. I got a lot of feedback when I was doing this best that working in my region or market was simply *different* than working in others. People felt engaged, empowered, heard. They felt *involved*…because they were.

You can do this too. You must let go of the notion that you're supposed to have all the answers, that the team can only learn from you, that they somehow always need you. They only need you to believe in them, inspire trust and courage, and set up an environment where they can get heavily involved in every aspect of their day: their coaching and development plans, the coaching and development of one another, their participation in meetings, and how they think about and plan their own work.

INVITE OTHERS TO KICK THE TIRES

Back in 1992, my uncle, Mark Chambers, won Toyota's National Salesperson of the Year award. Mark went through several rounds of auditions and competition, showcasing his sales skills, and finally landed on a national stage in front of several Toyota executives, competing against other finalists in mock role-plays. At stake was a free car and bragging rights.

My uncle passed away from ALS in 2015, an incredibly sad year for my family. One of the last things we did together was watch the video of Mark's performance in the competition along with the other finalists. The parameters of the competition were fun: minutes before each finalist went on stage, they were handed a sheet of paper telling them which car they would be "selling" and just one or two pieces of information about the prospective "client." In Mark's case, he would be showing a Toyota Camry—that year's most popular vehicle—to a woman with two small children. That was it.

Mark did an incredible job of immediately engaging the woman in conversation, asking what she was looking for and why. The people playing the roles of the potential buyers weren't making it easy on the finalists, but Mark found out in less than a minute that she was most concerned about safety, given her two small children.

Throughout the presentation, Mark involved the woman in conversation constantly, as he carefully observed his 20-minute time limit. Every statement he made about how great the car was, where it ranked in *Consumer Reports*, and how much trunk and back-seat space there was, *all* aligned with her concerns about her children. I'll never forget sitting on the couch in his Seattle home with our family, beaming with pride and laughing over aspects of that video, as Mark sat next to me in his wheelchair, a few short months from the end of his life.

Then, Mark did two things on stage I'll also never forget.

"This is my favorite part of the presentation!" Mark exclaimed to the woman, in a totally serious but friendly way. "Here, go ahead! Kick the tires."

"What?" she asked, a confused expression on her face.

Mark repeated himself. "Yeah, sure," she replied. Mark smiled, again motioning to the tires. "Kick the tires."

And so, the woman did. She kicked the tires. "What do you think?" Mark asked her, eagerly leaning in.

"They seem good!" she answered, starting to chuckle. Her chuckle slowly turned to a laugh. And Mark had done it—he'd gotten the first laugh that anyone had gotten on stage.

At the time I watched the tape, I wasn't familiar with the expression, but "kicking the tires" means to inspect something for industry standards or positive characteristics before buying it. The history of this expression, according to Wikipedia, comes from the early 20th century when "tires on early automobiles were made of thin rubber and were sometimes of poor quality, hence a prospective buyer might kick them to see how thick they were or if they would deflate."[5]

The next thing Mark did was to get the woman inside the car, behind the wheel, to do a multitude of things. She honked the horn, adjusted the seat, and looked in the rearview mirror. Of course, in a real-world presentation, this customer no doubt would have test-driven the vehicle.

As I watched the presentation carefully, a distinctive shift in the dialogue and relationship between Mark and this woman occurred. Mark had only met her on stage that day, but I could see their relationship grow and evolve in these two parts of the presentation. Ultimately, I believe it was these moments—and how she responded to him—that earned Mark the win that day. Mark was the only person who involved the prospective buyer this way. He was the only one who asked her to kick the tires and the only one who asked her to get behind the driver's seat and honk the horn. He was the only one to make her laugh. Mark was the also the only one who walked away in first place that day.

Mark *involved* his potential buyer on that stage. He put her—figuratively and literally—in the driver's seat of that car and the sale. Mark gave her the autonomy to experience the vehicle for herself and to sell the car to herself. Mark knew how important it was that other people be involved in things.

Mark lived his entire life this way. After leaving Toyota of his own accord, he went on to buy and then develop a large commercial real estate property in the Capitol Hill area of downtown Seattle, renting out units to both long-term tenants and short-term guests on vacation. He loved building things. He built his own home in Carnation, he built a wonderful marriage with his wife (my Aunt Oda), and he built incredible relationships with the 250 or so people who showed up to his memorial service in May 2015.

Perhaps what stuck out the most to me, as I observed the incredible legacy Mark left on the world and those who knew him best, was that he always involved others in everything he did. Inclusivity was a major theme in his in life, and when Mark passed away in his late 50s, he was still incredibly close and connected to his huge circle of friends he had made in college. That whole group stayed close for the four decades following college. Every time I visited Seattle, they were around, enjoying dinners and social gatherings together, helping each other with projects, involved in each other's lives. One married couple in this group even built a little getaway cabin on Mark's property.

Involvement works. Don't go it alone. In everything you do, invite people to kick the tires and get behind the wheel with you.

PRACTICE 5:
THE FEEDBACK LOOP—RECAP EVERYTHING

When I was starting out as a teller, I worked at a few branches where I practiced my newfound skills of referring clients to the mortgage and wealth management partners. Eager and excited, and wanting to do well, I worked tirelessly every day to look for leads I thought would be legitimately good candidates for these partners.

At one branch, I remember never hearing back from the partners. I became so discouraged. I'd refer and refer—and nada. I'd have to go *ask* the partners, "Hey, did you ever give Mrs. Jones a call on that lead?" or, "Hey, anything come out of that situation with Joe Smith? I really thought he was going to be a good one."

In some instances, the partner had already had a great conversation with the client, and things were underway. Maybe the business had even been written, signed, or sold. In other cases, it was a work in progress: they had planned to meet again and talk more, or the client was thinking about the proposal the partner had given her. In other cases, the partner hadn't been able to get a hold of my lead, had left a message, and was now waiting to hear back. In the worst of scenarios, the partner had forgotten to call and admitted it. In the *very* worst cases, it wasn't clear *what* had happened, but it *seemed* that the partner had totally forgotten about my lead and didn't want to admit it. That one always stung the most because, in addition to having forgotten to acknowledge the important work I had done (and what felt to me like a big effort), the partner valued me so little that they didn't want to build trust with me. This could have been done by Talking Straight or Creating Transparency (two of Stephen M. R. Covey's behaviors he discusses in his great book, *The Speed of Trust*).[6]

I can't quite put into words the dissatisfaction and loss of morale I felt when that happened, but it was major. Want to involve people in their work? Want more activity, more of the right behaviors, more engagement from people? Then here's a tip: *Follow up with them*. At all costs, every time.

If you're looking to really jump-start behavior and you have ideas of how you want people to interact and behave, then one of the most surefire things you can do is to reinforce, recognize, recap, and reward *anything* you see that *aligns* with that vision. People I've coached and trained are often shocked by how many opportunities there are to reinforce behavior in a given week. I've practiced this for years and continue to be surprised by how effective it is. Yes, it takes time to recap what you saw and loved (or didn't love), but it's a key way we can show people that their words and actions are noticed and get quick changes in future words and actions.

In many other moments, we could recap, recognize, and reinforce behaviors by completing the "feedback loop," but we don't take the opportunity. Here's a few examples of where, when, and how you could recap for people and close the feedback loop. One way is to recap for people after meetings. Ever been to a meeting and seen someone do something great? You've probably sat in a meeting, watched someone behave, and thought something like:

> "Wow, Tom is such a team player. He always says the right thing to affirm the contributions of others and really create more interdependence. We are so lucky to have him on this group."

> "Gosh, Mary is so creative and innovative. She comes to these meetings with so many great and new ideas. She obviously prepares for these meetings in advance. I wish everyone was more like her."

Rarely do we see these things and then *say something* afterward. Every now and again, we'll offer up some praise as the meeting is ending or directly after, saying something like:

"Hey, great job in there today. You really know your stuff." But feedback and recognition like this isn't specific and is often forgotten. If you know *exactly* what was so powerful in a meeting and you want to see *more* of that behavior, then I've got great news for you. Try this simple trick and watch more of the same great behaviors happen: Email the person and tell them TWO things:

1. Let them know what they specifically did that was so awesome.
2. Ask them to do it again.

If you're brave or *really* want to see better results, you can add a third part to this kind of email:

3. Ask them to help others demonstrate the same behavior as well.

Two important things to note here:

First, you can do this with just about *anything*. The format of this email can be used after meetings, but it can also be used in almost any situation. Anytime that someone finishes a project, gives a presentation, has a client interaction, makes a sale, or closes a deal, you have opportunities to reach out, either electronically or in person, and follow the format listed above.

Second, you can do this with almost *anyone*, not *only* your direct reports. You can do this with your peers, your boss, or even someone else's direct reports. We've already talked about interdependence and how anyone can play. If that's the case and we're in leadership not *only* to care about the people who report to us but *everyone* around us (including our partners and clients), then you can provide people with feedback on what they did or said that was so great from your vantage point—*anytime*.

We discussed earlier that "quotes make the best notes." When recapping for people, I've found what works best is to utilize one of the following two phrases: "You said" or "I heard." Somehow, hearing an exact quote that was previously said (especially when it was said by us) does something to us (and our minds). Often, it takes us *back* to that exact time and place where it was said and helps us reconnect our memory to ourselves.

Often, when we use quotes, people will recall the moment more clearly than if we only describe it. This is good. We want them to remember specifically what they said, what they did, and where they were. Most people like to be acknowledged in positive ways. Hearing we did something well makes us feel good inside, and we like to feel good. When you recap and reinforce things for people consistently, people *learn* that you do this, so they work even harder to deliver the behaviors and actions again that got them the specific praise and feedback.

Your email might sound or look something like this:

Hi, Jan! I wanted to drop you a short line to let you know what a fantastic job you did in the budget planning meeting today.

YOU SAID: "These are some excellent ideas, and I'm loving this discussion, but if it's okay with you guys, I'd really love to explore the revenue enhancement side of the equation and not just the expense reduction side with you all. I think we might be missing opportunities to grow our net income, and I want to explore that as a team." That was a PERFECT contribution to that meeting!

You used the words "we" and "team" and acknowledged what the group had done so far by saying that you didn't just *like* the discussion, but you *loved* it, which really showed that you want everyone to move forward as a group. At the same time, you voiced an opinion that was different and got us focused on where our attention really needs to be—revenue, which was spot-on in your thinking. After you did this, Bob spoke up, and he and Susie both shared new, great ideas that might not have happened if you hadn't said this. So, this meeting went much better thanks to YOU saying exactly this.

Please keep speaking up in the future, just like this. It is so important for others to hear your voice!

Also, anything you can do to help others to also have this kind of proactive, honest, and collaborative approach would be outstanding!

If you're Jan's leader, what are you doing by sending this kind of an email? First, you're showing Jan that you pay attention and "listen ferociously," as Liz Wiseman would say in her book, *Multipliers*.[7] You listen so well that you not only can recap the general gist of what others are saying, but you can actually *quote* people. When you use these powers for good, people become more deliberate and intentional about their word choice because they know it's being observed, and they begin to make better decisions with how they show respect to others in group settings and how they contribute and communicate.

Second, you create a call to action by stating that you'd like to see these behaviors again. If you do this consistently, you show people that if (and when) they do these things again, you'll recap and reinforce that behavior again. People love recognition, and once they observe when, where, and how to get it, they'll often do exactly what it takes to trigger that switch. They become more likely to act.

By adding a third section that also asks your employee or colleague to help *others* take similar action, you are starting to multiply your own leadership efforts because you ask others to help lead the broader group. You encourage your teammate or employee to not only think about *themselves*—as an individual contributor—but to consider the bigger picture and the greater good. You give them some responsibility for how the group performs, basically saying, "Your performance individually is great. But if you *really* want me to consider you a true top performer, one way you could do even better is to help *others* perform well too."

This might be an obvious charge to give someone who is already in leadership. In many organizations, it's explicitly stated that the true goal of any leader or manager is to help others— not only one's own direct and indirect reports, but their peers, colleagues, clients, bosses, and anyone with whom they come in contact in the organization. However, many people in leadership *haven't* realized that they're there to help guide, lead, mentor, coach, and unleash greatness in others—let alone have the ability to do it. Individual contributors are coached on this even less. Too many individuals undervalue the importance of helping guide other people. For many, topics such as influencing others or thinking organizationally simply isn't a part of an individual contributor's performance evaluation, meaning many people don't fully capitalize on their talent and create interdependence, but instead, let their teams stay somewhat stuck and siloed.

In great organizations, employees are invested in the success of other team members, even if they're not leaders. By sending an email or saying something to specifically affirm what someone did, and then setting up the challenge for that person to influence someone *else* to think or act in the same way, you could be putting this charge around teamwork and influencing others into that person's head for the first time. This could be the spark that enlightens someone's thinking about being a team player. Do this often, and this thought about leading by example and helping influence others might become front and center in your employees' minds.

Another opportunity to close the feedback loop is on field visits. By going out and observing people in their natural habitat, you'll find numerous things to recap for people so they know you were paying attention. During my decade as a district manager, I spent thousands of hours watching huddles, meetings, coaching sessions, and one-on-ones. In each of these situations, a manager or supervisor would lead something, and I would observe from the corner and take notes. I would stay true to my commitment of writing down specific quotes that people said, and later, I'd recap those for people. Whether you send a text, write an email, make a phone call, or talk over lunch doesn't matter nearly as much as your feedback being specific and that you share it with the person whom you hope to see do it again.

Sometimes, instead of asking the recipient of the feedback to "do it again," indicate that you hope to see them do it again. Saying, "I really hope to see more of this from you in the future!" or "I can't wait to witness this again firsthand!" conveys your genuine excitement about that person continuing their behavior in this way.

How does this all tie into the concept of involvement? I could've put this section on the "feedback loop" in other places in this book, but I couldn't ignore how well it ties into involvement. When we recap behaviors for people, we show them that we, as leaders, are involved in *them*. Not only are we truly involved in what they are *saying* and *doing* (in a particular moment), but we show them we are involved in their growth, development, progress, and journey (for the long haul). We show people that we value, appreciate, and care for them so much that we *want* to acknowledge what they're doing well and what things they can continue to do on their journey of being a top performer and how they can help others. It's a genuine focus on others over self. In more meetings than I can count, I've taken notes on everything being said around me because I knew I wanted to recap things for people later.

As you do this over time, you'll find that even the biggest of townhalls or the unruliest of groups can be molded and shaped, one piece of feedback at a time. Think of your team or organization like a bucket of clear water; imagine that every thought or idea you have about what it should look like is one drop of red food dye. Each time you shape a person's thought or behavior afterward by delivering feedback, you drop one eyedropper-full of red dye into your bucket. It's not noticeable at first, and it takes time to stand by the bucket holding your eyedropper, but as you do this practice over time, you will find that your bucket of water soon has a reddish tint. Keep up this behavior consistently, and soon, your water will be red.

VIRTUE 3:
Routine Regimen

"It's not what we do once in a while that shapes our lives.
It's what we do consistently."
– Tony Robbins

"We are what we repeatedly do. Excellence,
then, isn't an act but a habit."
– Attributed to Aristotle

There are countless leadership books on success: what it looks like, how to drive it, common pitfalls, etc. While many of these things matter, one thing, I've learned, stands apart from the rest: how *consistent* we are in our routines (assuming they're the *right* routines). Consistency and routines are *everything*. Executing on predictable, habitual routines doesn't only make a major difference in your ability to truly *lead*, but it will make a dramatic shift in your entire *life*.

What we do repeatedly—every darn day, in good times and in bad—*defines* us. I'd argue that what we do in the "bad times" defines us most. Many of us set goals. Many of us can even identify the routines, behaviors, and activities that will get us to that goal. Many of us start out with great intentions. However, few of us follow through. Why? Life happens. Think about all the things that happen in your life on a daily basis that influence your mood and strip away your desire to *want* to do those "right things":

- No one else is watching. You won't get credit for it anyway.
- It's pouring rain, so you can't go for that run.
- You had a fight with your spouse this morning.
- You got an unexpected phone call you had to take—and it set you behind on everything you were supposed to do and put you in a bad mood.
- Someone said something nasty to you, and you keep thinking about how wrong they are.
- Your kid's school called. Your kid is sick and needs to be picked up.
- Your parents have aged to the point where you need to step into a caregiving role.
- You simply don't feel like it.

When things happen unexpectedly, it's hard. These situations throw off our sense of equilibrium and send the plans we had for the day and ourselves into a tailspin. Often, our instinct is to feel upset, frustrated, or angry. That's normal. However, highly successful people recover from those initial feelings and move forward. What we do in these moments is incredibly defining. If you still act with consistent effort and action toward your goals, you become extraordinary. If you act in spite of bad luck and lousy circumstances, you build something so important, so concrete, so essential to being an exceptional leader that nothing can stop you.

I discovered the best example of this in Jim Collins' book, *Great by Choice: Uncertainty, Chaos, and Luck—Why Some Thrive Despite Them All*, where he describes what he calls "The 20 Mile March."[8] His story describes the different strategies of two similarly situated teams on a quest to be the first to get to the South Pole in 1911. The Norwegian team, led by Roald Amundsen, was successful. The other team of British explorers, led by Robert Scott, never made it, and most of them died on their journey. It's been said that both teams were equipped with similar skills, equipment, and experiences. And yet, the two teams achieved wildly different results. Why?

Collins' answer is simple: consistent routines and daily disciplines. In short, the strategy and approach of the two leaders (Amundsen and Scott) varied greatly. Amundsen's team made a commitment to march forward 20 miles every single day—and they kept it. Scott's team didn't. They took advantage of favorable weather and good conditions by marching upwards of 40 miles on "good days," but on "bad days," when conditions were tough, they took breaks, stayed in their tents, rested, and waited for more favorable conditions to return. In other words, they didn't develop a daily discipline of routines. They didn't live, create, and enforce predictable norms, ones they could set their watches by. They behaved differently in the good times than they did in the bad times, and thus, more bad times came for them.

We see these two kinds of approaches almost everywhere in life. Many of us have either known that person or *been* that person who crams for tests in college or pulls an all-nighter to knock out a term paper, even though the assignments were listed on the syllabus from the first class and everyone had weeks, if not months, to prepare for them. I think back to my college days and my "20-mile march" routines. One was going to the library for a few hours a day after class until dinner time. I was constantly asked by peers, "Why are you going to the library to study today? Nothing is due or coming up for more than a week! Hang out with us this afternoon! Let's watch TV and goof off!"

It wasn't that I *couldn't* do those things or was unwilling to do those things, but I had made a conscious choice to *not* do those things until my work was done. Yes, the work not due *yet*, but I knew it *would* be. A month later, these same friends would be shocked that I could go to a party when something was due in two days—or worse, the next day. "How can you go out?!", they would ask, somewhat judgmentally or enviously. "We have that project due tomorrow."

My answer was always the same: "Mine's done."

For me, studying each day was part of my 20-mile march. In good times—when no assignments were due—I worked for about 3 hours each day. In tough times—when assignments were due—I worked for the same 3 hours a day. If my classes ended at 4 P.M., I could finish studying by 7 P.M., have dinner at the dining hall before doors closed at 7:30, and then have the rest of my night free. Choosing this approach, I graduated magna cum laude while also finding the time to work out each day, lead an active social life, work three part-time jobs, take a leadership role in multiple clubs, and be in a romantic relationship. Because of the consistency in my routines, I was able to achieve success and balance without ever feeling anxiety or stress.

Consistent routines are incredibly important when it comes to health, diet, and fitness. Gym parking lots overflow in January, a month rich with people beginning New Year's resolutions. By late February or early March, they return to normal levels. Why? It's simple. Creating new routines and habits is really, really difficult.

I've never quite understood the concept of New Year's resolutions, especially when they're made in November but don't begin until January. There is no better time to correct a mistake, fix something you feel is broken, or start taking action to improve your life than the second you realize you *want* to do so. Waiting a week, a month, or even more to take action so you can start your journey on the first of the year is a loss of that time you waited. You're prolonging the inevitable, making your situation worse, and giving yourself time to make more excuses and rethink your plans. To be successful, it doesn't make sense to do this.

Nonetheless, we tend to take it easy on ourselves. In a 2015 study, *U.S. News & World Report* found that roughly 80% of New Year's resolutions are broken.[9] This makes sense. New Year's resolutions are often made by people who realized earlier than December 31 that they needed to change something but didn't *resolve* to do it in that very moment. People without immediate resolve often struggle to keep commitments, including the ones they make to themselves, which, by the way, are often the most important commitments we make.

Consistency is *hard*. Most people find consistency boring, tedious, painful, a drag. When we consciously attempt to change old habits, our subconscious minds often try to fight us. Our subconscious minds seek comfort in running old programs, doing the same habits we've taught ourselves over time. Our subconscious also tries to protect us. Since changing old habits can be uncomfortable, it will try to help us avoid pain by convincing us that a new routine that requires more energy, effort, and awkwardness isn't worth it. Often, our subconscious tricks us, talking us out of new and challenging things that might be great for us in the long run. Much of our mental anguish and emotional pain is caused by choices we make.

If you're struggling to make a change in your life, please reach out. There's nothing I'm more passionate about than this. I plan to release an entire book on the difficulties that come with habit formation and how we can overcome those, but until then, you can find me on LinkedIn, YouTube, Facebook, or via my website to initiate a conversation. For now, I'm here to say that having consistent routines and habits—and ensuring the routines you pick are the *right* ones—is an essential component of leadership. It's important that you assess your routines regularly. The right routines will support and drive the other 6 V.I.R.T.U.E.S. of leadership.

Because every business is different and every situation is unique, I won't be able to identify all the routines you'll need to be successful, but I'll share a few that are imperative no matter what kind of business you're in and actually drive all the other V.I.R.T.U.E.S. No matter what industry or sector you're in, these routines cannot be replaced. They work every time.

PRACTICE 1:
COACH YOUR PEOPLE, AND HERE'S HOW

Consider these 2021 statistics from ClearCompany's blog:[10]
- If a company invests in employees' careers, 94% said they would stay at the company longer.
- Retention rates are 34% higher among organizations that offer employee development opportunities.
- 74% of workers say that a lack of employee development opportunities is preventing them from reaching their full potential.
- Only 29% of organizations have a clear learning and development plan for their employees.
- 91% of employees want personalized, relevant training.

- 54% of employees would spend more time on employee development if they were given specific course recommendations geared toward helping them reach their professional goals.
- A well-planned employee training program would positively impact engagement for 93% of employees.
- Companies that spend $1,500 or more on employee development per year report 24% higher annual profits than organizations that spend less.

These statistics align with what I've witnessed during 20 years in corporate American culture. People desperately want coaching and feedback. Books such as *Crucial Conversations, Thanks for the Feedback*, and *The Speed of Trust* give us pointers on how to both give and receive feedback well, have tough conversations, and build relationships on the foundation of trust. I've spent thousands of hours coaching others and also being coached, and consistent, specific, individualized, observational coaching makes a *huge* difference in helping other people perform. As gleaned from the statistics provided, you have a dramatic ability to impact your team's engagement, drive, loyalty, motivation, and profits by coaching your people. Coaching others isn't always easy, but if you schedule it and engage in it routinely, it will make such a difference in your career and the career of others. Here, I'll demystify it for you.

Again, coaching should be individualized, observational, consistent, and specific. Let's dive into each one.

INDIVIDUALIZED COACHING

First, you need to coach people alone: just you and the individual. Too many managers depend on "management through group meeting," or worse, "management by email." Some do a combination of both, which isn't any better.

Our brains are complex, with a subconscious and conscious. Experts estimate that our subconscious can process information somewhere between 500,000 to 1 million times faster than our conscious minds,[11] showing how powerful our subconscious is. In many ways, this is great news. The ability of the subconscious mind to process information so quickly is what allows us to stop at a red light while simultaneously breathing and talking to our children in the back seat. But our subconscious minds can also pose a problem for us. In general, our subconscious minds do two things: (1) run old programs we've taught it and (2) seek to protect us. Because of these two goals, our subconscious minds can mislead us into fear, worry, and doubt. At different times, we fear change, not being good enough, learning something new, or getting outside our comfort zones. Our subconscious often prefers the comfort that comes from keeping things the same. It takes deliberate and intentional conscious choices to change that. For new habits to have any kind of staying power, it also takes constant checking in with ourselves to make sure we create new habits, follow through on them, and evolve and grow.

Many of us humans were brought up in wildly different environments. In the early years of our relationship, I didn't understand how differently my partner, David, and I were raised. We lived in different parts of the country and grew up in very different households. This led us to make very different decisions. My parents, especially my mother, hovered over me like a hawk throughout much of my childhood, questioning my every decision and guiding me to "do things *this* way, the *right* way," which I later realized was code for "*our* way." This never even dawned on me until reading works such as the *7 Habits of Highly Effective People* by Stephen Covey, *Mindset* by Carol Dweck, and *The Four Agreements* by Don Miguel Ruiz that *our* way was just that—*our* way. While my parents chose to stay together until long after I left the house at 18 (they split when I was 26), they weren't terribly happy as a couple and never dealt with that, which, of course, had an impact on me.

David, on the other hand, doesn't even remember his parents having been together. He didn't come home from school to find anyone asking him about his homework assignments or what his recent test grades were. He doesn't really recall having a curfew, like I do. Our parents believed different things, and because of that, we led different lives. After high school, I went on to college and finished in the typical four years. I was proud of that and initially judged David when I found out he took 10 years to finish college. I first thought, *What took you so long? That's too long.* Of course, this was simply a product of my ego wanting to believe that my way was the *right* way and any other way was wrong. As I learned more, I realized that David had experienced life in a completely (and potentially more fascinating) way. During his 10 college years, he lived in Munich, Germany, for a while on an exchange program; he worked a variety of jobs, including doing construction work in Las Vegas; he got a private pilot's license and glider pilot's license and not only flew planes for a hobby but competed in contests—which permanently changed his life.

After college, I went on to get an MBA and then spent years working in multiple leadership roles at numerous banks. I played tennis, rollerbladed, and eventually became a marathon runner. David became an engineer and worked for an airline, then a manufacturer. He played soccer and taught himself to ski and surf. For fun, I scrapbooked. For fun, David played video games. When we met, we were about as different as could be. David regularly donated blood to the Red Cross and got annual physicals. I hadn't been to a doctor in 10 years. The first book I saw David reading was *Oathbringer* by Brandon Sanderson. It might as well have been written in a different language. Back then, I didn't understand the content nor had great habits about learning new things. To protect myself from being uncomfortable, I scoffed that I didn't know why *anyone* would want to read a 1,200-page book with 122 chapters. However, David loved it. It takes me a great deal of courage to share here that when David and I met, I initially chose to be scared and uncomfortable by these differences. I could've chosen instead to be interested and impressed. Over time, I realized that neither way of conducting our lives was right or wrong, just different, and the best relationships are those that not only accept differences but value them.[12]

If you're married, have ever been on a team, traveled outside your state or country, or done business with an industry outside of the one you work in, you've probably observed that we, as people, are different. We are complex beings equipped with our own thoughts, paradigms, and emotions. As unique individuals, we often respond differently to the same things. It's for this reason that management by email or meeting simply doesn't work. If you're not looking to change the status quo or have breakthrough results, or if you're only in a role a short period, you *might* be able to get away with it. I repeat: *You might get away with it.* But this book is not about "how to get by." This book is how to dramatically change and shift people's lives.

If you don't coach people individually, you won't be able to experience dramatic breakthrough performance with them, and that's because you won't *know* your people well enough to know what their true strengths are, what they're really struggling with, and the reasons why. If person A and person B are both struggling with creating success and delivering results, it does not make sense to *only* solve this in a group. What's going on with person A may not be going on with person B, even though they literally sit side by side.

When you spend time with people alone, you build a relationship with them that can't be achieved when you're in a group setting with them. In a two-person dynamic, you learn more about the other person. You're more likely to learn what's going on at home, in their personal life, and what matters most to them. Do they have kids? How old are their kids? What are their names? By knowing these things, it then allows you to *ask* about these things later. You get to say, "How was Billy's T-ball game this weekend that you were so excited about?" Or you get to know that someone only wants to talk about work while at work. So instead, you learn more about them at work: what they love doing the most, what they're best at, what they dislike doing, and the things they're worst at and why.

I've had numerous private coaching conversations (both as the giver and receiver of feedback) that transformed my mindset, but one stands out. Several years ago, I was having a coaching session with a direct report whom I felt close to. She'd been working for me for three years and had called me one of the best bosses she'd ever had. We'd frequently talk about our personal lives. I always felt welcome in her office, and she was accepting and receptive to my feedback. I thought we had a nearly flawless relationship. I prided myself on being a boss with whom she could talk about anything. One day, my identity as that perfect boss was shattered.

Emily sheepishly told me she had something "embarrassing" to tell me. She had decided to go back and get her college degree. Until then, I didn't know that she never went to college. It hadn't come up. "This is something I've been wanting to do for a really long time," she told me. "I've wanted to talk to you about it, but I never felt I could—until now."

I was happy for her and immediately leaned in to ask questions to learn about her decision then share in her excitement and congratulate her. It was a lovely conversation, but as we were wrapping up, I asked her why she had never felt she could talk to me about this before. Because I wanted to become a better leader and a better friend, I asked if there was something I had said or done that contributed to this.

"I've always felt like you've talked about your experiences at Notre Dame and USC with such pride," she shared. "I felt kind of intimidated. It seemed like education was important to you, and so I felt like you'd think less of me if you knew the truth that I didn't go to school. So, I made sure I never brought it up with you. I also haven't really wanted others to know, so I don't bring it up in the group either."

I was about to ask Emily why she had decided to tell me now when she continued, "But now, it's different. You've changed. Lately, when we spend time together, it doesn't seem like education matters to you quite as much as it did before, and because of all our personal conversations, I now feel more comfortable to be myself around you."

There it was. A direct report whom I felt exceptionally close to had felt judged by me. She didn't feel "safe" telling me certain information for fear of what I would think. As I unpacked that conversation later, three things occurred to me.

First, I reconfirmed the power of private conversations. Since Emily admitted that she also felt uncomfortable sharing that with the group, I knew if we hadn't been alone that day, she never would have brought it up. It also had taken our other private conversations to help her slowly build comfort with sharing a detail about her life that she had previously been ashamed of.

Second, and far more importantly, I realized how likely it was that my views on having a traditional four-year degree had shifted because of dating David. This conversation with Emily came about two years into our relationship—long enough that I had started to recognize that my way of doing things in life wasn't the only way. My beliefs had shifted enough that something new had shown up in my language or behavior at work. Enough time had lapsed for Emily to observe it and decide it was now safe to talk to me. This reminded me how important it is that we spend time with people dissimilar to us.

Third, it took this private conversation for *me* to get feedback that I sorely needed. Often, as leaders, we think mostly about how we affect other people. A plethora of books detail how to provide better feedback and coaching; how to inspire and motivate; how to get great results. Far less books are written on what it means to *receive* feedback and how to put yourself in a position where people feel comfortable giving it to you and want to. The feedback Emily provided was probably feedback I had needed for more than a decade. As I listened to her that day, I wondered how many other people over the years had felt the same way but never felt comfortable saying it. It had taken my personal relationship with David to help me shift my viewpoints on what it means to have a college degree. David had shown me that brilliant, capable, and talented people don't always finish college in four years. He had helped me value differences and synergize with people dissimilar to me—to the point that it had shown up in my work relationships. I wondered, what if Emily had felt comfortable saying this two or three years ago? We'd probably be closer. She probably would have gotten better results. Earlier feedback might have helped me connect with other people better, helping me be a better leader.

We meet with people privately so we can build close relationships to them. Not only does this help us give them feedback that's appropriate for them and their specific needs, it helps them do the same for us. When we meet with individuals privately, they become more comfortable telling us things. We become more honest in telling them things. People begin to recognize that we really care about *them*. When they know we care about them, they're more interested in caring about us and learning the same things we care about. Think about that last big project you were talking about in your Monday morning group meeting. During the meeting, person A was stifling a yawn and thinking about their grocery list for the week, but in a private meeting with only the two of you, person A is likely to be more focused on what you're saying and asking them, especially if you've shown them that you not only care about them and their personal life, but also about their opinions and thoughts.

Furthermore, it's more obvious in a two-person meeting if someone isn't paying attention. In that setting, only one person is available to answer the question, "So what do you think of that?" In a group setting, folks can defer to the group as a whole and zone out. This happens all the time.

In a two-person meeting, you can ask questions and *really* test for understanding. Your request for feedback, especially if part of a consistent pattern of you asking for feedback, will feel genuine. Then people can talk about their fears, doubts, excuses, and reservations without fearing the group's judgment. With these out in the open, you can truly address them. You get to talk about it, help your employee through it, and continue to show you care. Two-person dialogue is personal, and it requires folks to answer, so it's far more effective than a large group meeting where communication tends to be more one-sided and some folks get lost in the shuffle.

Making time for private one-on-ones is key. The frequency is up to you, but for folks in frontline positions, especially if they're serving clients or customers, I think monthly is far too long. I recommend weekly.

OBSERVATIONAL COACHING

I'm going to make a bold statement here: If you manage frontline people, half of your coaching needs to be observational in nature. If you manage other leaders, you can get away with less, but I'd still recommend a third or fourth of your coaching should be observational. One of the biggest mistakes I've seen coaches make is that they don't put themselves in a position to provide truly helpful feedback, coaching, or guidance on someone's behaviors because they haven't actually *watched* them behave. It's so important leaders do this.

If you lead a sales team, then it's critical that you spend time observing them interact with potential clients out in the field. Ride along in their car and go to a sales call with them. You're not there to lead the interaction for them but to observe them do what they do. You are there to watch, listen, and observe. If you're a principal at a school, you'll sit in the back of class-rooms periodically and observe teachers teach. If you are leading attorneys, you could watch them argue in court. I don't care whether you lead cashiers at a grocery store or associates who work the makeup counter, if you want better results and want to understand what people are feeling, thinking, and struggling with, you must observe them.

If you lead other leaders, you should watch them in action too. As leaders, they probably run conference calls, facilitate meetings, and hopefully conduct their own observations and coaching of their team. Maybe they do field visits and run one-on-ones. Whatever you and they deem is part of their job, you should observe.

Why? When it comes to execution of *anything*, the easy part is *talking* about it; the hard part is *doing* it. But what do most managers observe? The talking about it. They send emails about it, hold team meetings about it, etc., and through these mediums, attempt to coach their people to do a better job at it…whatever "it" is. But they rarely watch their people in action in their natural habit.

I've unearthed three main reasons for *why* this is:
1.   It takes too much time.

2. The leader feels uncomfortable inviting themselves or asking permission to observe their direct or indirect reports execute.

3. The leader feels they shouldn't *have* to do this step; that if they've hired adequately and have good talent, they should be able to count on their good people to execute on their own.

I'll address these fallacies one at a time.

First, the time. As with most meaningful, worthwhile things in life, this *does* take time. Some say, "I can't *afford* to do that." However, if you want breakthrough performance, you can't afford *not* to. It's like John Wooden said:

If you don't have time to do it right,
when will you have time to do it over?

If you want to know what's going on and what your folks are struggling with, you can't depend on them to always be able to diagnose it on their own. Sometimes we're not self-aware. Sometimes we're struggling with things that we can't even see because we haven't been through them yet. That's the role of the leader! Many of us rise into leadership because we were promoted from the same roles that now report to us. We've already walked a mile in their moccasins and shouldered the same struggles. Because of that experience, we've found the solutions. But we won't know which ones to provide unless we're there to *see* what their struggles are.

It's amazing to me how many people smile, nod, and think they do something well, but they don't. I've seen people talk about how to do something in a training class only to be proven totally incompetent at it if we ask them to demonstrate it. If you don't want to take a few hours a week or a month observing your people, you could be coaching them on the wrong things. You might be walking around thinking that they know how to do XYZ when they really don't. In countless one-on-ones or meetings, you discuss why results aren't happening, but you're diagnosing the wrong things. If you watch your folks in action, you might find that XYZ isn't going well at all; instead, it's a disaster.

When coaching people on sales skills, I've seen how easy it is for people to drop buzzwords into conversations with their superior. They agree to ask "open-ended questions" about "financial needs," "uncover cues and clues," then "tailor solutions" and "overcome conflict," then "make sound recommendations" through a series of "benefit statements." Almost all my people would say they *could* do that, *would* do that, and *did* do that. They could oftentimes even give examples of these things. However, when I asked these same confident people to role-play with me, half of them would immediately show signs of less confidence. No doubt, role-playing makes people nervous, but they'd also be nervous because they were more confident in their ability to *talk* about doing something than actually *doing* it. I'll give you a secret: Doing things consistently and predictably, on schedules and with cadence, helps people be less nervous because (1) they know it's coming; and (2) it's a form of practice, and practice leads us to get better at things, which makes us less nervous. So, if people tell you that role-playing is a bad idea because it puts folks on edge, that's a telling sign that you need to be role-playing *more*, not *less*.

When I've asked the same people who had still been fairly confident in a role-play to be observed with an *actual* client, more than half that group became unconfident. Almost always, they subconsciously (or consciously!) *knew* that they couldn't execute on it as well as they'd said.

The time you spend diagnosing someone's *actual* strengths and weaknesses—not just *perceived* ones—is invaluable. An hour assessing someone's actual traits and skills and then talking about what you specifically observed is worth 10 hours of talking in group settings or going over action plans in a one-on-one. Observational coaching *is* time-consuming. It's the most time-consuming up front when you're learning someone's personality for the first time. It becomes less time-consuming later when you're building on an action plan that has already been created and you've learned someone's style. Make the time. Try it out. If you conduct individual and observational coaching with someone for six months, you will reap enormous rewards.

When you move past role-playing, which is table stakes, and into observing employees in *exactly* the scenarios they're in daily, this is where you get the toughest and most severe pushback. When it's time to see someone carry out their job with a client, patient, student, etc., this is where your average employee will hit the panic button.

5 EXCUSES FOR WHY WE DON'T DO IT

I've heard all the excuses and reasons why observational coaching of real-live scenarios doesn't work. Here's my responses to the top 5 excuses I've heard:

Excuse #1: This will be awkward and strange to our clients and customers. They'll either think we don't trust our own people and we're spying on them, or they'll worry that the person waiting on them isn't equipped to handle them.

Response #1: That's nonsense. Simply tell your clients and customers what you're doing and why. Again, the WHY matters. We don't observe our people in action because we don't trust them; we observe them in action because we care about and believe in them so much that we want to help them get *better*. To do that, we spend time with them to gather information on how they interact so we can create more highly skilled employees in the future, who will be more equipped to deliver an even better experience than the one we have today. Believe it or not, once this is explained, most clients love knowing that employees who wait on them are getting development and coaching.

Excuse #2: Our employees will feel that same way: It's awkward, strange; we don't trust them, and we're spying on them.

Response #2: That's also nonsense, and all the same responses to excuse #1 apply here as well. Tell your employees how much you care about them and want to invest in them. Share that you want *them* to get better, and you want to help *them* achieve their goals, hopes, and dreams of moving up or becoming stronger and more talented. Observing our people can be a great way of showing them we mean it when we say we care.

Excuse #3: Instead of feeling suspicious and untrusted, our employees feel uncomfortable to be on stage, modeling something for the boss. It creates anxiety. (This excuse is a cousin of #2.)

Response #3: We get more comfortable by doing things. Remember the first time you spoke in public? What about your first date? Or your first *anything* in life? How did you feel? Totally prepared and ready to go? Cool, calm, and collected? Or a bit nervous?

It's probably the latter, and that comes from not having done or rehearsed the action several times. How do you feel when you brush your teeth or put your socks on? No big deal, right? That's because you do those things every day, and you don't sense any kind of risk or danger. Again, fear often stems from our subconscious minds, and they don't often like change and the unknown. Here's how you get over that: You do something and show your subconscious that nothing bad is going to happen. Once your employees learn that you're not there to reprimand them, write them up, or fire them, but instead to develop, grow, and maybe even praise them, they'll probably be a lot more open to you *being* there.

If you want to get your employees over being afraid of being observed, it's important to make the overall experience positive. It's important that employees get something specific to work on, something that's personal to *them*, and something that ties into the struggles that they're having. But if you also deliver some reinforcement and praise for the things they're doing *well*, you'll likely find that your people will get over their fear, see what's going on as a good thing, and rewrite the program in their head—the one that says you watching them in action is a *bad* thing.

Excuse #4: You being present changes the interaction. It makes them act or do things differently than they would in real life, so you don't get an accurate picture of what's going on.

Response #4: Sure, that's likely true, and the way to solve to this is— once again—to do it more. We act most differently in front of an audience when we're already a little shaky or nervous doing the thing. Consider this: If your boss asked you to you brush your teeth, you probably wouldn't do it much differently than how you normally do it, right? Why is that? It's because you've (hopefully) brushed your teeth every day, maybe twice a day, for your entire life. If you're 30 and you started brushing when you were 3, and you brushed your teeth twice a day, you've brushed over 19,000 times. So, you'd probably feel comfortable having your boss observe you, right? Even if your boss is a dentist.

The reason we don't like to have our bosses watch us run meetings, talk to clients, sell to customers, or stock the shelves is that most of us don't undergo that kind of coaching *often*. If your people are terrified about getting feedback from you after seeing them in action, it's because you either aren't doing it enough or you're not demonstrating to them you really mean it when you say it's for their good. Or perhaps they don't believe your real intent is to help them grow, develop, and flourish. We need to remind them why we're there. We need to say it out loud. But we also prove it to them by showing them. Coaching our employees in this way makes it more likely they'll make more money or get a promotion, right? Especially if they've told you these are things they want, remind them that this will help them achieve their own stated goals.

Excuse #5: *You* don't feel you should have to do this.

Response #5: I'm going to say this bluntly: Get over yourself! Didn't you once need help too? If you think back to being a child, how did you learn how to do things? Let's stay with the example of teeth brushing. I distinctly remember both parents watching me brush my teeth when I was a child and guiding me through that process. Guess what? I've never had a cavity! I've also gone to the dentist every four to six months for checkups and cleanings throughout my life. I can't help but use this opportunity to point out that routines do, in fact, work.

So does observational coaching! My father didn't try to talk to me *about* brushing my teeth at the dinner table or while driving me to school. Instead, he coached in the moment, while I had a toothbrush in my hand, guiding me gently. "Hey, you missed a spot over to the left. Go back for it." "Hey, maybe not SO hard on the gums—you need to keep those!" and "Oops, well not *that* soft either." At some point, he signed off on my abilities to do that task, and we moved on to other things in life.

If you're a parent and you have teenagers, what big thing do you need to observe them doing before they're free to go off on their own? Driving a car, of course. There's no way you'd turn over the keys to your brand-new BMW if you hadn't ever *seen* them drive. You wouldn't hold a group meeting or send out an email asking them to agree that they know how to adhere to all the signs and signals on the road, right? You'd want to see them do it. Why?

Because there's too much at stake. They could crash the car, seriously injure themselves or another human, which could result in major medical bills for you, or even a lawsuit. And they could be seriously injured. Worst case, they could die or kill someone, which we can agree are bad things. So, what do we do? We teach, we show, we coach, we observe. We observe them practicing turns in parking lots until we feel they can venture onto side streets in a local neighborhood, then we graduate them onto the freeway before they take their driver's test and start driving (gasp!) on their own.

All of that makes sense, right? When we care about the people involved (our children) and the outcomes (our vehicles they're wanting to borrow), we get involved and observe them in the moment. Why, then, don't we do this in the workplace? Remember the Leader's Pledge? You agreed that if you're in leadership, you *care* about your employees in a truly deep, genuine, and authentic way. If you don't, you shouldn't be in leadership. Of course, it's also important that you care about your company's outcomes. If you don't, you shouldn't be with that company. But since you're still reading, I'll assume you do care about both.

Here's the deal: Most of us don't do this. When we don't make the time to ensure our employees are proficient, not only could they crash the car, but they won't develop the skills to be truly great at what you want them to do, carrying out that magnificent dream you're both working toward. Coaches of winning teams spend lots of time developing their teams through observation. It's why sports coaches "watch the tape" on Monday mornings… and take notes. It's no use coaching players in theory; what matters most is coaching based on observation of what's actually happening.

CONSISTENT COACHING

Too many managers coach their employees a few times a year: when big mistakes are made; either before or after a big event, like an important client meeting or a large presentation; or when it's convenient for them. We spent the first part of this virtue discussing how the things we do *consistently* are the things we really get better at.

In his 2008 book *Outliers*, Malcolm Gladwell estimates that it takes 10,000 hours of practice to become an expert at something or master it. Breakthrough performance requires that we have experts at the wheel. "Practice makes perfect" is a common idiom. I much prefer, "practice makes *possible*" or "*perfect* practice makes perfect." Only the right kind of practice helps us develop perfectly. This's why my father spent so much time observing me brush my teeth; he didn't only do it once or twice but repeatedly, until he knew I had it down. Practicing something incorrectly doesn't help us. Practicing the wrong behavior, or practicing incorrectly, actually *harms* us. Practicing bad behaviors repeatedly results in us forming bad *habits*, and then those bad habits work against us when we're trying to learn good habits later. When we've learned to do something the wrong way, we start to depend on those skills to "get by" or "survive," but then we must unlearn those behaviors before we can learn new ones that will lead to great results.

I didn't play sports much when I was a kid. Sophomore year of high school, I decided I wanted to change that. Maybe it was that one of my best friends, Patty, was an outstanding tennis player. She was on the tennis team, and going to practice after school looked fun. So, abruptly, and with no formal training, I decided to join the tennis team. My first year playing tennis, I did so with no coaching whatsoever, much less consistent coaching. I developed my swing all on my own. I was pretty terrible but somehow good enough to survive tryouts and make the JV team, playing low-level doubles. I played enough tennis that year, both in the regular season and throughout the summer with friends, that I became moderately decent using my self-taught swing. In general, it was enough to hit the ball over the net and periodically place it in a corner. I was stronger when I returned junior year for tryouts—strong enough that, this time, our tennis coach took notice of me and spent a few hours coaching me that season. Because I hadn't gotten individualized, observational, or consistent coaching previously, I had developed a swing that was good enough to keep me in the game but not good enough that I could make the varsity cut, play singles, or go nearly undefeated like my incredible friend Patty.

While I could hit the ball and keep it in bounds, I couldn't consistently place the ball with the accuracy needed to really shine. I wasn't as strong under pressure, and if I had to go to the net, it was somewhat hit or miss (pun intended). Our coach began coaching me with a bit of consistency and encouraged me to develop a more C-shaped swing with some follow-through that would have enough power to carry my weaker backhand shots to where they needed to go, which would also help me be more strategic in my aim and positioning. I was happy about the attention until I tried to change my swing.

Guess what happened? I got worse! Why? For one thing, it meant I had to stop depending on what I had been doing, start over, and replace my poor habits with something new. Since what I'd been doing had become so natural for me, and the new, "right" way of doing things was *not* natural for me, I got worse. I started losing more games, which of course, I didn't like. So, I attempted to revert to what I had been doing before. Because this particular coach was only coaching me with *some* consistency—spending most of his time observing and coaching his A-list players—my regression happened without much notice from him.

I'd try to take his feedback for a bit. I'd bumble through a game, eventually lose, get frustrated, declare things weren't working, then blame him and this new "way" of doing things. Back then, I had the incorrect viewpoint that he must be an idiot and my old way must be right, so I'd sneakily pull out my old behaviors at the next match, letting the bad habits creep back in. But a few meets later, he'd swing by my court, watch me play for a few minutes, and angrily coach me during the break that he couldn't believe I was back to my old tricks.

This went on for the entire season, making my junior year results even worse than sophomore year's lackluster performance. Fortunately for me, Patty noticed what was happening and finally gave me the coaching and feedback I needed that following summer. She played tennis with me regularly and coached me *while* we played, calling from her side of the court "NO, AMY!" as I was about to swing. Thanks to her, I was finally able to get my act together and dump some of my poor habits that summer. When I came back senior year, I had my best year yet, thanks to the individualized, observational, and consistent coaching I'd had. It took my friend's consistent coaching for me to really make the change.

When we're trying to replace an old habit with a new one, it's hard. It's incredibly common for people to fall back into old habits, retreat backward, and struggle to make forward progress. Without consistent coaching that acknowledges both effort and improvement, progress often is too daunting and doesn't happen. Because results often go backward before they move forward, it's easy for people to become extremely discouraged. In the beginning of making any kind of change, it's easier to go back to who you were before than try to become someone new. It's in these moments when people need us the most. Inconsistent coaches aren't there when people feel weak and are faltering. People with inconsistent coaches don't get the reassurance, recognition, and reinforcement they need to make it across the finish line.

3 REASONS CONSISTENT COACHING WORKS

1. Consistent coaches are more motivating than irregular coaches.

When we coach our people consistently, moments like mine from junior year in tennis don't happen. Folks can't (intentionally or accidentally) bring back old habits because the consistent coach won't let it happen. Just like my friend Patty calling me out *while* we were playing, as I was about to swing, consistent coaches are there to course correct while the game is going on. Folks who are taught by consistent coaches don't get the time to slip backward or say to themselves, "Forget this! This isn't working! I'm going back to my old ways!" because the coach is there to catch it quickly, before the next swing. When managers, leaders, or any kind of coach only correct and provide feedback *irregularly* (and often, *after* the game is over), backward regression and wavering can happen, and no real progress is made. Leaders who coach consistently show their people that they're watching and soon will come back, generating a lot of motivation to keep at the good habit—even during those tough times when it can be oh-so-tempting for the player to revert.

2.   *Consistent coaches are able to carry out the other parts of top-notch coaching more effectively.*

Consistent coaches are able to personalize and tailor the coaching to the individual more easily because they're present for every step forward or backward. They don't need to be general with their people because they know *exactly* where their people are at in the progress. When coaches follow the precise steps of coaching outlined here—they spend time with their people *individually*, *observe* behaviors in actual interactions, and do it *consistently*— then they know all the movements taking place at a micro level.

Let's look at an example with a sales coach. The coach knows when their employee has moved through the initial phase of an action plan around asking *more* questions of the client, to asking more *open-ended* questions of the client, to *responding* to difficult answers a client might give, to *handling the objections* a client might give in response to those responses. Because they're spending time and seeing things in the moment, the coach knows when their understudy has moved on from the plan around asking open-ended questions to asking better, more probing questions, to overcoming objections. They know these things because they're there to watch the tiny baby steps forward, like how a caretaker or parent can watch a baby progress from tummy time to crawling to standing to walking to running to running with scissors while talking to running with scissors while talking and stealing cookies out of the cookie jar.

These things don't happen overnight; they happen in steps. Adults can both progress forward and regress backward, and the consistent coach is there to course correct poor development before it becomes habitual, learned, and a dependency. My tennis swing took a year to undo and redo, and most of us can't afford to spend a year un-coaching a poor behavior, which is why consistent coaching works and is valuable to you and your people.

3. Consistent coaches lead by example.

When we coach people, we want them to develop good habits that we believe and even know will *work* for them, if applied consistently. We want people to do the "right things" consistently. Most of us agree that coaching our people is a "right thing." So, if we want our people to do right things consistently, why wouldn't we lead by example and do a right thing consistently? Making and keeping commitments and new habits is hard. Given all the conflicting priorities you have screaming for your attention, showing up and consistently coaching your people is hard. But when you do it, something happens: Our people get to see *us* in action. They learn the lesson that hard things *can* be done. After all, if we can do it, they can do it too, right? We show them what it looks like to act consistently, over time, and that makes it more likely they will develop those consistent habits too. As Stephen Covey has taught me, the three best ways to teach someone to do something are: Lead by example. Lead by example. And lead by example.

For many years, I led 15 large offices at financial institutions, overseeing roughly 250 employees. When I was on field visits, one of my routines was to peek into the branch coaching binders (because the best leaders not only had processes around coaching regularly but *how* they coached too). I'd ask managers to show me their coaching binder, a centralized place where everyone's coaching was kept. Most branches had individualized tabs for each person, and so it was easy to see that each employee of the branch was receiving weekly feedback.

One of the things I'd notice is that branches could be consistent for periods of time. Every employee would get coaching weekly for a period of weeks or months, until one day, the coaching would stop—never to be restarted. I never knew what had happened on that particular day or the subsequent days, but sometimes, it was like a shot was fired, changing everything in an instant. I'd want to find out *why*.

In the branches I visited most consistently, this rarely happened—probably because I, as *their* coach, was so consistent myself. But in branches I visited less often, this would happen. That taught me that habits are hard to keep, and without consistent coaching, it's easy to fall off. Once you've fallen off, it can be even harder to get back on, especially without external pressure (me).

I'd always ask the same question, "What happened this week?" so that we could trace our way back. Sometimes, we could pinpoint something, like the assistant manager had been on vacation, and the branch manager didn't make the time to run the whole branch by him or herself *and* do all the coaching. When the assistant manager returned, they spent extra time getting that person caught up, so it didn't happen that week either. By the third week, without my reinforcement and maybe because it's easier *not* to do something than it is to do it, and because new (bad) habits were already being formed, they just rolled with it. By week four, Presto! A new habit was locked in. In other scenarios, the reason why wasn't as easy to determine—maybe it was unexpectedly busy, or maybe it was raining. Who knows, but once it happened, it stuck.

Because coaching consistently is so hard, I wasn't always the most consistent coach. I've periodically cut corners on coaching or taken breaks myself, but every time I did this, I noticed my people cut corners and took breaks too. The more consistent I was, the more consistent my people were. Maybe they saw how much it mattered and set their watches by my inspection. Perhaps they learned better habits by following my lead. Perhaps it was because they received recognition as they made progress, and they were hungry for that reinforcement. Whatever the reason, your people will be more consistent if *you're* more consistent, and consistency *does* work, so don't shortchange your people on this. Be around enough to catch that magical drop-off day or week early enough that it's easy to get back on track, and you don't spend a half year with your folks restarting something that had been stopped.

SPECIFIC COACHING

Okay, so you're coaching your people on a one-on-one basis, you're observing them in action, and you're doing it consistently. The final component of great coaching is that it's specific. I've seen countless vague, unactionable action plans over the years. The piece I've most often seen overlooked is specific *action*, even though the definition of an "action plan" is that it ought to have ACTION.

The following are examples of unspecific action plans. These are literal quotes from action plans created by coaches working for me (until they were individually, consistently, and specifically coached by me to improve!).

SAMPLE ACTION PLAN STATEMENTS	MY FEEDBACK
Be more consistent.	More consistent with what?! How?
Ask better questions.	Define "better." What are examples?
Shadow Angela to learn how to do XYZ.	By when? For how long? How many times?
Make more outbound sales calls.	How many more? Per week? Per month?
Show more empathy.	How do we define empathy? What does that look like?
Participate more.	One time a meeting? Twice? Speak for how long? Share what?
Show improvement in ABC area.	You're kidding, right? Just "improve"?

Most of these, not just the last one, were enough to inspire my "You're kidding, right?" response. Even though I coached people consistently on these behaviors, the old habits of writing generic, unhelpful action plans with little action sometimes went down hard. The best acronym I've ever heard is the famous concept of SMART action plans, which means that action plans should be:[13]

- Specific
- Measurable
- Actionable or Achievable
- Relevant
- Timely

The lousy examples I've provided here are none of these things, but many action plans have *some* components of a SMART action plan but not all. If you're struggling to set goals for yourself or coach others effectively, know that action plans should answer the following questions:

- Who does what, how well, and by when?
- What does it look like?
- What does it sound like?
- How will we measure it?
- Will we know when it's completed/done? How?

During my years of field coaching, I would tell people that strong action plans should be written such that if both the branch and assistant manager went on vacation in Tahiti for two weeks and I came to run the branch for them—with no prior knowledge of what their tellers and bankers were working on—I could still come and effectively coach. I could pick up the last action plan, read it, then go observe—and know if the employee was successfully working on their action plan. There's no way I could do that with any of the sample plans above. If the plan is to be more consistent with demonstrating empathy but there's no examples of what the employee might *say* or might *do*, then I won't know how to assess performance because I won't know what was committed to, won't know what they were doing before, and won't know how unempathetic it was. I won't be able to answer the questions: "What does it sound like?" and "What does it look like?" We'd be left to go off my interpretation of what true empathy is, which could be different than what the coach and employee agreed that it was.

In the case of "Ask better questions," it's the same thing: I don't know what questions we've agreed to ask, and I don't know how ineffective the old questions were, so I won't know if things are "better." Without getting more specific, not only does the boss not know, but it's easy for the employee to not know too. We show the world and ourselves what's really important to us by writing those things down.

What gets measured gets done.

This quote has been said in numerous ways by numerous people, but it represents the most simplistic version of the third discipline of The 4 Disciplines of Execution, which is to "Keep a Compelling Scoreboard."[14]

As FranklinCovey notes: "People and teams play differently when they are keeping score, and the right kind of scoreboards motivate the players to win. People play differently when they are keeping score. If you doubt this, watch a group of teenagers playing basketball. See how the game changes the minute scorekeeping begins; it's not a subtle change."[15]

The first step to measuring something is to write it down. By writing it down, we take the first step toward committing to do it. We show the universe that we're serious. We show ourselves that we *intend* to do it.

"A dream written down with a date becomes a goal. A goal broken down into steps becomes a plan. A plan backed by action makes your dreams come true." – Greg S. Reid

Reid is right. When we write something down, put a "by when" date on it, and then break it down into specific, actionable steps, our imagined "end in mind" dreams come true, assuming we follow the plan.

We're all busy. Outside of work, many of us have families, children, and spouses. Many of us have nutrition and fitness commitments. We have hobbies and personal pursuits. We have friends. There are picnics, happy hours, basketball games, and fly-fishing. At work, numerous projects, deadlines, and meetings occupy our time. Professional development and learning to better your skill sets at work often take a back seat. It's easy to forget or shove aside what you loosely said you'd do this year to develop. But when we write down a specific plan of action, it becomes easier to remember what we said we would do, and it also becomes easier later to assess if we *did* it. It's us keeping a compelling scoreboard. What gets measured gets done.

When we write down *who* is going to do *what*, by *when*, and at *what* level of frequency, we start to assign boundaries. We truly set goals, describing exactly what it is that we want to see in the future world and in the future versions of *ourselves* and other people. We, the coach and those we are coaching, start to understand what success looks like and what's supposed to happen in the future. It then becomes obvious whether it's getting done.

When we spell out what something is supposed to look or sound like, we'll be able to answer questions like: "What should I be hearing if this is going well? What should be getting said?" and "What should I be seeing if this going well? What should be appearing before my eyes?"

To give this some clarity, below are the previous action plans reworded in a SMART format and answering the five questions I shared earlier.

SAMPLE ACTION PLAN STATEMENTS	REVISED VERSIONS
Be more consistent.	Be more consistent with standing up and shaking hands with members. Wear your name tag every day. Return from break and lunch on time instead of the usual 5 to 7 minutes late.

SAMPLE ACTION PLAN STATEMENTS	REVISED VERSIONS
Ask better questions.	Ask two open-ended financial questions in every interaction. Examples are: "Tell me about your financial goals" or "What are your top three payments each month?"
Shadow Angela to learn how to do XYZ.	Shadow Angela on Tuesday and Thursday from 9–11 A.M. Take notes on top three things she does well and work to implement those things in your own interactions. Also, bring those specific things to this week's coaching session to discuss why you chose them and how it's been going trying them yourself.
Make more outbound sales calls.	Instead of the 10 dials a day you've been making, make 25 dials a day. Protected time for these calls is between 4 and 5:30 each day. Remind Brandon each day to cover you, so you can make these calls with the door closed.
Show more empathy.	When a customer tells you anything negative, such as they've had a loss in their family or a health issue, say, "I'm so sorry to hear that. How are you doing now?" instead of just, "Oh, bummer."
Participate more.	In each morning huddle of 30 minutes, participate at least once. In our longer monthly sales meetings of 2 hours, contribute at least twice. Share your perspective, ideas, and thoughts on the discussion at hand.
Show improvement in ABC area.	Improvement can be specific behaviors, like the ones mentioned above, or can be results-bound. An example on results-bound: Achieve goal of XYZ unit amount or % increase by [date] versus current performance.

Using these plans, you can now see how possible it would for me, the coach of a coach, to walk into an environment and see if progress with an action plan is occurring. Armed with this action plan, I could go anywhere and coach anyone in a manager's absence because the coaching plan was so specific.

If success is happening and the action plan is being worked, I should see this employee shadowing Angela on Tuesdays and Thursdays from 9 to 11 with pen in hand. I should see this individual making outbound calls in their office with the door closed from 4 to 5:30, and Brandon should know about it. If I sat in and watched this employee wait on a customer, I should hear the two specific examples of open-ended questions or two similar ones in each interaction. During morning huddles, I should hear this person speak up. If those things aren't taking place, then the plan isn't working. I'd be able to coach the employee effectively.

All four components of coaching are hard; however, coaching works best when you do all four concurrently. Even if you do the first three steps, missing this last step of making sure feedback is specific is detrimental to your success and that of the person you're coaching.

You coach your employees individually, spending time alone with them. You can observe them and get a sense of what they're specifically struggling with. You can be there and speak with them and even practice with them consistently. But if you don't get specific in helping paint a picture of exactly what actions you want someone to take—what they should specifically say and do differently—then you will never experience breakthrough performance with them. Your employees might even know what the end result looks like— effortless conversations with customers, loyal clients who come back repeatedly, and great results—but they won't know how to get there or what it looks like on a day-by-day or minute-by-minute basis. Coaches of playoff teams don't just tell their players, "Throw the ball better" or "Score more touchdowns." They have predictable, strategic methodologies of how to get the ball back in their team's hands more often, how to take more shots, and how to communicate on the field more effectively. They talk about specific moves and motions and then run through them at practice again and again.

Have you ever been frustrated with your spouse for forgetting to do something or your friend for being late and making you wait *every* time you meet her? Maybe they say, "I know I need to get better at this!" Usually, just saying you'll get better at something doesn't work well because it's not specific. When someone is struggling with something, there's always a *reason* they're struggling with it. Specific action plans don't only address or describe the desired end results. Specific action plans address the root causes for *why* these things are occurring in the first place. They go deep, addressing the reason behind the bad behavior. The plan isn't so much around the results, but the behaviors—or rather, the actions (hence, *action plan*)—that will *lead* to those results. These action plans are focused on lead measures, not lag measures, because they *lead* to better results. They're also directly controllable by the person holding the action plan. They're predicable and influenceable.[16]

You'll notice in each of my revisions to the lame action plans, the focus was on the person's behavior and specific efforts they could take. In life, we can't always control end results. In fact, we *usually* can't control end results. But what we *can* control is our behavior. The person in this action plan can't control how much clients like her or how many sales she gets. But she *can* control how many calls she makes, how much time she spends with her top-performing peer, what questions she asks, or how well she demonstrates empathy by acting in ways widely accepted as being compassionate and caring. These things are specific, measurable, actionable, relevant, and time-bound. We know if she did them or not, to what degree, and we've set goals on when they're supposed to be done. They're controlled by the action plan owner, and if done consistently over time, they're likely to lead to her success.

When plans are written this way, they can be executed and coached to, and folks walk away with real direction over what to do. If you coach your folks but not this way and without checking in with them often on their progress, you're not likely to win.

PRACTICE 2:
SPEND FOCUSED TIME IN GROUPS

We've talked about how important it is to spend time with your people alone. Most managers tend to focus far less on that than the practice of spending time with their whole team together. *Both matter.* You can't do one and not the other. Both are critical to a team's success as well as the success of every individual member.

Why is it that managers tend to first "manage through email" then "manage through meeting"? Simple. It saves *time.* We all want more time, but we can't create more of it. We can't get it back when it's gone or buy another one. Because of that, it's a valuable commodity—perhaps the *most* valuable.

Saving time is attractive to leaders. Managers erroneously think that spending time in a group setting—where major initiatives and direction are shared and rolled down, updates and instructions are given, and group commitment is gained—can be a substitute for doing those things with people alone, independently. I hope, by now, you agree that spending time with people privately is essential. But thinking that solely spending time with your people alone will get you outstanding results doesn't work either. You need both.

Why? First, we, as human beings, are social animals. It's in our nature to crave interaction with other human beings. We seek this out naturally, even in childhood. Hyrum Smith, in his 1992 book *The 10 Natural Laws of Successful Time and Life Management*, describes these four major needs of humans:

- To feel loved, valued, and appreciated by others
- To feel important
- To make a difference
- To experience variety

Group settings help us achieve these needs. In a group setting, success doesn't all ride on the leader's shoulders because it's not only leaders who can help someone in the group feel valuable. *Any* member can. In Virtue 6, we'll explore how important reward and recognition is to humans. When we interact in a group setting, leaders can find opportunities to recognize and reward the whole group but also individual people in front of the group, which often matters to people. Also, group members can spread some of the recognition, especially if the leader creates an environment that supports that. You can even give away a segment of your meeting to the team to recognize one another for notable accomplishments and developments that day or week. When people know their actions matter, they try harder. When it's not just one person watching but the whole group, that not only adds motivation to the environment you're creating, but it also adds group accountability.

In Virtue 5, we'll explore how people on teams and in groups tend not just to learn from the leader, but from each other. Sometimes people will learn *more* from each other than the leader. When you allow time for group discussion and dialogue, people will learn from one another's questions and answers, and if the group feels safe enough and you create space for it, one another's mistakes, challenges, and failings. This is a beautiful thing, but your group will never feel close enough to you and one another (to do this) if they don't routinely get together. People want to test boundaries, seeing what flies and what doesn't. Sometimes, they're only willing to stick a toe in the water before placing a full foot in; they need time to build up their courage and believe that they're not going to get their hand slapped for saying or doing the wrong thing. This book expounds the value of group settings in many sections, but I can assure you, if you don't do it routinely, you'll never reap the rewards.

PRACTICE 3:
CREATE PRIVATE TIME TO STRATEGIZE AND PLAN

Notice that says, "Create"? That's intentional. Time is not found. It's made, and before we start on this practice, it's important that you understand that.

Every virtue and practice in this book requires time. Imagine how many of your problems you could solve with more time in the day. If you had an extra 10% more time than everyone else—2.4 extra hours a day, or 26.4 hours total compared to everyone else's 24 hours—imagine how much more successful you could be! You could apply those 2.4 hours to anything you want: creating your next masterpiece, running errands, seeing friends and family, or devoting more time to your health, diet, or exercise regimen. You'd be more organized, more innovative, more fit, more popular. Sounds pretty good, right?

Well, I'll let you in on a secret: You *can* find the time to do all these things in your life, no matter what that life looks like. Whether you have young kids at home, are going to school while working two jobs, or are caring for an aging loved one, you really can do it all. However, you *do* need to be focused on *how* you *choose* to spend your time. Making the right choices will be easier and work better if instead of waiting for the moment, you plan many of your choices.

Setting aside time before each week starts to PLAN it is not only helpful to your success as a leader, but it's also helpful to your success in life. The most successful people I know not only plan for their week, but they plan for their *day* in advance. They get up early and set their intentions for the day without fail. They do this religiously and don't deviate. They also have a plan for their *life*. These plans take many forms: a vision board of things they want to accomplish or have in the next year; a vision or mission statement for their life; a document that spells out what they want to accomplish over the next three to five years and their plans for *how* they will accomplish it. I've done every one of these things, and it's changed me. But this is more foundational: If you don't *make* the time to plan for your week, you won't be in control of and manage your time. Your time will control and manage *you*.

Many people who aren't experiencing success in life tell me, "I don't have time to plan and strategize." This is usually spoken by a person who doesn't *make* the time to plan and strategize. They complain they don't have the time for these things, yet it's the *act* of planning and strategizing that would afford them more time. These folks refuse to plan. Why? Because they have no time. And so, on the cycle goes, for months, years, or sometimes a lifetime. Don't be this person.

We all get the same 24 hours in a day, and if the proposition of having 26.4 hours (that extra 10%!) sounded intriguing to you, then get excited *immediately!* You don't have to wait for it anymore! No fairy or magical lamp required. You can reclaim control of your time, and your life, right now. But you have to establish a routine about planning your time, in advance, and stick to it *consistently*.

So, what am I asking you to do? I'm asking you to spend time every single week *by yourself* to just THINK, STRATEGIZE, and PLAN. Finding time to do this can be hard, and that's why this works best when you put it *on* your calendar somewhere. Create a routine of when, where, and how you'll do this.

I always do this on Monday mornings. I write out my weekly "wildly important goals" (WIGS),[17] both personally and professionally. Then, I share my WIGS with my accountability partners—others who are following the same process—so we can hold each other accountable. In the past, my direct reports and some of my clients have followed this routine and sent me their weekly WIGS. Anyone who shares their WIGS with me gets mine back in return. As I've done that routine, I've realized that it's not only *fair,* but it's insanely *helpful* to have other people know what your wildly important goals and tasks are for your week. They can help keep you on track. They're another person checking in to see if you're getting things done.

As part of this process, you decide, before the week starts, what and where you'll choose to spend your time. Stephen Covey talks about this process as putting "big rocks first,"[18] meaning that you schedule time to complete all the most important things—the big rocks—in your life that you want to make time for. Questions you need to ask yourself are:

- What are the most important things in my life right now?
- What are the things that if not completed, then nothing else matters?
- Where and when can I devote time toward those things—before I plan anything else?

- What things do I need to do *today* to have the life I want *tomorrow*?
- What things, if done consistently, starting now, would really make a difference in my future?
- What one to two things can I do this week to get me closer to my longer-term goals?

This process works with every aspect of your professional life. You know what the long-term goals are, right? Regardless of the industry you work in, it's quite common for leaders to have annual, quarterly, or monthly quotas, targets, or goals. Perhaps it's about becoming safer and reducing the number of mishaps or accidents. Or becoming more efficient and reducing costs. Maybe it's attracting more followers or clients. But whatever you do, if you have a metric you're wanting to improve, this process is for you.

"Working *on* the business is just as important as working *in* the business." – Russ McAtee

Perhaps you want to become a better leader and get better results. This month, you want to crush all your goals, have zero HR issues, and feel you've led a team of happy campers. You will do far better at achieving all that if you take time to strategize and figure out your best uses of time—in advance. When we consistently make an hour (or more!) a week to take ourselves *out* of the business to work *on* the business, we think differently. It is so easy to get lost in the hum of the day-to-day minutia that we don't notice certain things or think outside the box. Scheduled strategy time allows you to breathe deep and tap into parts of your brain you might not be using in your daily auto-pilot mode. It's a chance for you to be creative and innovative but also more observant as you think about what's going on in the world around you. The following things might dawn on you in your scheduled weekly strategy time:

- Betsy didn't say much in last week's project update meeting. You decide it's wildly important to ensure she's with you—she's the most experienced player you've got. You decide you want to schedule a one-off meeting with her to learn more about what she was thinking. If nothing else, she'll know how much you care about her individually and as a person.

- Morale feels lower than usual lately. You decide it's wildly important for your team to be fully engaged going into the final push of the big project. You decide to plan a recognition event to show your team some appreciation and love. It might be just what they need.
- It's been a while since you talked to any clients. You decide it's wildly important for them to hear from you so you can do some quality control. You decide you want to call your top 20 clients to see how they've been liking your team's service lately. You also might learn something.

Strategizing in your professional life, consistently and routinely, changes everything. But this process works for your entire *life* as well. Those of us who have balance in all areas of our life tend to be happier, more productive, and more successful, so I highly recommend figuring out what's most important at home too.

Perhaps it feels important to see your best friend and take him or her to dinner this week. Great, figure out when that's happening and get it on your calendar. You might need to email, call, or text this friend to determine time. I'd recommend doing that *after* strategy time. Too often, I've seen people start to strategize and never finish because they get overzealous about one of their WIGS and immediately start working on it.

Perhaps it feels important for you to lose weight and you've mentally committed to working out five days a week for that to happen. Awesome! Get it on your calendar. Plan which days you'll work out in the morning and which days you plan to exercise after work. Plan the details of the workouts too. Will you go to the gym to lift, or are you planning to run outside? Maybe you want to play tennis with a friend. Terrific—sending the text to the friend also goes onto your WIGS.

Perhaps it feels important to you to devote quality time toward your relationship. You want to have a date night with your significant other to have dinner or watch a movie. Great. Figure out what day that is and put *this* on your calendar too.

Perhaps it feels important for you to give back to the community. Or you're working on developing yourself through going to school, taking a class, reading a book, or heck, writing one! Get it on the calendar. Right now, it's a

Sunday afternoon, and David and I have plans to "hang out" this afternoon. However, one of my top personal goals this week was to write 10,000 words of this book. So, I'm writing right now because I made a *plan* to write now. I'm doing what I planned to do, and it feels good. Once I do what I planned to do, hanging out with David will feel even *more* rewarding because I'll feel that I earned it.

Life moves fast. As Stephen Covey notes in *The 7 Habits of Highly Effective People*, "What matters most in life is not what happens to us, but how we respond to whatever happens. Our basic nature is to act, not to wait to be acted upon." If you don't act, you will be acted *upon*. If you don't have a plan around what's most important to you, then other people's requests, demands, desires, and asks of you will run your whole week. If you want to become a famous author, get in the best shape of your life, travel more, or get that promotion at work, you've got to plan (in advance) what you'll need to do with your time to get/have/acquire/earn/produce those things. Things in life are typically *not* granted or gifted to us. We must chase after them by controlling and managing our own time well. Time management doesn't happen magically or accidentally. Those of us who seem to have it all together often planned to have it all together, by deciding in advance what was important to us and then by following through on those things.

The grass isn't greener on the other side of the fence.
It's greener where you water it.

For something to grow or flourish in your life, it needs care and attention. Figure out what your most important priorities are each week and plan for them. Great relationships everywhere—in the workplace and at home— require love and attention. Great results in *any* area of your life—your health and fitness, hobbies, development—also require time. These priorities should all have spots to live—on your actual calendar. Without *first* making time to determine what things are most important to you, and then ensuring those things have scheduled time slots, you simply will *not* make forward progress in anything you want, including your own development. Great achievements won't happen accidentally in life, at least, not repeatedly and consistently over the long haul. Luck can come and go, but true sustained performance belongs to those who act intentionally and deliberately. Strategy time ensures you are planning your future moves in advance.

TIPS TO HOLD YOURSELF ACCOUNTABLE AND ENSURE SUCCESS

You can improve the effectiveness of your strategy and planning time. If you adopt the following habits, they'll enhance this process and strengthen your chance of success.

TIP #1: ALWAYS HAVE A PEN AND PAPER IN HAND WHEN YOU DO THIS OR A KEYBOARD.

Writing things down manually—with pen and paper—help us absorb, remember, and retain them better. According to a 2018 *Forbes* article, we're somewhere between 20% and 40% more likely to achieve our goals when we write them down, and "study after study shows you will remember things better when you write them down."[19] When we do that, we're *involving* ourselves in the process of learning, so strategy, planning, and prioritization is best done with some kind of tool. So, whether it's on a Word document, on your calendar, or on a piece of paper, make a plan for your upcoming week's top priorities in *writing*.

Of the many reasons to have a routine around strategizing, planning, and prioritizing, one critical one is to hold yourself *accountable* for accomplishing the things that matter *most*. It's much harder to break a promise or a commitment to someone else if you put it in writing, right? That's why most deals no longer are made on a handshake. It's easier to flake on something you only verbally said you'd do. This includes promises or commitments that we make to *ourselves*.

As mentioned, our subconscious minds want to help us avoid pain and often prefer the path of least resistance: the *easy* way. Because our subconscious knows that committing to excellence and then pursuing it is hard, it sometimes wants to help us avoid that. Thus, it can be tempting to *not* put your commitments in writing. That way, if you later feel unable to execute on them, change your mind, or something else comes up, you don't feel so guilty for not following through. So, not writing things down prevents you from feeling pain if you're unsuccessful. Avoiding pain can make us feel good.

Do *not* fall into this trap. The act of writing something down makes it more real. It signals our brains and bodies that we're serious about it. Why *wouldn't* you be serious about your plan to be successful? Why wouldn't you be serious about what you need to do to make your dreams come true and achieve your goals? You absolutely *should* be serious about it! Not writing down your plans and commitments for success because you're afraid you might not do them is a recipe for disaster—it's almost a guaranteed way to fail.

"There is no reason to have a Plan B because it distracts from Plan A."
– Will Smith

Allowing yourself the "out," before you even get started, tells your mind that you were never that serious in the first place. It's a self-fulfilling prophecy. Telling yourself, *I might not be able to do this, and that's okay. If it doesn't work out, it's not that big of a deal*, makes it *far* more likely that it won't work out. Since you've already mentally prepared yourself for failure, you don't try as hard. You're not as confident. You don't proceed with gusto. You don't think of every single possible way to make the dream a reality. Some are afraid of the pain they'll feel if it doesn't work out. Others fear failure or looking stupid for trying unsuccessfully. There's no way you can think this way and concurrently apply yourself wholeheartedly. So, thinking this way makes you stay stuck.

Make time to reflect and understand yourself. Figure out what's most important to you. Then, plan to win and be successful. Don't leave it to chance. Writing down your goals on paper or electronically makes them more real and signals your mind that you are serious about achieving them.

A final note: Organizing your most important priorities and writing them down is *not* the same as making a To-Do list. If anything, to-do lists can sometimes disrupt actual productivity. Often, to-do lists are reactive lists of tasks that need to be completed but don't truly transport us closer to our most wildly important goals. There's a big difference between what you'll do in strategy time and making a to-do list.

TIP #2: GO BACK EACH DAY OR WEEK AND ASSESS HOW YOU DID THE PREVIOUS DAY OR WEEK.

One of the beautiful things about having your plans, priorities, and goals written down is that you can go back and score yourself. You can easily evaluate if you *did* what you had planned to do. You get to evaluate what worked for you and what didn't. From this comes much meaningful learning, allowing you to adapt for future days and weeks. Successful people constantly evaluate if their well-laid plans worked out. They don't run away from the process of finding out. They want to know if they are creating success or not. They don't have their identity tied up in how they look or if they experienced any success in one day or one week; rather, they recognize that success can be a gradual process. It is the result of consistent execution of the right behaviors and practices, day after day, week after week, month after month, year after year. Successful leaders want to *know* if they're deviating from their plan and then figure out ways to adapt, amend, or improve on the plan. They ask themselves questions such as:

- Was I successful this week in pursuing this strategy or these goals?
- If so, what made me successful, and how can I replicate those results again?
- If not, what stood in my way, and how can I overcome that obstacle next week?
- Am I happy with this week's outcomes? Am I satisfied with this week's results?
- Am I happy with my efforts this week? Am I satisfied with my behavior?
- If so, how can I keep this up?
- If not, what can I adapt, shift, or change next week to get more of what I want?
- Are there any pitfalls or blind spots holding me back that I don't readily see?
- If so, what am I doing about those?
- What factors am I *not* considering? What questions am I *not* asking myself?

Top-performing leaders and people aren't afraid of this process because they know that life is just that—a *process*. They don't expect to be an overnight success. Instead, they know that success comes with a lot of hard work, sweat, and persistence—in other words, consistent habits and routines.

Let's say that you have decided, as part of your strategic planning time, that you want to read two books a month. If you read for 45 minutes a day on weekdays, you'll be able to do this. So, you set a plan to read for 45 minutes each night before bed. As you're checking in with yourself each week, you notice that you're still not having success. Here's how your weekly check-ins might go and some hypothetical adaptations you might make:

- Learning from Week 1: I shouldn't plan to read at night, right before bed. I'm finding I'm too tired to do this. I will make an adjustment to read first thing in the morning when I get up.
- Learning from Week 2: I'm finding I don't really have time to read when I get up either. I will set the clock 45 minutes earlier going forward and start my day earlier to read.
- Learning from Week 3: I'm finding that I struggle to get up when I hear the clock go off at 6:15 instead of 7. I will go to bed an hour earlier at night, set a second alarm, and put that alarm across the bedroom so I have to get up and walk to turn it off.
- Learning from Week 4: OK, I'm getting up on time and making it to my desk to read, but I am finding that I immediately get distracted by incoming email and notifications on my phone, and my 45 minutes when I planned to read is vanishing on me. I will make a rule that says I cannot look at my phone or email until the reading is done.
- Learning from Week 5: I'm now reading my book each morning for 45 minutes but am starting to lose motivation. I'm finding that I really like setting up rewards systems for myself. I've asked my husband to take me to dinner to celebrate every time I finish a book, and he's agreed. Now, in addition to looking forward to finishing the book, I get to look forward to dinner to celebrate the finished book.

When you check in on your past written commitments and how strongly you adhered to your plans, you start to learn about yourself. You become more familiar with and aware of yourself. We're talking about "knowing thyself," which includes learning what makes you tick, what motivates and inspires you, what distracts and impedes you, where your soft spots are, what kind of things are most likely to throw you off track, and what things you can do to stay on track.

In the example, this person goes through multiple revelations about themselves over a six-week process. This person learns they have more energy in the mornings than in the evenings, they struggle to get out of bed, they can easily be distracted by emails and notifications, and they like to be rewarded after an accomplishment (especially before it becomes a habit).

Because this person was committed to success with their reading goal and had written down a specific commitment, they didn't stop at the first sign of struggle. Instead, they took the meaningful learning about themselves and their tendencies, adapted the plan over time, and stuck with the process until they found a system that worked.

Without having a goal written down on paper, routines to assess how things were going, and adapted plans to experiment with possible solutions, this person would have likely fallen off course a few times and perhaps given up entirely. You've probably met (or at some point in your life, *been*) a person who says out loud or thinks, "Gosh, I would really like to do X someday!" but someday never comes. Usually, when people aren't achieving their stated goals, they aren't going through this process:

- Making strategy time to truly assess what they want out of life and making a plan to get it
- Choosing actionable behaviors and putting those actions on their calendar each week
- Writing the commitments and promises they want to keep down on paper (or somewhere)
- Holding themselves accountable by going back and checking in to see how they did
- Making adjustments to the future plan based on learnings they've had previously

Change this one thing, and you'll change everything. Follow this process on a weekly basis, and within a month, you'll notice improvements in your life. As with everything, this must be a routine. These are daily and weekly disciplines, and they must be practiced as such for them to have the desired (and proven) effects.

TIP #3: EXPECT IT TO BE HARD.

Doing these things is hard. You must make commitments around your actions and behaviors, and those commitments are often in conflict with doing what's easy, natural, or comfortable.

"A goal is a planned conflict with the status quo." – Hyrum Smith

It is far easier to sit around on the couch, drink beer, watch television, and scroll through social media on your phone than do the things I've described. Doing these things will feel (and be) *hard*. Do these things anyway. Life is hard, but you can do hard things. Doing hard things leads to a better, easier life in the long run. If you *expect* these things to be hard in advance, then you'll be able to stick with them longer, have more success, and over time, they won't *feel* as hard.

"If you do what is easy, your life will be hard. If you do what is hard, your life will be easy." – Les Brown

When we prepare our brains for what's coming next, we are better equipped to handle it. This probably has to do with our love for predictability and patterns. Our brains tend to like structure and routine, so it can be hard to handle unexpected events or surprises. If you tell yourself that what you're about to do is going to be hard—and then it *is*—it's easier to handle than when you tell yourself what you're about to do is going to be easy—and then it's *not*. Anytime you're changing a routine and forming a new habit in your life, it's *going* to be hard. You're starting a new process, from scratch, which will feel unfamiliar and awkward to you. But you have a choice. You can choose to tell yourself it's normal to feel this way and it's okay that it's hard. You can even decide that doing hard things makes you a better person, or you set a goal around doing hard things. If you do this, you will be able to "embrace the suck" with more gusto, energy, and vigor than if you expected it to be simple and then got caught off guard when it wasn't.

Making time to strategize and plan your week and days will be hard. At times, especially early on, you likely won't see any rewards from doing it. The big rewards from staying true to this process tend to come over *time*. Staying committed to the process and choosing to believe in it, before you've stuck with it long enough to prove to yourself that it works, is hard. But if you expect it to be hard and plan for that, you'll be more prepared when the difficult moments come. You'll get to say to yourself, "Oh yeah. I totally knew this was coming. I prepared for this. I've got this. I can do this." You'll also be more likely to stay the course.

TIP #4: FORGIVE YOURSELF WHEN YOU SCREW UP (AND KNOW YOU WILL).

No matter how good you are or how long you've been doing the process of setting specific weekly goals, checking in with yourself, assessing yourself, and adjusting for the future week, you are going to have moments when you screw up. Perhaps you'll have a week where you don't feel like staying on track and you accept a friend's invitation for a happy hour instead of going to the gym like you planned. Perhaps you'll let the pressing, more urgent needs of others get in the way of your wildly important goals at work. Perhaps you'll realize that you misjudged how much time something was going to take, and even though you do your best all week, you still fall short at finishing a project because it's more complicated than you originally realized.

Forgive yourself. Love yourself. Be kind and patient with yourself. These things happen to all of us. You won't do yourself any favors by being overly harsh and critical of yourself. Recognize that progress and success is not the shape of a straight line but rather a weaving, windy one with peaks and valleys. Not every day can be amazing, and the most important thing you can do when you fail to meet your own expectations is allow yourself some grace, dust yourself off, acknowledge the progress or improvement you have made, and then recommit once again. Dwelling on the mistakes of your previous week is a surefire way to become highly disengaged in this process.

"Never miss twice." – James Clear

In his 2018 book, *Atomic Habits*, James Clear explains that the most successful individuals at creating new habits and routines aren't necessarily any more disciplined. They don't fall off track any less. However, when they do, they are better at getting back on track faster. His rule of "never miss twice"[20] is a great call to action for what we can do when we've made a mistake. Let's say you had a bad day. Work hard to not let it happen again. If you didn't meet the previous day's commitments, resolve to do better the next day. This advice has been especially helpful for me in relation to my fitness and health journey. When I'm about to become discouraged or frustrated that I missed a workout or a day of eating right, I make a point of not missing it two days in a row. I vow to have a better next day, and often do.

Let's review. Consistent strategy and planning time is a necessary routine. You use that time to determine what behaviors and actions are likely to have dramatic effects on your desired outcomes and results. You can't possibly keep it all straight in your head, so you've got a pen in hand. The next step is to check in on your progress. Don't be disappointed or disgusted by yourself if you fail at delivering on your plans, even if you fail more than once or repeatedly. We don't write things down and go back to evaluate ourselves to feel guilt when we weren't successful. We do this to evaluate what's really happening to us, and around us, to learn from our mistakes. Then, we can use this learning to make different decisions in the future.

THE QUESTIONS YOU MUST ASK TO LEAD OTHERS WELL

You might be wondering what this has to do with leading others. You might be thinking, *Alright, I get that planning my time in advance can be helpful for organizing my life. How does that help me run a better team or group? How does that help me* lead *other people better?* That's a fair question.

This process is all about deciding where in your life you want to spend your time and effort and why. It's about determining where investments of your time will have the highest return on investment. This process is just as important for you professionally as it is personally. One of the most important components of strategy and planning time is that you ask yourself questions— not just *any* questions, but the *right* questions. To ensure you're really focused on the correct "big rocks" professionally, you might ask yourself questions like these:

- What's one way I could push myself to grow, evolve, or learn something new this week at work?
- Where does my team really need me the most?
- What has my team been struggling with lately? How can I help them with that?
- What has my team been doing extremely well lately? How can I recognize them for that?
- Who on my team could really use some of my love and support this week?
- What bottom performer on my team could I help this week? How would I do it?

- What top performer on my team could I help this week? How would I do it?
- Where can I get some "bang for my buck" this week?
- Who is one person I could send a short, simple email to and it might change their week?
- Who is one person I can build a better relationship with this week, and how can I do it?
- What's one meeting I need to have this week that could dramatically shift or alter my business?
- What's one crucial conversation I need to have this week?
- How can I build more interdependence at work this week?
- What's one activity I could do this week that could lift performance in a big way?
- What use of my time this week at work is likely to make the greatest impact on our performance?
- Do my desired results and outcomes match the actual ones I'm having?
- If not, what is one thing I can do about that, starting today?

These are sample questions you might ask yourself when planning for how to use your time at work. There are many more. If you're entrusted with the gift of leading or influencing others, then they're the kind of questions you ought to be asking every week. They boil down to a few themes:

1. How you can learn new skills, upgrade your own talents, and grow even stronger
2. How you can build better relationships with those around you
3. How you can deliver better results by helping *others* deliver better results

These themes are listed in this order intentionally, as explained next.

ALWAYS START WITH YOURSELF.

First, one of the most forgotten activities of many leaders is to start with themselves and upgrade their *own* talents. Remember the concept of lowest common denominators (LCDs) in math?[21] Quite frankly, most leaders are the LCD of their teams. Often, teams can only grow and evolve to the point of the leader. In a scientific chemical reaction, we might call this the "limiting reagent." Generally, when this happens, strong individuals leave their leader. A past boss of mine, Johnny Montes, often used to say:

"A talent will never work for C talent. At least, not for very long."

Johnny was right. The most common reason why is that A talent knows it can do better, and because A talent players are proactive, look for learning opportunities, and constantly want to upskill themselves and their contributions, they'll quickly recognize that there's little (or nothing) their boss is teaching them that they can't find elsewhere or on their own. They'll also recognize that their growth will be stunted if they stay. So, they move on. Over time, C talent leaders tend to only be able to recruit and keep C talent players, which, of course, doesn't lead to breakthrough results.

In today's ever-evolving business culture, you absolutely *must* help others become stronger. To do this, *you* need to become stronger. You need to upgrade your own skills, knowledge, and talent so you can help others. You can't pour from an empty cup, so it's critical that you do some of the following:

- Invite your employees to read books to help with their development and growth.
- Ask your employees to research their own strategy ideas and thoughts.
- Invite your team to invest in their own passions, pursuits, and dreams.
- Ask your team to find new sources of information and question their previously held beliefs.

You must do all of these as well. It's important that some of the questions you ask yourself in your weekly strategy and planning sessions have to do with this topic of becoming stronger yourself. By the way, I'll add that exceptional leaders are not the LCDs of their teams—they intentionally help others around them get better, stronger, more capable, and powerful, and that's because they follow all the V.I.R.T.U.E.S. in this book.

RELATIONSHIPS MATTER.

You may notice that several of the questions listed have to do with relationships. This shouldn't be a surprise because, as a leader, you constantly cultivate and develop relationships. Without strong relationships with your team, you can't effectively lead them. But I want to make a few points here.

First, you'll notice the relationship questions didn't *only* focus on your own internal team. It was relationships with *others* too: your peers, your boss, maybe colleagues or vendors in your industry. As a leader, communication with *everyone* is key, and making time to meet with people who have ideas and thoughts dissimilar to your ideas and thoughts is *critical*. How else can you learn all you need to know to get better and stronger in your field and help others do the same? It's important to talk to all the right people, meet with the right people, and spend time with the right people for you to win and be successful.

Second, within the questions that focused on your own team, you'll notice that some questions focused on *all* types of performers: folks who are doing well, folks who are not, and folks in between. It's a common practice in leadership to focus most on your bottom performers. We do this with so many things in life. We think, *What's holding me back? What's getting in the way? Okay, I need to go address that.* We do this so naturally and subconsciously that we sometimes forget to focus on what's going *well* and how to keep those balls afloat or moving through the air with style and grace. Remember bringing home your report card in school? If your family was like mine, your parents did one thing before anything else: they scanned the report card for the *lowest* grade and always asked the same question: "What happened here?" They'd immediately be trying to put a plan together for how to remove or tidy up any of the blemishes or ugly spots on that report card.

Bosses everywhere commonly do the same thing. "What parts of our scoreboard or metrics aren't going well? Where are we failing? Where's the red? What's holding us back? Who are the outliers? What's the plan here?" These are usually the first questions asked in someone's weekly or monthly coaching or business line review. When we spend focused time planning on how to solve for these things and answering these questions, we sometimes forget to make time to celebrate or acknowledge what *is* going well. When we forget to do this for too long, it *stops* going well. We can't solely focus on the parts of our business that are struggling or in disrepair.

Think of the most athletic or buff person you know. Have a picture of them in your head? Great. Now, think about what their daily life looks like. Chances are they *do* something to *earn* that body. They go to the gym, they lift, they eat well, they exercise. It's likely they spend a lot of focus, love, attention, and energy on it. All of it takes *time*. That's how they're getting some of their results. I don't care how endowed they were at birth or how "lucky" they got—if they're truly at the top of their game, I can assure you they're devoting some level of effort to keep it there.

Now, imagine if they *stopped* doing those things, ceasing their nutrition and exercise routines. What would happen? Well, probably nothing—at first. You might not notice any real difference in them within the first week, but what about in a month? You probably would. Within a year? You definitely would. It doesn't matter if it's Arnold Schwarzenegger we're talking about. Consider the following excerpt from a summary article by Tim Denning about Arnold's book, *Total Recall*:

> **Arnold worked out five hours a day, six days a week. Most of us train 45 mins (sic), and we're exhausted. All at the same time he was working on his mail order business, on his acting classes, going to college, training for three hours a day and doing construction.**[22]

Thirty hours a week, or 1,560 hours a year, is a *lot* of time training. Arnold is pretty spectacular, but he *is* so spectacular because he worked to *make* himself that way. He lived by Virtue 3 and established a dedicated regimen of routines. He put together a plan of what he wanted his life to look like—and followed it. It worked, and the results came, but only because he invested the time in the right places.

Good things don't just "stay good." Most people who have been married and then divorced will share that they had high hopes for their success on their wedding day. Most people didn't stand at the alter with a plan to fail. Most people believed that things would continue to be as joyous once they were married as they had been during the courtship. The reality is that most things tend to move toward a state of decline *unless* we exert effort and action upon them. All of it is hard work, so it's not surprising that many marriages end. If we don't show the people who are important to us that we love and appreciate them, they don't tend to work as well for us as they did when they were new to us. It's the same with inanimate objects. Think about the cleanliness of your house. Or the state of your car. Or the food in your refrigerator. Houses collect dust, cars collect rust, and food collects mold unless we care for these things properly and give them time and attention.

This is also the case with top performers. You can only depend on that rockstar employee who's coming through at 200% of goal for so long. For them to keep delivering results, you have to spend time with them and give them the same personalized coaching you give your bottom or midrange performers. Your spouse will stay with you only so long if you don't invest quality time with them too—supporting and championing their dreams, encouraging their pursuits, listening to them, and helping them create time for their wildly important goals and hobbies. People change over time; they have new experiences that alter and shape their beliefs, and if we don't continually invest in the people who matter most to us, then they'll change in ways we don't understand. No one likes feeling misunderstood. So, not only is it important to spend time with people who are struggling, it's important to spend time with people who are *not* struggling to ensure that they don't *start* struggling.

Finally, almost anything in life can be improved. That top performer you're depending on to carry the bottom of the team? Even if that person *doesn't* go into a state of decline because you're not helping them grow and develop, you miss the opportunity to help them get even stronger and better. We sometimes look at people who are great at something and forget that even they, too, can get better.

I learned this lesson the hard way. In my early years as a regional manager at the bank, I made all these mistakes. While my overall team's performance was often strong, I'd focus my energy and effort on folks who weren't doing the same for me—*they* weren't putting in the energy and effort. Because I was too timid to have the right kind of crucial conversations with them, their performance would perpetually fluctuate, up and down. I would go back to their branches and spend repeated time with them, in sort of a dance routine where they would improve *only* long enough to get themselves off corrective action and get me off their case, only to return a month later to their prior state of being. The most consistent managers I had working for me, at the top, were visited far less frequently, and I leveraged their performance to round out my numbers for the whole region. It wasn't fair, and while they did earn the well-deserved rewards of high performance review scores, the best annual increases, and the best bonuses, what they missed out on was development from me. Perhaps my lack of focus on helping them become even bigger superstars prevented some of them from their own regional manager roles. It took me a while to figure out that everyone needs love, even people who are already doing well, so that they can keep doing well and do even better so they can aspire to something more.

If you're not interested in that, then you are using your people. You're not taking seriously the commitment that you *should* have made when you stepped into leadership. Again, we should go into leadership because we want to help people—not just *some* people, but *all* people. If anyone deserves your development, feedback, and coaching, it's the people working the hardest and getting the best results. So, don't leave them out of your weekly plan. Don't strategize where to put your time and forget the golden goose. The other V.I.R.T.U.E.S. in this book will assist you on your way. As you plan and strategize your week to ensure you're doing what really matters most, you might recognize that you're ignoring your top folks. You might then realize it's because you're spending too much time with bottom performers. If you've followed consistent routines around communicating your vision, involving them, coaching them, developing them, and spending time with them in group settings, then it's probably time to toughen your conversations with them and prepare to cut them loose.

RESULTS MATTER.

Finally, you'll notice that the third theme of questions was about results. Why? Because in leadership, and with anything in life, results *matter*. So many folks confuse behaviors with results. You have to find time to match up your behaviors, efforts, activities, and actions with the desired and actual results you're getting and ask yourself if you're satisfied. If you're not satisfied, then it's time to figure out what to change.

PRACTICE 4:
MAKE AND KEEP COMMITMENTS

In early 2011, I started a new job at a major commercial bank. It was the first time someone had given me a shot at regional leadership, and I was excited to learn as much as I possibly could but also transmit any of the learning I'd already had to others. During my first several weeks, I was teamed up with a peer in a neighboring region named Randy Wang. Our boss asked him to mentor, coach, and guide me through some of his best practices as I was figuring out the ropes.

For the first few weeks, Randy spent time with me almost every day, helping me learn to use our systems, look through reports I'd need to pull, and understand our company culture and the various routines, scheduled calls, and meetings we had. By the end of my first month, I was off on my own. I did my own branch visits and ran my region. As we made this transition, Randy suggested that we put a weekly one-on-one on our calendars so we could touch base with each other, and he could answer any questions I had.

I still remember being caught off guard when he called me for our first scheduled appointment. Wanting so badly to perform and do well, but already swimming in a sea of reports, deadlines, and deliverables, I had completely forgotten about our scheduled 1 P.M. call. I hadn't been paying attention to the few appointments and meetings I had on my calendar. When Randy called, I wasn't sure why and asked him what was going on. I'll never forget his response:

> "Well, I'm just keeping this commitment we had made to each other to check in on your progress. Your success is important to me, and so I wanted to make sure we kept this routine so I can help you."

It was one of the first times in my career that a peer had held me accountable. I had become accustomed to bosses holding me accountable. Perhaps I had also created a few good habits to hold myself accountable. I always wanted to excel at the things I was doing, and at work, I knew my team and our clients were depending on us. Often, I kept the promises I made and did the things I said I would do. But I wasn't as used to doing this with peers.

For Randy, it was simple. Randy had essentially said: "I made a commitment to you, and to myself, to be here today at this time. Speaking with you right now is what's on my calendar. We didn't cancel it, so I intend to have this call because I said I would."

Randy also had shared with me that *my* success mattered to *him*. He had been tasked by his boss to help me. As I got to know Randy much better over the coming years, I learned he didn't have to be tasked with helping a peer to help a peer. It was in Randy's nature to help his peers, and Randy cared about the success of everyone around him. I also learned that Randy lived by routines, and scheduling strategy and planning time was one of them. In that time, Randy thought a lot about who he wanted to be, as both a person and a leader, and then would schedule time to *do* the things he thought would help him with that. Helping grow and develop peers into the outstanding regional leader that he was, was a huge passion and goal of his, so his call that day wasn't entirely about *me*. It was also about him. It was him being the person he wanted to be in business and in life: organized, disciplined, and a man of his word.

I never forgot that call. In the moment, I was ashamed and somewhat embarrassed that I hadn't taken that calendar appointment seriously. I had seen it on the calendar but hadn't had faith or trust that it would occur. When Randy called me, right on time, prepared to talk about my week and its obstacles, my learnings from those challenges, and my successes, I wasn't ready. I knew I had failed him. Fortunately, Randy forgave me, and I vowed to never let that happen again. After that incident, we continued a routine of checking-in for years after that. Long after we were required to—and probably long after we needed to—we continued to talk on a schedule. At some point, we moved our routine from weekly to monthly. The biggest thing I learned from Randy is that if you say you're going to do something, you sure as heck better do it.

Randy's never-ending commitment to his word led him to a lot of success. Because Randy would make commitments *often*—to himself and to others—and then *keep* those commitments, he developed a reputation for being highly dependable and credible. Everyone knew it, including the senior executives. When big projects came into play, Randy was repeatedly asked to work on them. When it came to his ability to lead others, Randy was just as consistent. If he said he was going to visit a branch for the day, swing by a huddle, or go to a community service event, he'd put those commitments immediately onto his calendar *as* he was making them. Then, Randy would follow his calendar every single day. He was always where he said he would be, becoming predictable because of that.

The many leaders and managers who worked for Randy over the years also benefited from this. When people consistently keep their word and do what they say they'll do, they show us that they value us, our time, and the relationship. We like to be valued and appreciated by other people. It goes back to our four basic needs as outlined by Hyrum Smith. When people repeatedly make time for us, it shows us that they care about us and love us. We want to return that feeling and do better for them too. Because Randy always came through for people exactly in the ways he promised, his team all felt valued and loved by him. They wanted to deliver results for him. They didn't want to let him down. Randy had low turnover in his region because of the loyalty people felt toward him. Randy's folks were also highly successful. Randy led by example and showcased for them what it looks like to set expectations and keep commitments. I noticed that his team followed in his footsteps. They kept commitments. They consistently delivered results. Their region was always a top-performing one. This meant fewer corrective actions or write-ups, little discipline, more bonuses and incentive money, and lots of time left over for reward and recognition. Randy's team was well coached and involved in much of the decision-making and communication. It was a great work environment, and everyone knew it. Doing what you say, keeping commitments, and delivering results was part of that region's culture, and the more everyone executed on these things, the more fun it became to be part of that team. I still admire and respect my peer and friend, Randy.

In today's world of constantly competing priorities, many of us feel exhausted, stressed, overwhelmed, or even depressed. Many of us don't get enough sleep, don't eat healthy enough, don't relax, don't spend time pursuing our passions and hobbies, and because of that, we lack a sense of joy and fulfillment. As a result, we have lower energy than we should. When we feel drained, it's easier to break our commitments.

Great leaders don't do this. If they've committed to doing something, being somewhere, or spending time on something, they adhere to it. They simply have the courage and confidence to say, "Gosh, I'd *love* to do what you're proposing, but I've already made a commitment to be somewhere at that time." or "I'm already scheduled to do something that's wildly important at that time. Do you have another day or time when that works for you?" Like the other practices I've shared with you, this can be hard. But if you show up for the things you said you'd show up for, people will learn that you're good for your word and will trust you. With that trust comes better relationships with your team as well as better results overall.

Great leaders keep commitments for several reasons:

1. They have routines around strategizing what's most important in *both* their personal and work lives and live by those. They schedule personal time at home for the things that help them renew energy, relax, and recharge. So, they're less likely to feel drained in the first place.

2. They know that many times, in business and in life, the key to success is doing a certain number of things you don't really want to do so you can have what others can't have. As Stephen Covey has taught us, they recognize that saying NO is easier when you have a greater YES in mind.

3. They recognize how important keeping commitments is and the consequences of not, so no matter the pain of keeping a commitment, they'll dig in and do it anyway.

4. They've already reaped the rewards and seen the spoils of keeping commitments—even when it's hard—and know the value it brings. They remember those case studies and use that data to find the strength to persist.

When you set expectations with people about what's going to happen, and you prove to them that you always live up to those expectations, you get more action out of *other* people too—a beautiful thing.

When Randy called me for our first scheduled appointment, he was prepared and I wasn't. This was because I hadn't yet learned the routine around keeping commitments, even when you're not being "watched," and so I didn't expect Randy to follow through. When I quickly learned that Randy always follows through on what he says he'll do, I got much better at preparing for our calls and meetings because I knew they were going to happen. The more I practiced keeping my commitments, the more I noticed others around me would keep *theirs* too. As I became someone who stopped by offices to observe things when I said I would, people who reported to me knew to expect it. They'd have forms ready for me to see and debrief, reports pulled for us to review, or a coaching session scheduled and ready for me to watch. Whatever we had agreed on would be done. Because I had showed them, over time, that I always delivered on my commitments, they knew they had to as well.

It gets awkward and uncomfortable quickly when two people are scheduled to meet regularly but only one person routinely keeps the commitment. Unless there's a flagrant lack of respect for you or the individual is incompetent and doesn't have the skills to complete the task (and the courage to say so), this kind of lopsided arrangement doesn't happen often. Broken commitments shouldn't be tolerated. I remember an instance where one of my direct reports attempted to test me on this a few times. When I arrived at his branch for a second visit in a row and the agreed-upon deliverables we had planned to review and inspect together had not been prepared for me, I simply left the branch and refused to do the visit. I stated that if that happened again, I would apply written consequences. Then, I walked out. It never happened again.

VIRTUE 4:
Talk Terrifically

"The single biggest problem in communication
is the illusion that it has taken place."
– Attributed to George Bernard Shaw

ant to be an exceptional leader? Then be an exceptional communicator. When I started the outline for this book, the first thing I wrote in my notes under this section on "TALK" was, "You have to be exceptional here. Ordinary will not cut it."

If you haven't viewed yourself as a terrific communicator, don't panic. I have good news for you. *Anyone* can learn to communicate well. Communication isn't about delivering electrifying speeches in front of large crowds that always inspire standing ovations. We've probably all heard a message or a speech where we've thought, *Gosh, that sounds great! I should do something about that!*, but afterward, forgot all about it. This isn't effective. Truly effective communication inspires others to *act*. If you want to be a great leader, it's imperative that people not only *hear* your message, but *do* something with your message. Thus, effective communication has as much to do with the receiver of the message (the audience) as it does with the sender of the message (the speaker). Ensuring people are inspired to take action or change has less to do with how charismatic *you* are and more to do with how engaged *they* are. As long as you're willing to challenge yourself a bit and adopt the following practices and behaviors, you'll find your effectiveness as a communicator expands greatly.

PRACTICE 1:
BECOME AN EXPERT QUESTION ASKER

Strong leadership is noticeably absent in many companies around the world, and sadly, because of that, strong leadership *training* is also noticeably absent. Far too few companies study the art of leadership and then train other leaders well. In many companies, top performers are often promoted into leadership from staff level or individual contributor roles. These kinds of promotions—where strongly performing individual contributors skilled at *doing* the work are promoted repeatedly until they are supervising, managing, or leading *others* who are *doing* the work—can be disastrous and are some of the most common "Peter Principle" failures I've seen. The "Peter Principle," explored in Peter and Raymond Hull's book of the same name, is where members of a hierarchy are promoted until they "reach a level of incompetence: employees are promoted based on their success in previous jobs until they reach a level at which they are no longer competent, as skills in one job do not necessarily translate to another."[23]

Many companies don't study, observe, teach, train, coach, and then discuss leadership constantly. At companies like these, a terrific senior engineer might get promoted because they've done well—*so far.* Eventually, that promotion will be to management—the charge of leading other people. As great as this senior engineer might be at engineering, that doesn't necessarily mean they have any skills at leading others to be great senior engineers, let alone be a cultural fit for the organization, which might include anything from "team player and collaborative" to "an innovative visionary" or "self-directed, transparent, and accountable." However, so many companies do this and view it as a no-brainer because they assume the following: Who better to teach someone to do their job well than someone else who does *that* job well? Therefore, star performers get promoted to develop and cultivate other star performers even though they might have zero training in how to develop and cultivate others.

This is where many of our world's leadership problems arise. People who are put into leadership roles under these circumstances are under the impression that leadership is about having been highly skilled at a certain job (and having tremendous knowledge) that other people need. They conclude that it is *their* job to dispense the knowledge they've gained through their experience and intellect onto others until others are as great as them. They think that's their primary responsibility. Because of that conclusion, and with no formalized leadership training, they tend to follow the way of the boss that came before them. In companies with no real understanding around what makes great leadership, the examples that came before them aren't very good either.

Many of these "leaders" view themselves as the answer giver. They spend their days calling meetings to explain things, answer questions, direct, and instruct. Typically, they do most of the talking in meetings while their understudies take notes. They give updates from the "important" meetings they've gone to. They relay information about things happening at levels above their group. They shed light on things that are coming down the pike. They ask questions only about the work being done. They ask for status updates on key projects, about how things are progressing, and when XYZ project might be completed. They also *give* status updates on important projects they are working on. If there's a problem that someone shares with them, they offer up a solution, which of course, they feel equipped to do because they are hearing about the same problems they faced when *they* were in that role. They set deadlines, and every now and then, they offer up a "Good job, team." They keep things together.

Our world is full of these kinds of low-level managers. In many organizations, where people haven't had the benefit of working for a truly outstanding leader, it's almost unnoticeable. Assuming these kinds of managers have decent personalities and are reasonably likeable, it's possible that years or even decades can go by with few people (if anyone) even noticing that their "leader" is incompetent at the actual role of leadership. Because what I just described is an incompetent leader. I know because I've worked for them and also used to be one.

Don't get me wrong. The previous description is one of a competent staff-level employee or individual contributor. As the Peter Principle suggests, people are *not* promoted because they were incompetent. These people who were promoted into leadership (but haven't the foggiest clue how to truly lead) were often *highly competent* in their previous roles. They often *do* have much of the knowledge and many of the answers that their staff needs to be successful. It's understandable why so many of these leaders naturally conclude, as did the leaders that came before them, that they should disperse and dispense knowledge onto others. *That's what they're in leadership to do, right? Teach?*

No. The best leaders in the world don't just *teach* things to others. They help *guide* others to learn things on their own. They promote self-discovery. They promote an environment and culture where those under them can embark on their own journey of learning. They unleash talent in others. That's a big difference.

"Give a man a fish and you feed him for a day. Teach him how to fish and you feed him for a lifetime." –Attributed to Lao Tzu

Leadership is about teaching other people how to fend for themselves, how to be more resourceful, how to find their own answers, how to push through pain, how to solve their own problems, and how to develop the mindsets and beliefs that help them endure. Sure, leaders can give people the answers to simple questions, but leaders who do this create a dependency of their people on them. They teach people: "Come ask me about this one problem you're having. And I'll tell you what to do about it. Then, you can go back and fix the one problem. When you have your next problem, you can come to me, and we'll do the same exact thing again."[24]

These kinds of leaders never create any real bandwidth for themselves because they don't develop their people. They don't cultivate and grow a team that possesses ever-expanding decision-making abilities, critical thinking skills, judgment and reasoning skills, knowledge, resourcefulness, and experiences of their own. They keep their team stagnant and dependent on them, as the leader, to provide all the answers. They give their people the fish but don't teach them *how* to fish. They *answer* questions instead of *asking* the questions, so their people remain stuck and dependent. Sadly, for the leader, this means they'll never be able to multiply their own time. They'll never be able to do the many activities and behaviors that are addressed in this book because they will always be busy delivering messages to their teams and communicating to them—in totally ineffective ways—because they haven't taught their teams how to think for themselves.

We've already talked about how planning and strategizing your time is critical. We've also talked about how much more time exceptional leaders have than their mediocre counterparts. How you talk and communicate with others is one of the most make-or-break V.I.R.T.U.E.S. of being a great leader because of what it frees you up to do in *other* areas.

The biggest way around this is to stop answering questions. Instead, great leaders *ask* the questions. Instead of thinking of themselves as the person who should solve their team's problems, they should recognize that they are there to talk *through* their team's problems *with* them and then often allow their team to make their own decisions.

If you lead other people, then it's likely that sometime today or tomorrow, someone is going to come to you with a question or a problem that needs solving. Often, these questions sound like this: "What do you think I should do about X?" If you immediately want to be a better leader, then you can start answering that kind of question by saying something like:

- Wow, that's a great question. What do *you* think you should do about that?
- What have you already done so far?

- What steps have you taken?
- What were you thinking about doing next?
- What are some of the possible outcomes you've considered so far?
- Who do you think could help you with that?
- If you were me, and you got to make the final decision, what would you say?

Remember Trish from the "Anyone Can Play" section? Remember how good she was at involving others? This is exactly what she did. This is a simple shift in your leadership that you can start today that will change everything for you.

If you haven't been responding to questions this way, I want to provide you with a warning. The first time you switch your routine from answering people's questions to doing this, you'll feel like you're pulling teeth (in the beginning). Your employees or team might look at you as if you have four heads. Anytime you practice a brand-new behavior out of nowhere, your team won't know what to do. Don't worry. They'll recover, and so will you, no matter how awkward you feel in the moment.

Your team is likely to lack answers (at least any good answers) to these questions, especially if you've never asked them questions like these before. People who aren't routinely put in environments where they have to practice critical thinking, strategic thinking, reasoning, or decision-making on the fly are not usually superstars at being able to do that. That's okay. The worse your team does at knowing the answers to any of these questions, the more desperately they need *you* to change your leadership. The great news is that you *can* change.

Competence at anything comes as a direct result of practice, which means, the more you ask these kinds of questions of your team, the more they'll learn to expect it (recall the "Make and Keep Commitments" section). When you do things repeatedly, your team comes to expect it, and then they adjust their behavior to be ready for you. This is what you want. So, if the first time feels disastrous, no worries. The second time might not be much better. Your team might still assume you're just having a bad hair day and it's affecting your brain cells. But by the third or fourth time you ask them for what *they* think, they'll probably start to understand that this is part of a new routine you have and it isn't going anywhere. Plus, you can use your communication skills to *tell* them that you're wanting to become a better leader, and you're trying something new.

If you want to build a more competent team, respond to questions with ones of your own. Send them back to do their own research, find the information from a peer, or think through it on their own. Then, follow up on how that went. Ask about what they learned. This builds competence in others, which is exactly what great leaders do. Your team will get better at it. Believe in them. They will start to show up more prepared for your questions. The beauty of creating this kind of environment—where people know your expectation is they do their own research and find their own answers—they will start to *deliver* on those expectations. They will do the work in advance of coming to you. They will find more of the answers independently. They will start to get stronger, which means, wonderfully, that sometimes they won't even come to you. Why? Because they will fish for themselves. That frees up an incredible amount of your time, which you can devote to the other leadership practices described in this book.

I'm not recommending that you never answer questions. I'm recommending that, as a general rule, you ask your team questions and they answer them, which provokes *their* thinking, *their* understanding, *their* reasoning, and *their* researching abilities and desires. If you're always the answer person for your team, your team learns to view you as the solver. If you push back on your team with statements like, "I've got some ideas on that, but let's talk about it together. What are *you* thinking so far?", your team will start to recognize that your role is *not* to fix their problems and solve things *for* them. Your role is to help them grow, learn how to fend for themselves, and solve their own problems.

We've talked about this in the Involve Others Virtue, but I want to dive more into what it means to be an expert question asker. It's essential that your team sees the overall, long-term future vision you have for the overall team and for each person individually. However, it's also important that what they *do* or how they *think* on a daily basis is a joint effort and one they get to weigh in on. We've talked in Virtues 1 and 2 how much more excited, engaged, and proactive people are when they have a say in self-directing some of their own work. So, when it comes to matters of the *how*, it's important that you engage your team in dialogues, not monologues, about what's going to happen. Here's some sample questions you might ask:

- What was everyone's biggest learning this week?
- What are you going to change as a result of this learning? What will you do differently?
- What were some of the "Aha!" moments you experienced?
- Let's go around and have each person share a challenge they faced and how they overcame it.
- What are you still struggling with?
- What's on your mind these days? What's keeping you up at night?
- What are you doing about those things?
- How did that [meeting, client interaction, project, committee, presentation] go?
- What were the results of those things? Were you happy with the results?
- If you had it to do over, what (if anything) would you do differently?
- What are some of our great successes this week? What are we proud of this week?
- What were your biggest accomplishments this week? What were your small wins?
- How can I support you this week?

Within these questions, you'll notice a few themes, which is intentional. These questions are designed to elicit certain kinds of thinking and to *show* your team what you *value*. They show what you regard highly and what you deem important in top performers. These questions imply that problems can always be solved, that you expect mistakes and times of struggle, and you value proactive effort, action, curiosity, and learning.

THE BIG 5: THE 5 KINDS OF QUESTIONS YOU MUST ASK

The questions above are not an exhaustive list. Top performing leaders regularly ask hundreds of questions. However, if you review the sample list, you'll notice five big themes that show up repeatedly. In my experience, these five kinds of questions, when asked consistently, drive exceptional performance in teams. The five big themes are:

1. Self-solving, learning, and growth

2. Checking for clarity and congruence
3. Delivering results
4. Practicing courage and showing humility
5. Reward and recognition

Let's dive into the importance of each one.

#1: SELF-SOLVING, LEARNING, AND GROWTH

Here's the questions in the sample list that can directly be tied into self-solving, learning, and growth.

- What was everyone's biggest learning this week?
- What are you going to change as a result of this learning? What will you do differently?
- What were some of the "Aha!" moments you experienced?
- Let's go around and have each person share a challenge they faced and how they overcame it.
- What's on your mind these days? What's keeping you up at night?
- What are you doing about those things?
- If you had it to do over, what (if anything) would you do differently?

In the questions about learning, aha moments, and challenges, there's an underlying understanding that people worked through these things either on their own, with the boss, or with a peer, but that they somehow found a way to overcome it. The questions don't say, "share one *if* you have one," but they imply you *ought* to have one. They suggest that every single week, you *should* have a learning, and it's normal and expected to have challenges. Some managers won't tackle these questions because they don't want to believe that their team should struggle ever. They view this as a sign of weakness; they believe that life should be easily and always solvable. That's not how life works. Life is messy. That's not how growth works. Growth is messy too.

When we're working toward peak performance, we need to be constantly changing, evolving, growing, learning. None of those things can happen without setbacks, struggle, mistakes, failure, or moments of sheer frustration. The questions don't say, "*Did* this happen to you?" The questions automatically assume that it did, and when asked *this* way, in one-on-one or group settings, the leader gets to show folks "it's okay."

When we socialize challenges, struggles, mistakes, and failures as positive teaching or learning moments, the expectation becomes that people will have these situations but find ways to overcome and solve them. This approach entirely changes teams. People are no longer afraid to try new things. People are no longer afraid to admit they've made a mistake or failed. People become more innovative and creative because they know they can be accepted as they truly are. People no longer feel they have to disguise or hide their tough moments. That's a wonderful thing. So, ask questions about their challenges, shortcomings, obstacles, mistakes, and failures. When they tell you about those things, teach them to be self-sufficient and brave by asking them what they learned from it or what they did about it. Ask if there's any help they need. You are not there to work through those things *for* them; you're there to work through those things *alongside* them.

#2: CHECKING FOR CLARITY AND CONGRUENCE

Lots of managers believe their team has tremendous clarity when, in fact, their team lacks it entirely. Sometimes, only certain individuals lack clarity. Other times, typically aligned teams lack clarity on one particular task, assignment, or project. Great leaders are constantly checking for these times when not everyone knows what is going on. Oblivious managers, on the other hand, toil for weeks, months, or sometimes years wondering why their teams are only mediocre. They wonder why their team barely delivers on time or why they can only get to 102% of the goal but nothing greater.

Some leaders don't even *know* their teams are only adequate since they've never seen breakthrough performance. They haven't been in environments where people accomplish truly exceptional things, so they don't know what it looks like. In many cases, teams lack the clarity, coaching, and structure that we've been discussing to do it anyway. So, even if their leader *did* aspire for the team to accomplish more, it's unlikely.

This is a major failing of most environments. We are so conditioned to make our lives easy and comfortable that we settle for average. With more clarity, up front and every day, what could we accomplish? What could the results be? What if you're striving for more?

"The greater danger for most of us lies not in setting our aim too high and falling short; but in setting our aim too low and achieving our mark."
– Michelangelo

Establishing clarity with your team is not a one-and-done assignment, approach, or task. You don't walk onto a team as the new leader and talk about the vision and mission once at the first meeting, assume the team has it, then never discuss it again. Head coaches of winning teams don't walk onto the field or the court and talk about the dream of going to the Super Bowl or championships at the first practice of the season and never again. They talk about it EVERY. SINGLE. DAY. There's not a day that top-performing leaders and teams don't talk about the magnificent dream or quest they're chasing after (the WHY and the WHAT) and also talk about the steps to get there (the HOW). Here's the questions on the sample list that tie into clarity:

- What are you still struggling with?
- How did that [meeting, client interaction, project, committee, presentation] go?
- What's on your mind these days? What's keeping you up at night?

In these questions, the leader is checking for understanding, wanting to ensure that if someone is not on board with the overall strategy, or even the day-to-day tactics, there's a chance to speak up about it. A chance to socialize it, in a group setting or in a one-on-one setting with the boss, allows the leader to bring clarity to their team. This is a chance for an employee to say: "Things are going well overall, but there's one thing I still don't know if I agree with" or "I'm struggling with why we're doing this. I ran into this pitfall this week, and it seems like this is really slowing us down." Most leaders avoid these questions because the answers can be scary, intimidating, or threatening. Most leaders feel that asking questions like these is inviting dissent into the room that wasn't there before.

That's nonsense. Misunderstanding, dissent, disagreement, confusion, and unalignment are going to happen anyway. You don't avoid it by avoiding talking about it. By talking about it in a group setting, or tackling it with your employees at their one-on-ones, you prevent these same conversations taking place by a watercooler, behind your back, and without your knowledge. That's even riskier. In those scenarios, you're not there to redirect the group and be the voice of reason. They're left to figure it out totally on their own. Without your guidance (again, *not* your instruction, but your *guidance*), they might not figure it out. You also create a divide between you and your team. If you never tackle questions that check for clarity, alignment, and congruence between your master plan and theirs, you essentially show your team that certain topics are off-limits. Your team concludes, on their own, that some "undiscussables" should not be brought up in front of the leader. Your team concludes that either you couldn't handle it, you would prefer not to know, or it's not culturally acceptable to talk about those things in a group setting.

None of this will help you or the team when folks get stuck, trapped, have worries, start to veer off course, or feel that the group should veer off course. The scariest part of this is that you actually lose brainpower. What if your team is *right*? What if they have ideas for how to achieve the goal better? What if some of their worries are founded? What if things are going wrong in the process that you don't know because they don't feel they can share them with you? Checking for clarity, alignment, and congruence is a key part of a leader's job. Making sure your team has bought into the objective of any project as it progresses is a constant drum beat that needs to happen often.

#3: DELIVERING RESULTS

The questions in the sample list that have to do most with delivering results are:
- How did that [meeting, client interaction, project, committee, presentation] go?
- What were the results of those things? Were you happy with the results?
- If you had it to do over, what (if anything) would you do differently?
- What are some of our great successes this week? What are we proud of this week?
- What were your biggest accomplishments this week? What were your small wins?

When you ask your team about results—the results of their work, what they're proud of, what they've accomplished, how specific meetings or projects have been going—you show them that results matter. And they do.

Being "busy" or "working hard" is often confused with performance. People often feel they're doing a great job at work because their desk has stacks of papers, their calendars are full of appointments, their schedules are packed with meetings, and their days are long. That doesn't mean a thing. Without great results, someone's long hours or busy schedule is even *more* concerning because it means they're not competent enough to select the right wildly important goals or priorities for their day.

"Do or do not. There is no try." – Yoda

Whatever you do in life, it's important to not just *try* to do it, but to actually *do* it. When you ask your teams about outcomes, you're showing them that while trying is a good first step, what really matters in life, in business, and what you value in your relationship with them is how well those efforts materialize into results. So, if someone on your team plans to have a crucial conversation with another person, is making a presentation they're nervous about, or is going into a tough sales call with a client, it's important you ask them after: "How did that go? What were the results? Were you happy with the results?"

If you ask these questions often, people will learn quickly that you will ask these questions again. You show your team that you care about results, and you're going to inquire about results. When the results weren't what you and your people expected, you are there for them, to help them think, reflect, ponder, and identify how to achieve greater success in the future. You show them that the practice of tough self-assessment doesn't have to be overly painful or life-ending, like too many people act like it is. Instead, it's a part of getting better.

When things have gone well, you're there then too. You're there to celebrate with them, to cheer them on, to encourage them to stay the course, to keep going, to try again. You show them that both their sucky results and their terrific results matter to you, and you aren't going to throw them out the window when their results are in between as long as they're going through this active process of self-evaluation and meaningful learning. We recognize when learning is happening and know when that learning is meaningful when we see people taking different steps or actions in the future. They'll change their behavior. When we're not getting results but we change our behavior, we tend to get different results. If you go through this often with your team, they'll start to care about improving their own results as much as you, and guess what you'll get then? Better results. At some point, they may even (and likely will) be breakthrough results.

#4: PRACTICING COURAGE AND SHOWING HUMILITY

The questions on the sample list that had to do with practicing courage and showing humility are:

- Let's go around and have each person share a challenge they faced and how they overcame it.
- What are you still struggling with?
- What's on your mind these days? What's keeping you up at night?
- If you had it to do over, what (if anything) would you do differently?
- How can I support you this week?

Many other questions on the list could also turn into opportunities for folks to be courageous enough to show humility and admit struggle or defeat (even if that defeat is only perceived). Anytime we ask someone to tell us about how something went or about learning, we open the door for them to admit that they had moments of weakness and challenge. Typically (unfortunately and sadly), most people in society don't view these things (challenge, adversity, struggle, weakness) as good things, but rather bad things. While much data, science, and research suggest these things are only bad if we make them so in our minds, most people don't buy that. Only truly successful people know better—that adversity, struggle, and pain can help us grow and develop if we let it. For more information on these topics, I highly recommend you read *The Obstacle Is the Way* by Ryan Holiday and *Mindset* by Carol Dweck. They changed my life.

Back to the questions: You're asking your team to talk about struggle, tough moments, what they're unclear on, and things that aren't going well. For the average person, most of these moments are unpleasant and uncomfortable. That's exactly why you should discuss them! Want to know how we make things that we fear or don't like more comfortable for ourselves? Practice.

Yes, we do them again and again. This comes straight from Virtue 3 on routines. Asking questions and communicating well is such an important routine that it got its own chapter. When you ask your team to talk about when they felt most weak or uncomfortable and then don't dive off the deep end or ram your head into a wall, you show them that *it's okay*. You teach them that having tough moments is a part of life and a part of whatever pursuit they have in life (to be a great salesperson, teacher, athlete, surgeon). It doesn't matter whether you are trying to lead people to world-class performance in banking, baking, or boxing—having the grit, perseverance, and discipline to get excited instead of exhausted when things are tough is necessary to succeed. Doesn't matter the field or profession. Being able to embrace these tough moments in stride *does* matter.

By talking about these things repeatedly, your people will begin to be more real with you. They'll tell you about their real struggles—the ones that need solving. As with everything else we've discussed, while you won't give them the answers, you can help them through the answers. You can find the answers together, even if you thought you already knew what to do. Heck, you may learn something too! They'll recognize that you're not there to put them in detention, you're there to help. They'll bring you the big stuff—the things slowing them down or impeding their progress—and you'll tackle those as a team. They won't be hidden in the shadows. They won't be talked about in the evening hours when the parking lot is going dim by a few employees standing around their cars. Your folks won't need to do that because they'll be able to say to each other: "Just go to Amy. She'll know what to do" or "Have you talked to Tina yet? She'll help you through that" or "What did Devon say about that? Did he have any ideas?" You'll culturally set up an environment where your team sees you, the leader, as *part* of the team, a safe place and sounding board where real solutions can be found. The team, because it is humble and willing to look at its weaknesses and errors, will then correct mistakes they made before. The team will grow and get better. Results will get better too. That will feel good. People like to feel good, so they will bring new problems, struggles, and challenges in the future, allowing the cycle to repeat.

When people are willing to be humble and say what's on their heart, which takes courage, and those things end up improving their situations, they learn that humility and courage are good things. They end up practicing both attributes. Invariably, those who are both humble and courageous have more success in life than those who are not. So, make sure to ask questions that allow your team to practice these skills. It'll change their lives.

#5: REWARD AND RECOGNITION

People like to party. Bars, lounges, nightclubs, vacation resorts, cruises—much of it wouldn't exist if people didn't like to celebrate. Many people celebrate their birthdays not just when they're children, but for a lifetime. Married couples celebrate their wedding anniversary. Many folks celebrate holidays: 4th of July, Memorial Day, Christmas, Thanksgiving, New Year's Eve. We remember moments in our lives or in our country's history that were big—everything from gaining our independence to celebrating the veterans that fought to keep our freedom, to the advent of another year in our own life or the calendar. We use these days as reasons to feel good, be happy, and do so with the people we love.

Celebration is a key part of any team or workgroup too. People want to celebrate. They want to know that their work and their contributions are valued. They want to know that the pain they've been going through is worth it. If you've already been implementing the behaviors we've been talking about, you've asked your team to talk about their struggles and challenges—and solve them; to learn new things and apply them; to practice courage and humility. These things don't come easily to most. So, it's vital you find reasons to reward and recognize your people for the journey they're on and all they've been doing—not just once a year or at the end of big projects, but often and on an ongoing basis.

The questions on the sample list that tie into an opportunity to reward and recognize folks are:

- What are some of our great successes this week? What are we proud of this week?
- What were your biggest accomplishments this week? What were your small wins?
- How can I support you this week?

Unlike some of the other questions, which although important and helpful to ask can be uncomfortable in nature, these questions are positive in nature and pull your people toward good memories or discussion of what's been going well.

It's essentially asking your people to wear the Yellow Hat in Edward de Bono's *Six Thinking Hats*.[25] People crave positive affirmation for the things they've done well, and by asking these questions, you allow them to have their moment in the sun, bragging about how well they've done. If you're consistently asking your people about what isn't going well, what stumbling blocks they've been facing, and what learnings they've had to get over this, it's really important you spend time asking questions that cause them to celebrate themselves too. Everything in life is best in balance and moderation, and if you're forcing your people to go through much critical self-reflection, allowing your folks moments to highlight and share their successes will balance that out. It allows the seesaw of feelings in our brains to go from lopsided to balanced. For many, thinking about what isn't going well can be overwhelming, especially at first, so getting balanced time to think about what *is* going well can be cathartic and necessary for the average person.

Thinking about all the research done on positive reinforcement, science tells us that people will habitually learn to do things, over time, that lead to more of the positive effect they want. In other words, if celebrating success and being rewarded and recognized for hard work feels good, people will figure out what it takes—and then *do* what it takes—to put themselves in that situation again. So, if you recognize folks for a job well done, you are more likely to get a job well done more often. Taking time to ask these kinds of questions of your people is a valuable tool, as it increases their desire to accomplish more, so the next time you ask, "What are your proudest accomplishments?", they have something to talk about. You also get to show them what you value, desire, recognize, and measure. It's what leaders show that they appreciate, want, and will track that gets done.

GO FISH! A FRESH LOOK AT OPEN-ENDED QUESTIONS

In any formalized training for sales, how to interview better, how to resolve conflict, how to negotiate, or how to be a better conversationalist, there's a section on open-ended questions and how important they are. It's all been said and done before, and when you saw this heading, you let out a giant yawn. I totally get it, but bear with me.

Open-ended questions serve a real place in leadership. Without them, no leader can be effective, just like it's nearly impossible for consultative or advisory sales folks to function without open-ended questions in their inter-actions with clients. Yet I see managers ask primarily closed-ended questions to their team all the time. Here's a list of questions I constantly see in one-on-ones with staff or group meetings:

- Can everyone agree to that?
- Does that sound good?
- Anyone have any problems with that?
- Does this make sense?
- Did that get completed?
- Are you okay with that?
- Does anyone have any questions?
- Is that why this happened?

The problem with questions like these is that you generally limit your answers to "Yes," "No," "Sure," "Good," or "Fine." You don't provoke and incite people's thoughts, feelings, and reasoning. You don't even give yourself the chance to learn *how* people are thinking, feeling, and reasoning. You don't get information so you can accurately assess the character and competence of those around you (which Stephen M. R. Covey says are the two critical components of trust in *The Speed of Trust*).

Have you ever played the game, Go Fish? It was one of my favorite card games growing up. In the game, you're limited to asking Yes or No questions that all the start with the words "Do you...?" Players might ask, "Do you have any squid?" or "Do you have any grouper?" with the hopes of matching another player's card with their own cards to make the necessary matches and win the game. Of course, an extra wrinkle in the game is that by hearing what people are *asking* about, you learn what they're likely to *have* in their own hand. If you can remember that, then you get an advantage because when you draw the card they were previously looking for, then *you* can now ask about that card and steal theirs to complete your own match.

The reason the game isn't over in a matter of minutes and can go on for some time is that the questions are quite limiting. Imagine how much better you'd do if you could ask *any* question you wanted. What if you could say, "Tell me about all the cards in your hand"? Or even, "What cards do you have? Describe them all." On your next turn, you'd be totally equipped to ask for what you need because you'd have tons of information about what your opponent is holding in their hand. You'd be able to use the information you had gotten from your first open-ended question (perhaps you learned your opponent had a jellyfish, a shark, and a whale—all of which you have and want) to go after each of those cards in consecutive order. You'd be able to shift your strategy to take all their cards, put them in your own hand, and win the game. You could get there faster and design your every move around the full awareness of what your opponent is working with.

What someone holds in their hand in the game of Go Fish would be great information, but the game would likely end quickly and not be all that fun. But in leadership and in life, we're not playing Go Fish. We're not opponents; we're on the same team, and we *want* to know what our teammates possess and hold in their hands. We want to know where they're at. In fact, we want to know *all* about them. When we know these things, we are better equipped to design our next best move. We can alter and shift our strategy. We can ask about different things in the next question. We can make headway faster.

When we know what our people fear, what they want, what they're excited about, and what concerns them, we can build better action plans for them. We can set more realistic goals uniquely designed to *them*. We can engage and empower them more effectively. Asking questions that start with "Do you..." is a bad idea. Yet so many leaders around the world operate this way. When we ask someone, "Do you have any problems with that?" or "Do you have any questions about that?" or "Do you have any concerns or worries?", what do you think most people's natural response is? It's "No."

Most people don't want to rock the apple cart, especially with their boss. If you're the boss, and you're in the habit of asking closed-ended questions that start with "Do you...," you probably don't get a lot of dialogue in your meetings. Meetings without much dialogue are boring. You might believe yours are different because your team really likes you and you have so much great information to share, but don't fool yourself. No one is all that interesting or entertaining on a repetitive basis, and even comedians ask open-ended questions of their audiences and then use that material to engage with the group in better ways.

Meetings where teams don't engage in dialogue stink. If you want to truly keep your team's energy and engagement and have them taking notes on what you're talking about rather than writing their To-Do list or grocery list for the week, you better get your team talking. Not only can you ask better questions of them, but you can create an environment where they can ask questions of each other, themselves, and of you. You can have the courage and faith to do that, no matter what they might say, because through your other outstanding leadership practices, you'll be leading a highly charged, highly engaged, highly talented team, and nothing they'd bring up would be something you couldn't—or wouldn't want to—handle and tackle.

If you haven't done this previously, it's likely you're not getting the real story from your team because they've become accustomed to not saying anything. They haven't been asked much for their opinion, so over time, people tend to become uninterested and unaccustomed to giving it. Also, having the courage to speak publicly, especially when it means expressing a different viewpoint than the group or leader, is really *hard* for most people. It's also hard to admit that you don't know something, are confused, or missed something and want clarification. For others, it's hard to speak at all—expressing thoughts, feelings, and working through things out loud can be intimidating for people. Which is why we must give people the chance to practice the skill of speaking up as often as we can. I'm a fan of doing this every day. Having the courage to speak truthfully, transparently, and from the heart—all with humility—is a practice. Thus, it requires practice for it to improve. So many leaders talk about how important it is that their team speaks up. They say ridiculous things like, "I have an open-door policy," and they *do* physically leave their door open. But they never ask themselves why no one ever comes knocking on it. They conclude that everything must be okay, that "no news is good news" or "silence is golden."

This thinking is erroneous and shortsighted. No news is NOT good news and silence is NOT golden. These things are very scary. They are dangerous. When your team isn't talking—pushing back on each other and you, expressing dissenting viewpoints, admitting mistakes but also talking about their proudest accomplishments, learnings, results, and successes— something is very wrong. This should be happening all the time, and the only way that you'll train people to do this is to show them you value it and by creating an environment where they *get* to practice it constantly. It's true that creating an environment that requires people to contribute means that they *have to* practice it. But the reality is that they *get to* practice it. Over time, when done right, they'll view it that way too. They'll love practicing it and want to practice it. As humans, we want to be seen and heard. Having dialogue results in this.

We've talked about how your team might say "No" to closed-ended questions about worries, fears, doubts, or issues because they've become accustomed to not speaking up and because you haven't created the right environment. You'll also get "No" if your team isn't really paying attention—at least, not enough to know if and when the answer *should* be "Yes."

I wasn't entirely kidding when I mentioned employees working on their grocery list. I've done it. I've done it at a time when I was considered a top performer by my results. It's unlikely that anyone would've suspected me of organizing my personal To-Do list during a meeting, but I did it because I frequently sat in meetings where I never learned anything new, never was asked for my opinion, and wanted to make use of the time. If you're leading meetings that don't have dialogue and open-ended questions to test for understanding, thoughts, and feelings, you'd probably be shocked how little your people are hearing what you say. So, when you ask if there's any questions, concerns, or worries and the answer is "No," the reality is that half the time, it's because your people don't *know* what you were talking about. A fun exercise (although it's not one that necessarily will build trust) is to ask specific and various members of your team to repeat back what you had been talking about, and what it is that you're wanting their opinion on—and see if anyone (or how many) don't know. I've seen this done a few times, and the results are often staggering and embarrassing for both the leader and the individuals being asked.

I've searched several sites online trying to determine what most research says the average attention span is for an adult. I found answers ranging from 8 to 12 seconds (these were the most common) to 20 minutes and everything in between. I found one article that says humans are now lagging behind the humble goldfish in our attention span, which felt especially relevant given my Go Fish analogy. No matter the true attention span, if you're going to run an hour-long meeting, or God forbid, a multiple-hour meeting, without full blown participation from your audience, most of your people aren't picking up most of what you say. To ensure that you never have a room full of zombies who are smiling, nodding, and pretending to be on board, you need to ask open-ended questions.

Let's go back to the list above and figure out how we might reword these questions to ensure that we get full participation and engagement from others. You also want to learn about their thoughts and feelings, which allows you to then work through those thoughts and feelings with your team- so you can make better decisions, and maybe even adjust your strategy or your game plan. Just as you would in 'Go Fish', if you could see and know everything your opponent saw and knew about their cards.

PREVIOUS QUESTIONS	REVISED QUESTIONS
Can everyone agree to that?	What do you all think about that?
Does that sound good?	What do you think about that?
Anyone have any problems with that?	What concerns do we have with this?
Does this make sense?	Tell me what your understanding is here.
Did that get completed?	How are we doing with that?
Are you okay with that?	How do you feel about that?
Does anyone have any questions?	What questions do you have?
Is that why this happened?	What happened here?

When people see how much more engaging work is when they have a voice, value the skills they're practicing around speaking up, and find their voice (and *using* that voice), they often notice how much that can enrich all of their relationships. When this happens, people no longer view it as an obligation but, instead, develop a deep desire and passion to contribute in this way. This will come with time. It's helpful that the nature of these questions requires people to give you more information. It would be flat-out weird if someone answered the question, "What do you think about that?" with one word. It's nearly impossible to answer the revised list of questions with "Yes," "No," or any other kind of one-word answers. The questions call for people to *tell* you what they're really thinking and feeling. What does this do? It causes people to actually *think* about it. If we want to know what people think and we ask them to tell us (instead of just asking them to agree with us), then we provoke thinking. That is *always* a good thing, regardless of what those thoughts are.

If we're truly paying, employing, or enlisting people to think, we should want to hear and know what those thoughts are. If you're saying to yourself right now, *I don't know if I really want to know what they think!*, then you've recruited, hired, enlisted, and employed the wrong people.

Regardless of what kind of team you lead—whether a professional one in a workplace or an athletic team—hopefully you can say that recruiting top talent was part of your game plan, and you have a process around that. But if you feel that you are bringing great talent onto your team, then hopefully you are enlisting people who are either smarter, better, or more talented than *you* are at some things—or at least as smart or talented as you are. If that's the case, then you should absolutely want to hear what they have to say. You should want it so bad that you behave in specific ways that get it out of them—until it's such a norm they *expect* you to ask them for their opinion, they would find it weird if you stopped asking one day, and they offer up those opinions willingly and without being asked.

I'll add something here. The best leaders don't expect to *be* the smartest, most capable people in the room. Exceptional leaders have a philosophy that the essence of leadership is not what *they* contribute individually, but what they help others to contribute. They believe they are there to unlock others' potential. They do, in fact, hire and recruit great talent for their teams, and they're not afraid of finding people who can do things *better* than them. The best basketball coaches in the NBA or the best NFL coaches are often not the best players. Much of the time, the players on winning teams are more talented, and in some cases, *far* more talented than their coaches. These coaches know their job isn't to excel at being a lineman or a point guard. It's to excel at coaching, setting vision and culture, strategically leveraging the talent of others, building great teams. The coaches of pro teams are not afraid of their players being "better" than them. They know that's a good thing, not a bad thing, because they're clear on their own role, which is to help others *around* them be the best.

When that happens, leaders do all the things we've been talking about. They devote time to involving others (Virtue 2), coaching others (a big part of Virtue 3), and not only communicating well with others but ensuring that others have a place to practice communication well too (Virtue 4) because they know they literally can't do it without others. Great leaders don't focus on what they can do; they focus on what *others* can do. These practices are all designed to impact others in huge ways. If the people you're hiring or enlisting for your mission aren't more talented in some ways than *you*, then you've got big problems. If you don't walk into interviews or your recruitment processes with the expectation of finding the most talented, most spectacular people—with the expectation that you're then going to care about what they think, what they want, what they know, and what they do—then you've got even bigger problems. The biggest problems will come when you don't also understand that your role is to set up environments and create cultures that foster their growth and development. You can't do it all as a leader, and you're not there to do it all. So, if you don't get comfortable at hiring people better than you at the things you used to do, then you will struggle eternally.

When we as leaders know how much others have to offer (because that's why we selected them), we're always interested in their feedback. Questions and dialogue are needed so we can cover our own blind spots as leaders and help us think in ways that aren't strengths for us. None of us are so brilliant and infallible on our own that we don't need the help of those around us to set us straight and to think of the things we're missing. I've never met someone who thinks about every last component of a decision, including the marketing piece, the finance piece, the technology piece, the human resources piece, the client/customer piece, the risk piece, and the communication and rollout piece. "It takes a village," as is often said.

Let's say your company is planning a large-scale year-end celebration to acknowledge the company's success. The person who evaluates the impact of that decision to a balance sheet is not usually the same person who does an amazing job creating the theme of the event and thinks of the perfect decorating details. In 2019, my company planned a major initiative rollout that coincided with the 50th-year anniversary of America landing a man on the moon for the first time. While I was intently involved in the design of the initiative and wanted a large-scale rollout, it wasn't in my wheelhouse to design an event. So, we gathered individuals with unique talents in a room together, several times, and I asked a heap of questions like: "What do you guys think we should do?", "What are more ideas on how we can bring this to life?", "What about other thoughts?" Ideas from one person led to ideas from another person, and soon, the group around me was envisioning the Styrofoam moons hanging from the ceiling, a life-size cutout of Neil Armstrong, a dessert of cookies and cream ice cream, and tie-ins to John F. Kennedy's speech. Together, through communication, we discovered similarities of NASA's 1969 mission to what we, as a company, were trying to do in 2019.

It was awesome that we had talented individuals on our team whose minds work differently than mine, who made what they envisioned come to life.

By the way, it was shocking how closely a scoop of cookies and cream ice cream resembled the moon with its craters. Before, I didn't understand how that was relevant. But when I saw it on the day of the event, I saw it the work of a genius it was. If it were me, I probably would've simply served a sheet cake and called it a day. Thank goodness we practiced both Virtue 2 and Virtue 4: involving others and talking terrifically.

The goal with these revised questions is to set expectations with others that you want their true, candid feedback and you're not going anywhere until you get it. Even the question, "What questions do you have?" suggests that there *should* be questions. Asking your team, "What haven't we talked about?" at the end of a meeting or brainstorm session shows them you're aware that you (one person) couldn't possibly come up with all the answers. The question, "What concerns do we have?" suggests there *are* stones unturned, things the leader has forgotten to think about. The invitation to weigh in on those things, if offered consistently, becomes a genuine one, not one for show.

An important note: Just because your team weighs in on something doesn't mean you'll always go with their opinion. It doesn't mean you'll necessarily change your mind. Sometimes you'll be making group decisions, and you'll allow the group's input to sway you. Other times, you'll make a decision that is counter to the advice your team gave you. Your team needs to understand this is going to happen. However, what they should also understand is how much you appreciated their input while you made that decision. A key part of communication means that you never leave people wondering. You never let people draw their own conclusions about your intentions or how you're feeling. You want to know what people are thinking, how they're feeling, and what they're experiencing, right? Well, it makes sense that your people should know what *you're* thinking, feeling, and experiencing too. You might say something like:

"I really want to thank you all for your feedback. In the end, we've decided to go in this other direction, and here's why we decided that. I can't tell you enough how much we valued and appreciated the feedback from this group. Please keep speaking up."

Sharing with your group that their feedback was considered, valued, absorbed by others (or by *you*) and that it did have an impact is vitally important if you want people to give feedback again. In all kinds of relationships—whether with a family member, best friend, spouse, boss, or colleague—it can be hard to be asked for an opinion, to provide it, and then have that opinion not followed. It can feel like full-blown rejection. You want to ensure that no one licks their wounds for too long. Instead, the emphasis should be placed on the dialogue that was had and the teamwork and camaraderie generated by such dialogue. By creating a culture that teaches people that you will always *consider* their opinion but can't always accept it, you increase your chances that you'll get quality input *again*. And again. Which matters, since doing this repeatedly means you'll get more real, more truthful, better information from your team, allowing you to make better decisions as a leader.

As long as people believe, feel, and know their feedback was heard and taken into account—and you gave them the chance to discuss it (the "psychological air" that Liz Wiseman discussed in her book *Multipliers*)—folks are often more willing to get on board with a decision, even if they didn't necessarily support it at the outset. Somehow, getting to weigh in and contribute helps people support decisions after the fact that they might never have championed or supported had you not let them be a part of that decision-making process.

To review, here's what you *do* to talk terrifically and communicate exceptionally:

1. Recruit and enlist great people, who are insanely talented, and settle for nothing less.

2. Expect them to delight you but know that you play a part in extracting their genius.

3. Care about what they think, feel (including what they fear, what they worry about, and what they want), know, and do.

4. Create an environment where they know those thoughts and feelings (including their doubts, fears, worries, and wants) can be expressed, as well as expressing what they know and don't know.

5. Do so by routinely—nearly constantly—asking them for their opinions. Use open-ended questions to check for understanding, invite them into the discussion, and invite them to disagree with you and one another to ensure you're truly tapping into all their brainpower to make the best decisions.

6. Require their participation in this activity at first, recognizing that over time, you won't have to. Over time, they'll want to willingly participate.

7. Communicate the results of their feedback to them; share how they've influenced you or helped you or share how much their feedback was at least valued in your decision process.

PRACTICE 2:
BECOME AN ACTIVE LISTENER

"When you talk, you are only repeating what you already know. But if you listen, you may learn something new." – Dalai Lama

As mentioned, being a strong communicator is necessary for strong leadership. Being a strong communicator requires being an active listener and a strong question asker. These tasks can be tough, with constant pitfalls. But don't worry: I'm here to address some of those.

7 CARDINAL SINS OF LISTENING AND QUESTION ASKING

#1: YOU FILL THE SILENCE.

Have you ever been in a meeting where someone asks a question and there's not an immediate answer from the group? Just when you're about to answer or say something because you've been thinking about it, the question asker rewords the question or asks a new one? I've seen this happen countless times. It's as if we have an expectation that when leaders ask questions, people are supposed to have *immediate* answers. If they don't, we're so uncomfortable with that silence that we *fill* it. We assume our audience didn't understand the question, so we rephrase it in an effort to get an answer.

Why do we ask questions? Is it to get answers? Of course. But the best leaders ask questions to *stimulate thinking*. We want our audience to *process* what we've said. Thinking about something and processing what's been said doesn't always happen in a moment. For many, it takes several minutes. So why would we jump in and save the group? Not only do we not really *save* the group, but we also disrupt that thought process. It cuts off thinking and processing at its knees.

Truly tremendous communicators don't mind silence. If you're on a conference call and talking to a group of people (or even with one individual) and ask a question that's initially met by silence, you can choose not to have a hard time with that. If you're uncomfortable with the silence, put yourself on mute. That way, you won't feel as compelled to speak. It'll remind yourself that it's no longer your turn and you're waiting for a response. It shows your team that you're serious about getting an answer to *that* question. For anyone on the line who got distracted, started multitasking, hasn't been paying attention, or didn't hear the question, the silence will scare the heck out of them. These people will think you might've called on them and start worrying that they've missed something. Do this enough, and it'll inspire people to pay better attention, since no one enjoys those moments of pain or fear.

When we allow for silence after questions, we allow people to get further down the road with their thoughts. The people who don't do their thinking out loud but process thought internally actually *get* to process thought. So, if you let the silence hang without filling it with another question, you'll get *better answers*. You'll get answers to your initial question, which probably was the right one. In all the times I've seen leaders ask a follow-up question or reword a question because they weren't getting quick enough answers of their first question, the secondary question wasn't as good as the first question. The leader had it right the first time. So don't get scared when there's not an immediate answer. It has nothing to do with your leadership abilities, and if anything, it only shows weakness when you can't handle the silence that comes after a question for which people are really thinking about and trying to get to the true root cause before speaking.

The belief that you're a bad leader because the airtime isn't 100% filled with words is nonsense. Great leaders don't mind when a room goes silent for a full minute or longer while people think about what you've said. In this case, silence *is* golden. Worst-case scenario, no one is answering because no one was listening to you. If you wait, it'll come out that no one heard you or was paying attention—which is a great clue that you might need to work on your own communication skills using many of the practices in this book.

#2: YOU ACCEPT THE FIRST ANSWER AS THE RIGHT OR ONLY ANSWER.

Want to shut down participation, dialogue, and engagement from all in a group setting? Asking a question to a group, taking the first answer, and then moving on is a great way to do that. I've seen so many settings where multiple answers to a question exist, but many of them aren't ever explored. Leaders will ask, "Why is this happening?" or "What are we seeing out there this month?" and someone will answer. They'll give one perspective of life as they know it. The leader will then take that answer and move on, saying something like, "Okay, then what do we do about that?", or worse, give their idea and answer about what to do about it (instead of letting the group self-solve that problem). Here's the trouble with that: It's probably not the *only* thing going on; it's just how *one* person feels.

Usually when we're asking questions about landscape, environment, or things happening, multiple factors are at play. What is going on with one employee might not be what's going on with another employee. Let's say you're talking to a group of managers of various offices, and you're wondering what's causing a slowdown in the business or an inability to crush that month's goals. One person might say it's seasonal—it's December, and everyone is on vacation. If you start tackling what to do about that, then you miss all the *other* answers. Maybe another person feels like the marketing department hasn't done a good job of putting out promotions lately. A third manager might point out that their team is short-staffed. A fourth person might argue that it's the interest rate environment, the political climate, or recent news that is causing customers to be afraid. A fifth person might cite that there's new competitors in town at the same strip malls or locations as your business. Perhaps a sixth person isn't seeing any kind of slowdown, or they were, but they already found a way of handling it and overcoming it. Maybe that person has a solution that could help the group.

Oftentimes, multiple things are going on. If you want to be a great leader and help your people develop multilevel thinking, you've got to get used to asking, "What else?" It doesn't matter if you're with one person or in a group setting. You're wanting to promote that there are multiple ways to look at things, accomplish things, and solve things. If you're looking for root causes—WHY something is occurring—there could be multiple answers and more than one thing at play simultaneously.

You also have to keep in mind that one person's root cause and reason for struggle may not be another person's, and what one person is seeing might not be what another person is seeing. If you're asking your people why there was low attendance at an event, and you accept the first answer of "I think we did this event on the wrong day of the week. Saturdays aren't a good day; people already have plans with their families," you might spend the rest of your meeting diving into that. Then, you might only change the day of the week when you plan your next event. But what if the real problem was the *time* on that day or the time of *year*; that you didn't market the event with enough notice, market it the right *way*, or market it to the right *people*; or the price point for entry was set too high. Maybe it's a combination of *all* those things.

Unless you ask, "What else?", you'll miss the different possibilities and the chance to *really* evaluate your business. After hearing multiple answers from multiple people, you might instead decide that Saturday was the perfect day of the week, but that Saturday of Labor Day weekend isn't; you need to get the word out more than a week in advance; a $100 ticket for a plate of BBQ food was too steep; and only posting the event on Facebook without leveraging other social media platforms wasn't casting a wide enough net. Maybe you'll realize that a start time of 5 P.M. is too early or too late. I have no idea what you'll find out, but I do know that if you don't ask, "What else?", you won't find out nearly *enough*. You'll only find out what *one* person thinks.

Always ask for second and third opinions. Ask for more opinions until there's nothing more to add. Learn to say things like, "What about the rest of you? Any different perspectives? What else is going on?" As with everything, consistency is key, so show your team over time that you are *going* to do this. You want your team to realize that second and third opinions are going to be requested. This keeps people's heads in the game after the first person answers. Show people you'll want multiple answers on any question, and you'll also help people search for multiple answers and angles when they leave you. When not with you, they'll learn to come up with an answer to their *own* questions and then think, *Okay, but wait. That's just ONE answer. What else could be causing this? What else could be going on? Am I sure I know everything?*

If you do this, you'll get far better and more robust dialogue. You'll cultivate thinkers who evaluate things, even in their personal lives, from many angles. You'll help people grow into deeper thinkers. Make sure to hear from multiple people and explore multiple differing points of view before you move on.

#3: YOU PLAY FAVORITES.

Another great way to shut down healthy group dialogue is to let the same person or few people always answer the questions and be talking. If you've got a group of people you frequently engage with, and you can easily think of a few who dominate the discussion, then you have a problem. If this is repeatedly happening, then *you* (as the leader) are part of the problem.

Every group is going to have people who are naturally more engaged, talkative, assertive, and extraverted than others. While we want to accept and love people as they are, it's also your job to manage people's personalities in healthy ways. The folks on your team who rarely speak need your help. They need your prodding. They need you to stop letting the superstar talkers run the show, and they need you to help the group balance things out.

When you ask questions of your group and the same minority of people are always the first and last to speak and you let that continue, multiple things are happening. Your quieter folks aren't getting the chance to *practice* public speaking and express their ideas. Because of that, they might not even be learning to practice *having* ideas because they're so used to Talkative Tom or Verbose Victor dominating the show. Talkative Tom and Verbose Victor are also not learning to *listen*. They aren't practicing crucial skills of showing respect for others, being influenced by others (instead of doing the influencing), or recognizing there are *other* people with something to contribute. The best answers and discussion come from *everyone* participating. Our brains all work in complex but different ways, and the best decisions and solutions will come from diverse people sharing diverse viewpoints. It's likely that the folks who are most quiet or laid back on your team *do* see things differently than the folks on your team who are most talkative and involved.

So, you're seeing this dynamic: What do you do?

First, *invite* your quieter folks into the discussion. View group discussion like a dinner party. You wouldn't expect people to come to your dinner party if they weren't invited by you, right? As the leader, it is *your* responsibility to invite people to join. If you ask a question and your typical talkers are quick on the draw to speak, you can still take their remarks but then say,

"Next, I'd like to hear from a few others who haven't spoken yet." If you're not getting what you're looking for when you do that, call on people by name. "Sally, I would love to hear what you're thinking" or "Rhonda, tell me about your perspective on this topic." Again, consistency is key. The more you do this, the more it will become a norm and culturally accepted that you want commentary from *everyone* in the room, not just the same two or three people. Over time, with practice, people will either get more comfortable speaking in front of the group or simply learn it's expected. If you've got the right people, they'll rise to the occasion.

Second, manage your top talkers. Perhaps you even pull them aside individually and say, "I love how much you contribute, and I want to continue to hear from you, so please don't hold back or go silent on me. But I'm really trying to get others to speak up as much as you. Can you help me with that?" Issuing a challenge like this can lead to amazing results. When you don't dictate what it means to "help with that," you leave the answers up to them. I've issued challenges like this to my top talkers and seen them go talk to the quieter folks on the side, saying things like, "I'd really like to hear more from you in the group. Is there anything I can do to help you speak up more?" In other instances, top talkers simply stop feeling the need to have the first comment and hold back to clear space for others. I've heard some individuals say in the group setting, "I have a lot of thoughts on this, but I also know that Julie has been thinking about this one a lot, and I'd love to hear from her first before I make my remarks" or give encouragement to others: "I really love what Mario just shared, and I want to go back to that." Asking your top talkers to either pull back or help you with pulling out others in the group can do wonders.

Again, your job as a leader is to unleash talent and leverage the brainpower of the *whole* group, not just part of the group. So, make sure everyone gets in there. You won't necessarily be able to drive the group toward equal participation, and you don't need to. Some people will always naturally contribute *more*. But the key is that everyone should contribute, and if you've got some folks dominating the show, it's likely your group needs your help to curtail that.

#4: YOU DON'T ACKNOWLEDGE WHAT PEOPLE HAVE SAID.

The greatest facilitators and leaders I know *value* the verbal and written contributions of their team, and they want people to know it. They know that valuing people's behaviors, actions, and overall great work is how to get *more* of those behaviors, actions, and overall great work. One of the best ways we can show people we value their contributions, especially during a verbal conversation but even in writing, is to show them we are listening. The best way to do this is to acknowledge what they *said*. When we do this, people are more likely to speak up again in the future.

Let's say you're in the process of gathering multiple opinions in a meeting. You keep asking, "What else?" until you have heard multiple opinions. You need to show them you've heard all the remarks. You can do this individually after each comment, saying things like, "Sounds like we're thinking we should close early that day. Thank you for that idea, Marcy. What other ideas are out there?" Then, "Sounds like Bill could help us with this project. That's a great point, Phil. How do others feel about that?" Then hear from the group and say, "Okay, got it. What else?" Then, "Sounds like we also need to issue a notice to our clients that we're going this direction. Terrific point, Karen. What else?"

Or you can gather everyone's comments and then acknowledge them as a group. "Okay, so I've heard we should close early that day, we can have Bill help us with this project, and we should issue a notice that we're going to do this. Thanks Marcy, Phil, and Karen for those comments. What else?" You can also go back to things people have said in earlier parts of group dialogues and meetings. When done often, this is effective and really shows people you care. You might bring something up that was said an hour earlier by saying, "To Don's earlier point, about this being more about strategy than tactics, I'd really like to make sure we stay focused on the big picture here. That really resonated with me personally."

Over time, you'll notice that other people learn from *you* and start to do the same things. If you're leading other leaders, this is especially effective because they learn to follow these tactics with their own teams. That, in turn, will drive better dialogue and help inspire people to keep contributing because they know they get that little reward every time they do. However, even if you're not leading other leaders, you'll open the road up for people to respond to each other in these ways as well. As peers, people will say these same things, like, "I really like what Ernesto said earlier. I'm dealing with that same thing," or "I want to go back to Sandra's point. Sandra, why do you feel that's what's happening? Have you tried talking to this person you're having this issue with?" When you set the rules of the road like this in a communication setting, you show people what's acceptable and what isn't, but you also pull the group up to higher communication standards. You show people it's important to truly listen to what's being said, not just for the sake of *hearing* it, but truly understanding and remembering it. You show people it's important to value and acknowledge others so they know they were heard. You teach them to listen better and more intently to each other. Because of this, they can become better listeners at home and value the opinions of their friends and family more as well. Then you're helping your team become better communicators in every area of their life. The best leaders always impact our personal lives.

If you don't do this, you'll notice over time that people aren't as engaged or excited to share. When they make their comments, if you move right onto the next comment, your folks will often feel like their comments are going straight into a black hole. That's not fun for anyone. So, respond to people—again and again.

#5: YOU DOUBLE- AND TRIPLE-STACK YOUR QUESTIONS.

Have you ever been asked two or three questions at the same time? We've all done it. The problem is, when we do this, usually only one question gets answered. And usually, it's the last one. Remember, great leaders ask questions because they want people to *think* about the answers. At some point, you want answers because answers contain information. You need information to make decisions, find solutions, and move forward. Business and life are all about moving forward and progressing—not staying the same. So, you need people to *think* and *answer*.

When you double- or triple-stack questions, you put people in a tough position. The human brain can only really focus consciously on one thing at a time. (Even though our subconscious minds can process numerous things at once, our subconscious is not where we make the best decisions.) If you really want people to think about what you're asking and also answer you, then you can't throw out multiple questions at once and expect the average person to think about *all* of them and answer *all* of them. Usually, our brains operate with some level of recency basis, so we'll answer the question we heard last—the one after which was finally silence, allowing us time to think.

There's probably lots of reasons we do this, but one is nervousness. We might ask a question that makes *us*, the asker, uncomfortable. We want the information, but maybe we feel the question is too invasive or it's the first time we've asked a question of its kind. Perhaps we're new to management and this is the first time we're trying to hold someone accountable and ask them directly, "What the heck happened here?" To deal with our nerves, we sometimes double- and triple-stack questions. In this scenario, we might say something like, "So, what happened with this? Was the expectation not clear? Or were you short-staffed?" We essentially jump in and start doing some of the work for our audience.

You'll notice the first question was an open-ended question, designed to elicit thought and reflection and something from the respondent's heart. However, it was then followed by closed-ended questions. This is the most common way I've seen people stack questions, and it's highly ineffective for a few reasons.

First, when we do this, we start filling in the holes for people. When we start giving options of possible answers to the first open-ended question, our respondents are likely to take one of them, which may or may *not* be the real or complete answer. It also might not contain the information we really want and need. In the scenario, the person might say, "Yeah, I'm short-staffed!" Then, our next question will likely dive into that concern. But if we're asking why someone didn't hit their sales goal, the real reason might have nothing to do with the person being short-staffed. We'd be much better off asking about what happened and letting our respondent fill in their *own* blanks.

Second, when we do this, we're back to a game of Go Fish. We start narrowing the scope of the question, and what we really want to know gets lost. If you're wondering *What happened?*, then why wouldn't you simply *ask* that? When we give people possible answers, we're only perpetuating stories we've started to form in our *own* minds, filling voids of silence with nervous energy about how our respondent *might* react, what they *might* think, what they *might* say. The best thing you can do to stimulate real and meaningful dialogue is ask one question at a time, starting with the question you really want to know the answer to, and leave it at that until your audience responds. Then, you can determine if another question is necessary.

#6: YOU INTERRUPT PEOPLE BEFORE THEY ARE DONE SPEAKING.

This is the ultimate sin of listening, and yet it's something we do every day. We ask people questions and don't wait for the answers (or the full answers) before we start talking again. Great leaders who make an art form out of asking great questions also wait for the answers. They don't cut their people off. They don't interrupt. They let their people finish. They do this not only out of respect, but because they genuinely want to learn from the people they're talking to.

Our egos and our impatience often get in the way and prevent us from doing this. When it comes to ego, it's often a matter of thinking we know better. We often wrongly assume that, because *we're* the leader, we have all the answers. Well, gosh! Then why ask any questions at all? Perhaps people who do this out of ego feel that they *should* ask questions. Perhaps they read in a book somewhere that it's the right thing to do, and so they do it for show, to "check the box." Perhaps they're self-aware *enough* to know that asking no questions of other people—ever—makes them a tyrant. But they don't ask questions with the intent to actually *listen*. They only pretend to listen until they can get the mic back and go on with the rest of their monologue.

Two reasons seem to drive our impatience when we're listening. First, time. We're always trying to conserve it and to create more of it. We want people to get to their points more quickly to save time. And second, we're so self-absorbed that we want the floor back, not necessarily because we know better, but because we *think* we know the full extent of what the other person is going to say. Someone will start talking, and when they get a few sentences in, we hear something that we want to respond to. We'll wrongly assume where the other person is going with their thoughts—entirely. So, we'll swoop in. Sometimes, we do this unintentionally; we get so excited by something someone else has said, it spurs new thoughts in our brains, which we feel the need to immediately disperse—to show interest, to stay engaged, to not become bored. Whatever the reason, it's really a lack of patience and, perhaps, self-awareness that prevents us from hanging in, waiting for the whole story, and allowing the person to finish.

Often, we're wrong when we think we know what someone is going to say. When we cut someone off because we think we know where they're going, sometimes we're right, but sometimes we're not. Problem is, when we cut someone off, we don't get to find out. We make assumptions as if we have a crystal ball telling us how every person is going to behave in the future. But we don't have a crystal ball. If we're good leaders, we know that people are learning new things, growing, evolving, and expanding their mind every day. (If you don't see your people that way, that's a major shortcoming on your part, and perhaps your people aren't doing those things because you're not enacting the V.I.R.T.U.E.S. in this book.) If you're doing it right and the people around you are constantly upskilling themselves, then you can't possibly ever be sure you know what they're going to say because what they might have said yesterday is not what they'll say today. You don't know what they learned or decided yesterday. Allowing people to speak out loud and express themselves verbally is a true gift you give others; for many of us, it's like the air we need to survive, and it's how we often advance our understanding. I'm one of those people. It's important for me to speak my thoughts out loud. Saying them verbally aids the understanding and internalization process for me, and so when others don't let me speak, I'm stuck in place, and stagnant isn't good for anyone. When we let our people talk, we open ourselves up to the possibility that they might teach *us* something—a truly great gift.

> **You ain't learnin' nothin' when you're talkin'.**
> **– sign hung in Lyndon B. Johnson's office**

We're ingrained as leaders to believe we should always be teaching, and we tend to believe we can only learn from those who are senior to us. Great leaders have debunked this myth, knowing they can learn from *anyone* around them. They also know that they can only be learning when they're not speaking. When we're talking, we're often only repeating and sharing what we already know. The only way to learn something new is to listen. When we are quiet long enough to hear about the struggles, challenges, experiences, ideas, thoughts, and feelings of others, something amazing happens. We expand our ability to influence others because we've opened ourselves up to being influenced.

Whatever the reasons—you think you're smarter and have the answers, you're eager and get so excited by what someone else is saying that you don't let them finish, you get bored and impatient, thinking you know what someone will say, and cut them off early—not actively listening to others makes you a lousy leader.

"You can't fake listening. It shows." – Raquel Welch

People have a real need to be heard. When you don't listen to them, you show them that you don't appreciate, value, and care for them. You don't believe they have anything to teach you. You might not *think* that's true, but if you're cutting people off and not truly listening to them, your behavior is showing them you don't value them or have interest in what they're saying. Perception is reality, and I guarantee you that if you make a regular habit of cutting people off, you'll eventually be seen as arrogant and no one will have any interest in talking to you. You might not notice that others don't have much to say because you'll be so busy filling the space with your own thoughts and ideas, which makes you feel good. But it won't make people around you feel good, which is what matters most. That's what leadership is about. It's not about you. Great leaders help ensure that everyone knows they have a voice and that their thoughts and contributions matter. Not only are they interested in making people feel that way, but they're interested in showing people that it *is* that way. You need to harvest the intellect of others. No matter how sharp, bright, or brilliant you are, you're not an island, and you can't function independently. You need your team to help cover your weaknesses and blind spots, to shore you up where you're not as naturally strong and gifted. You need the intellect and perspective of others who don't see things the same as you. So, listen actively when your people are talking. Let them finish, and great things will come.

#7: YOU ONLY ASK THE QUESTIONS THAT DELIVER THE ANSWERS YOU WANT.

Great leaders seek out conflicting information. They recognize the true point of dialogue and asking questions is to help others reflect and process and for all to learn. Great leaders count on their people to teach them things, to give them the real pulse of the ground floor, to escalate and bubble up not only real ideas and solutions, but also real problems and issues.

When leaders only ask certain kinds of questions—ones that make them feel good, ones that help them feel that everything is going great, ones that make them feel intelligent and important—a major disservice is being done. When that happens, they only have *that* intel to go on, but it might not be the *right* intel. I recognize how tempting it can be to gather information that only makes us feel good, but a great life (and great leadership) is not about feeling good. Sometimes, it's about feeling bad (and being okay with that). We can only fix problems we're aware of, so hearing about what we don't want to know or what we wish weren't happening—but being able to handle it—is a critical part of our role as leaders.

When we're willing to ask about the tough stuff, actively listen to the answers, and then show we can handle the information, we build credibility with our teams. Our teams see our true desire to gather honest and real information. Because they see that our quest to learn about real life is legitimate, they're more likely to give us legitimate answers and even share additional information we haven't asked for. Then, you build a team that doesn't only speak when spoken to but speaks freely all the time. This means you'll never be in the dark. What a great place to be!

VIRTUE 5:
Understand How Learning Works

"We sent them to training…right?!" – countless leaders

wish this quote was a joke. I can't tell you how many times I've heard a manager say these words. In fact, some managers say these words *anytime* someone makes a mistake, doesn't know something, fails in some way, or isn't having success. Since many like to find scapegoats and blame others for problems, this statement is a way to cover our tails for people who roll up to us who don't know something. It's a way to say, "It's not *my* fault that my employee doesn't know how to do X. I'm just their leader. I sent them to training, and I should've gotten a fully functional employee back who was perfect in every way and ready to apply all that great training they received in whatever course, class, seminar, or certification program."

This kind of thinking is ridiculous—but pervasive. Why wouldn't it be? Most companies have whole departments, like Learning & Development (L&D) or Training, solely focused on the training and development of employees. New employees or newly promoted employees often go through training classes—sometimes weeklong or multiple-week programs with many layers—to learn how to do their jobs better. In customer service or sales organizations, it's not uncommon for employees to take a host of classes to sharpen their skills. Many companies have full menus of training classes or programs that employees can take, and it's not uncommon for employees to have full transcripts of what classes they've taken at their company since the beginning of time. When these programs exist, most managers send their people to training, and in many cases, these programs are great. The classes are interactive, engaging, and from a content perspective, well-designed.

So, what's the problem? Adult learning is a tricky thing, and it requires *far* more day-to-day involvement and reinforcement on both the learner's part and their manager's part, *after* formalized training is done, for *real* learning to take place. When a manager says something like, "I sent my employee to training. An expert taught them, and my employee completed all the prework, postwork, and attended the class. I'm told they even spoke up and participated. We're good!" real problems begin, for both the manager and their employee.

If you're reading this book, I assume you want to learn something about leadership. Great leaders don't teach people things (or send their people to training) to fulfill a requirement, check a box, or to say they did it. They don't even do it because they want their people to learn things. Great leaders teach people things because they want their people to *practice* what they've learned.

They want to see their people *execute* on their newfound learning. It's not enough for learning to have occurred, but that it's *applied*. Great leaders want their people to not only learn but to remember what they've learned and to use it. For that to happen, leaders must be actively involved.

By no means am I implying that formalized and structured company training programs don't work. I'm also not implying that the sole responsibility for the learning of an employee falls on that person's leader. However, formalized training won't cut it *alone*, and too many leaders seem to have no clue what it takes for learning to take hold. In this chapter, we'll explore how learning really works and provide some practices to ensure learning *sticks*.

PRACTICE 1:
DON'T TEACH CALCULUS BEFORE YOU TEACH ALGEBRA

The biggest mistake I see leaders make when they're trying to teach someone something is they don't invest time up front understanding what someone already knows and doesn't know. It's equally important to understand what someone is already able to do and not do. One of the most important truths of learning is that, in general, it must be a stepwise progression where complicated, harder topics build on previous, easier topics and aren't introduced *until* those previous topics have been learned. And by "learned," I mean not only understood but *practiced*.

When you think about the concept of "learning," what do you think of first? Most people think about school. In elementary school, multiplication and division aren't taught until *after* addition and subtraction are taught (and learned). And before children can even be taught addition or subtraction, they must understand the concept of numbers first, right? They must know that numbers exist and what a number is—a mathematical representation of a quantity or amount.

Imagine how difficult it would be to multiply or divide numbers if you didn't know what a number *was*? Imagine how equally difficult it would be to multiply or divide numbers if you understood the concept of numbers but didn't know the *order* of numbers? For example, you hadn't yet learned that 72 is a greater number than 27? It would not only be difficult, it would be impossible.

For the most part, our primary educational system gets a lot of this right. We teach children the alphabet before we ask them to learn various words and know how to spell and pronounce them. We ask them to spell and work on pronouncing certain words before we ask them to read full books. When we do ask them to read books, we start with books designed for children, with lots of pictures and simple words. We wouldn't hand them a copy of *this* book before they have mastered Dr. Suess.

We do this because we have an understanding and expectation with children that we can't teach harder concepts before we teach the basics. Learning is progressive, and harder concepts require the mastery over simpler concepts first. We don't always do this in the workplace. We sometimes throw facts, figures, and concepts at our team that they're not prepared to digest. We talk *at* them instead of *with* them. We don't always test for mastery and understanding over previous material before moving onto new things. Why?

The top five reasons that stand out to me are:
- We think it'll take too long, and we don't want to invest the time.
- We treat our adult colleagues and employees differently than our children.
- Our egos prevent us from meeting people where they are; we'd rather they come to us.
- We're afraid of what we might find out.
- We haven't been taught how to teach.

It *does* take time to figure out where someone is in their learning instead of throwing everything you know about the topic at them. It *does* take time and patience to meet other people where *they're* at in their understanding instead of expecting them to meet us where *we* are in our understanding. We understand with children that things need to move in a progressive order, but in work environments, dealing with adults, we delude ourselves into thinking they can handle it, and so we forge ahead. We also have egos. We delude ourselves into thinking that if a nugget of information helped us, there must be value in sharing it with someone else. So, we talk over people's heads, throwing tons of information at them that they're not understanding. Sadly, too many employees are too afraid to speak up and say they don't under-stand or that they're not following along, often for fear of looking stupid. This only perpetuates the cycle—with the manager thinking all is well and their people are coming right along with them. This often worsens the cycle, as managers become even less aware of what their people don't know or are only pretending to know, and as the cycle repeats itself in future meetings or classes, the gap between real knowledge and perceived knowledge only becomes greater.

This is rarely, if ever, effective. When we don't take the time to dig in and find out what our employees do and don't know, we can't possibly structure a learning plan around *them*. We don't meet them where *they* are. This causes us to lose so much time in the long run. We host meetings and coaching sessions where we're so eager to teach them "everything we know" so we can "get them up and running faster!" However, we don't stop in and check for understanding. We don't notice the "deer in the headlights" look on so many of their faces. We don't pay attention to the verbal and nonverbal signs that our team is lost. Sometimes these signs are obvious; other times, not so much. Often, because we haven't created an environment safe enough for people to speak up and share how lost they are or ask clarifying questions, we press on and never realize that whatever pep talk, coaching session, or meeting where we dispensed a ton of information wasn't effective at all. This creates a huge problem because the longer our employees stay with us, the scarier it becomes to admit that they don't "know" something. So, the chances of them speaking up to say, "I have no idea how to do that" or "I have no idea what you're talking about," become smaller. With that, errors, mistakes, issues, and even a lack of engagement or ability to grow and develop become more likely.

The bottom line is that we can't know *what* to teach others until we know what they already know.

PRACTICE 2:
ASK AND OBSERVE

"Trust but verify." – Russian proverb often attributed to Ronald Reagan

President Reagan, who popularized this phrase in America, was onto something. While it's critical that we truly extend trust to our people, it's also critical that we, as leaders, check in periodically to understand and ensure that our mission is on course. People aren't always going to deceive us intentionally. It's easy for this to happen accidentally. But given our expertise and experience, there's no one better than us to check in to ensure that our people are really understanding, progressing, and coming along with us on our journey. There are a few simple ways of verifying what your people know, and the first is to *ask*.

Don't just say, "Hey, do you know about XYZ? Oh, you do? Great!" We can *really* ask by asking our employees to teach *us*. We can say, "Oh, that's great. Would you mind explaining it back to me? I'd love to understand how you're thinking about this." Or "Hey, would you mind teaching that to others at our meeting this Friday morning? I think Jack is struggling with that." We can test, verify, and confirm that our employees know as much as they think they do by asking what they know and finding ways to see those answers in action. Asking an employee who *does* know something to *teach* another person about that thing is a great way to enhance learning too. After all:

"To teach is to learn twice." – Joseph Joubert

The next best way to understand what someone knows and doesn't know about something is to *observe*, to *see* them do it. The power of observation is great. If someone knows how to do something and they're good at it, they'll have no problem demonstrating it for you. For employees who feel they're in a safe environment where mistakes aren't just tolerated but are encouraged and applauded because of how much personal growth they lead to, they know that demonstrating something in front of you, the leader, is a great way to grow and get better at it. If you're trying to understand how much someone knows about a key component of their job, and they say, "Oh, I absolutely know that," ask, "Would you mind walking me through your process then? I'd love to learn from YOU!" or say, "Would you mind demonstrating that in front of me today? I'd love to see you in action." This is similar to the process above except you're asking someone to demonstrate what they know in action, whereas previously you were asking them to explain what they know in words.

Over the years, I've had employees tell me, "Of course, I know how to do that. I'm a master at cold-calling," "Asking open-ended questions is my strong suit," or "I feel very comfortable closing loans that have this special paperwork associated with them." But when I asked if I could sit in and watch my employees do the things they had just confidently told me they "knew" all about, I'd identify plenty of knowledge (and execution) gaps in their delivery. We'd find that they didn't always know what they didn't know. In some cases, this was innocent; they truly thought they had absorbed all the complexity or detail around a certain concept or topic. This reminds me of one of my favorite quotes:

"I would not give a fig for the simplicity this side of complexity, but I would give my life for the simplicity on the other side of complexity."
– Oliver Wendell Holmes

In other cases, I discovered employees who didn't feel comfortable "telling" on themselves and putting themselves in any position of perceived weakness. In too many corporate cultures, people believe that for them to be respected or valued, they have to know everything. Setting up an environment where it's okay to not know something or admitting that you're still in the process of learning too will help people be more truthful and forthcoming about where they are in their understanding, which then helps you know where, when, what, and how to teach. So, as much as you might trust your team, don't just take their word for it.

If you're honest with yourself, you might realize you're afraid of what you might find out by asking what your team knows and doesn't know and asking them to demonstrate it. I can assure you that it's far better to inquire into where your team truly stands than to take their knowledge for granted and assume everything's fine. Not delving into where your team truly is with their knowledge and skills is an easy way to get burned when you least expect it. I had to learn this lesson the hard way. In my first few years as a district or regional manager, I felt uncomfortable quizzing people on what they knew and asking them to demonstrate it for me. I felt like I was being an invasive pest by wanting to dig into their skill set or knowledge base. So, I didn't. I took the word of my direct and indirect reports that they had read whatever recent memorandum had come out; fully understood whatever new policy, procedure, initiative, or incentive plan had rolled out; or fully grasped whatever recent training they had been to.

"Here's how adult learning works: Step 1: You read it. Step 2: I ask you about it. Step 3: You tell me about it." – Johnny Montes

Fortunately, I was lucky enough to have some great bosses who weren't as naive and had no problem appearing nosy in asking what people knew or didn't know. I still remember learning how to practice this behavior myself.

In a few instances, I invited my bosses out to my branches to get to know my teams. One time, we hadn't even been there 10 minutes before the facade came crashing down. My area executive, Johnny Montes, and I stood on the side of the morning huddle and watched as the branch manager did what I had been doing (they probably were learning it from me). The branch manager said, "So, everyone's read and understands the new policy around X, right?" Every branch employee nodded in unison. "Does anyone have any questions?" the manager continued. Every branch employee shook their heads in unison. "Great!" he responded, putting that page of his stack aside, about to continue onto his next topic.

Johnny wasn't so quick to believe. Embracing the spirit of Wendell Holmes and Reagan, he asked me and the branch manager permission to chime in, which we happily gave him. "I'm so happy you guys are up to speed with this new policy," he said as he scanned the room. "It was initially somewhat complicated for me to understand, and I'm still learning things about it every time I read it," he admitted with a sheepish smile. The room chuckled. "I'm finding that the branches that are doing the best with this change are the ones really talking about it," he continued as his eyes landed on a name badge affixed to one gentleman's suit. "Jose, would you mind enlightening us on the policy? Just share the most important one to two changes that stood out to you about this new policy?"

Jose couldn't do it or tell us a single thing about the new policy. My boss, Johnny, then asked if someone else wouldn't mind sharing. In one of the most memorable moments of my career, I watched as not one single person in this branch could tell him anything about the policy. Not only had this team "fooled" their branch manager, but they had fooled me too. I was more than embarrassed. In fact, so much so that it was the last time I allowed this to happen. Whether Johnny was actually learning new things about the policy every time he read it was irrelevant. He had disarmed others by saying it was complicated for him too. He had made himself vulnerable before asking others about it. What a perfect example.

I won't lie to you and say it's never uncomfortable to ask people to teach you something you already know or demonstrate something for you. If you don't build the right rapport with your team, by using all the other V.I.R.T.U.E.S. and practices in this book, your team can and likely will feel distrusted or spied on. However, as discussed in Virtue 3, things often become more comfortable (for all parties involved) when they're practiced habitually. So, if you want to make this process more comfortable and expected, choose to do it more. Also, when done right and well, this practice doesn't have to be uncomfortable. It does require the following:

- You've built great relationships with the people you're asking. They see you often, and you know each other.
- You have pure intentions when you ask. You truly do want to test for understanding for the sake of ensuring there's understanding, learning, and development taking place—not to "catch" them in the act. You express that, you show that, and it's seen and felt by others.
- There aren't consequences when people tell you the truth. It's important that people don't feel they get chastised for admitting they don't know something or need more help. If you don't create a safe environment for people to admit where they're at, you haven't set them up to be honest about it. (Obviously, if consistent teaching and training are in place but learning still isn't taking place, that's a separate conversation.)

The reality is that if you've created an environment of learning and growth and routinely ask questions about how that's all going, learning becomes a team exercise. It can be enjoyable and fun, and your team won't mind putting their knowledge (or lack thereof) on display if they know that they'll learn something new or increase understanding.

PRACTICE 3:
KNOW WHEN TO GET INVOLVED AND WHEN TO HANG BACK

Sometimes learning what people know and don't know can be frustrating. I remember once during my years as a regional director, I invited the company's COO to come out and watch me do branch visits with my team. Although my boss had observed me doing site visits before, his boss never had, and at the time, since I was trying to climb the corporate ladder, I wanted him to see how capable I was. Wanting to prove my own capabilities became a major downfall that day.

One of my branch managers was hiring an assistant manager, and we had both separately interviewed the candidate in the days prior. Talking about our (well, what *should* have been *her*) hiring decision was on the agenda for that day's visit. In addition, I would be observing her coach one of her personal bankers. As my guest, our COO would also be sitting in on those two interactions.

I remember that day like it was yesterday. I was so excited to showcase all that I knew to our COO. I had been conducting branch visits as a regional manager for years and felt confident in my ability to run a great visit. For years, I had gotten feedback from my branch managers and, frequently, their staff that my visits to their offices were great; they always left smarter than before, learned a great deal, and got clear direction on how they could improve. Since I had held every position in a bank branch, I was quick to find solutions to every and any problem.

That day was no different. In both interactions with the branch manager, I found myself eager to coach and teach her everything I knew from having walked a mile in her shoes. With regard to the assistant manager position, I was surprised to hear that she liked the candidate tremendously and planned to hire her. I asked questions about why and listened, as I was accustomed to doing, but was eager to share my own opinion with her—which was very different from hers. When it was my turn to talk, I shared with her how concerned I was about several aspects of the candidate's personality and statements the candidate had made. I encouraged the branch manager not to hire her and to keep looking. "I'd be really careful with this or that," I advised her. "I've never seen *that* end well." My branch manager agreed and told me she'd keep looking, and I internally patted myself on the back for saving us from making a shoddy hiring decision.

When it came time for her coaching of a personal banker, I found myself overly involved again. When her employee didn't seem to be embracing her ideas of how to ask better and more provocative questions with his clients, I jumped in, eager to show everyone how it's done. I asked her personal banker to role-play with *me*, taking over the entire coaching session until I gained his commitment to ask the questions we had practiced. After he left, it was just the branch manager, myself, and our COO, and I led us through a discussion on *why* I took over, where things went awry, and how she could've better prevented it. She thanked me, once again, for my "tremendous feedback," and I felt like a superstar.

The day ended smoothly, and I walked our COO to his car to gather some feedback on what I thought was a great performance in how involved and perfect I was as not only their regional leader, but also as a trainer and coach. "I'd love your feedback," I said to him as we neared his car. We talked about lots in that conversation, many of which were positive. But I'll never forget what he said to me on the topic of training and learning—which became such a part of *my* training and learning and could only have been stated after *he* observed *me* in action.

"Amy," he said, looking me square in the eye, "they're not you. And when you assume they *are* you, you rob them of their journey."

I was heartbroken. "What do you mean?" I asked, desperate for feedback.

"You've got to let them make their own mistakes," he responded. "Today was all about you. You overtook the show. They're the cast and characters in the play, not you. Let them struggle and fail. If you always solve their problems for them, they'll never learn how to solve their own problems."

But I'm the boss, I thought as I drove away. *I'm supposed to be helping them through their journey, by sharing and giving them the benefit of all the wisdom that came from my own...aren't I?*

I had to think about that *a lot*. But finally, I realized our COO was *right*. I had become so accustomed to wanting to help other people, I had started to violate some of my own principles. What do we do when our child is struggling with a tough math problem at the kitchen table? Do we rush in, take the pencil, and solve it for them because we know how to do it with ease?

No, most parents let their child struggle for a bit, for the sake of learning and growth, then gently ask questions and coax from the sidelines. That year, I was faced with a challenge of personal growth as a leader. I went back to that branch manager a couple of days later and encouraged her to make whatever hiring decision she wanted for her branch.

"But what if it doesn't work out?" she asked. "You said you didn't think it would."

"Then you're probably going to learn something," I told her. "And you'll learn it exactly the same way I did—trial and error."

Turns out, that branch manager *did* make the hiring decision she wanted and brought the candidate I was so concerned about on board. A year later, something interesting had happened. One of us *had* learned something, but it wasn't *her*. It was me. That candidate worked out wonderfully, and I had been wrong. I learned that while it's important to figure out where people are at with their knowledge and learning, we must be careful. Sometimes we're wrong. Sometimes the best way to help others with that learning is to allow them to go through it on their own. To make errors and mistakes. To allow them to go through what we went through and form their own identities as leaders.

When people are learning (including yourself), you have to allow for a certain amount of discomfort, which comes in many forms. Sometimes it comes from embracing mistakes or failures. Sometimes it comes from the anxiety of believing that a mistake or failure is *about* to happen. Sometimes it comes from allowing someone else to make a decision that you, as the leader, disagree with. Since learning happens best in environments where people are allowed some leeway and space to experiment, to err, to try and fail, or to struggle through something before they figure it out, this means you'll have moments where you have to stand back patiently and bravely and wait for it to happen. If you don't, people rarely learn anything, including yourself. You also limit people to only learning what *you* know. If you've hired great people and trained them to think critically, you should be able to allow them some space as they learn from their own mistakes. Sometimes, as I did with the hiring decision, something you think will be a mistake actually isn't. Sometimes things you imagine will be failures turn into successes. This allows you to learn too, but it also supports a learning environment where people feel free to use their own brains, think creatively and innovatively, and chart their own course. So don't prescribe every single course of action, dictate every single decision, and provide every answer. Let people learn.

I'm by no means recommending that you empower the wrong people. I'm not recommending that you let everyone, at all levels, run loose. When you extend trust, create space, and provide room for people to err and make their own mistakes, it should be because you've carefully evaluated your talent. It's important you've first seen a level of capability and competence in your people. You'll know what members of your team have earned the most freedom and latitude by adhering to the other V.I.R.T.U.E.S. and practices in this book. You'll have spent time with them, engaged and involved them in dialogue, communicated regularly with them, asked them lots of open-ended questions, and observed how they think and reason. For completely new team members with zero experience, training, or time with you, you might need to stay more involved and hand them problems and challenges with increasing complexity until you recognize they're capable of more. The more you give people latitude and they don't let you down, the more you can extend grater challenges in the future.

I realized later in the situation with the branch manager I had been overcoaching in front of my COO that she wasn't deserving of my overinvolvement. This was a leader who had been with us for years. She had been in a management role for a few of those and was running one of my largest offices. Later, when I talked about the situation with my boss, he asked, "Are you going to rate her over a 4 this year?" (Our performance ratings only go to a 5.) "Yes, she's been rated over a 4 every year I've had her," I responded. "Does it ever make sense to make a decision for someone you consistently rate over a 4?" he asked. That question was a major wake-up call for me. I realized, it rarely does. While my behaviors with her might have been more appropriate for a brand-new, first-time manager, they weren't appropriate for her. Understanding your people—who they are, how they reason, and where they're at— is a key component of knowing when to jump in or when to hang back. Great leaders don't paint everyone with the same brush.

PRACTICE 4:
DON'T LET THE END JUSTIFY THE MEANS

Even a broken clock is right twice a day.

I play blackjack. I love it. Blackjack is my favorite game in any casino, and I find it to be one of the most interesting games on the floor. What I find most interesting is the human interactions I witness at the table, especially when a seasoned player is trying to teach the game to a new player.

In blackjack, it's quite common for newbies to show up at the table and often be accompanied by a full-blown coach. When, I say "coach," I don't mean an "official" coach. They're simply there with a spouse, significant other, family member, or friend, but these "seasoned" blackjack players who coach their partners or friends who are playing the game for the first time *really* like to coach. To varying degrees, they're eager to explain what's going on (from their perspective) with every hand. They're full of predictions on what's going to happen and why. They teach their loved ones how to play based on their own rules and preferences about the game. They don't like it when other players at the table have a different set of rules and preferences about the game. While their ideas about the game may vary, the one thing they all seem to share is that they don't like to be *wrong* in their explanations.

Of this bunch, my favorite "coaches" are ones who refuse to play by the book (on choice hands, or at all), make risky decisions at the worst time, and look to justify poor decisions by the outcome. I'm not here to teach anyone to play blackjack the way I do, but the "book" instructs that you hit a 16 when the dealer is showing a 10 (because the dealer isn't likely to bust and, instead, is likely to end with 20 or 21). This same book, used by blackjack experts, also says that assuming you have at least 12, you don't draw when the dealer is showing a 6 (because the dealer is most likely to bust with a 6).

Every now and again comes along a person who will stay on 16s regardless of what the dealer shows and hits their own bust hands when the dealer is also showing a bust hand. It tends not to work out, and people who play this way tend to lose more, but blackjack is a form of gambling for a reason.

There's no guarantees. Sometimes, the dealers bust when they shouldn't. Sometimes, the players bust when they shouldn't. Sometimes, the dealers pull out 21 when they should have busted. Sometimes the players pull out 21 when they should have busted. When I say "shouldn't," all I mean is "when they're not expected to." Blackjack is a game of probabilities, and masterful players are simply playing the odds. The game involves some skill, but it also involves a bit of luck. This isn't dissimilar to leadership, business, or life.

Sometimes, coaches who make these poor decisions (poor by usual standards anyway) and are teaching others to do the same will go on a winning streak. Things will happen on the table that aren't expected to happen, and I'll watch as the "coach" gleefully explains to their understudy why their strategy "works." "See," they'll say as the dealer pulls out an 18 from a 6. "It paid off for me to hit my 12. I got a 20 and beat the dealer. I saved my hand!" The lesson they're teaching is that it pays to hit 12s when the dealer shows a 6, but that's not a lesson most experts would want a new player to learn. It makes me cringe when several bizarre outcomes like this pop up in a row. The coach touts the ridiculous luck they're having as talent and skill, and another newbie learns a terrible methodology for approaching the game of blackjack.

When we're teaching people how to think about something, it's important we direct people's focus toward the things they can control, not the things they can't. Sometimes a person or a team will have great results. It's important that we don't hail the merits of that person or team based on results alone. We should dig in and understand the practices, behaviors, and activities of the person or team. It's critical that we understand *how* that person got their results. To ensure we're teaching people correct principles so they can eventually govern themselves,[26] in ways likely to make them successful, we have to look at their methods.

There are two reasons this is critical. First, we want to make sure that results aren't simply happenstance. Especially when we're going to put something on stage as a teachable moment—where others can learn from it—we need to know it didn't occur because of luck or chance, but rather, through hard work, discipline, and with a model of success that can be replicated and will likely generate more success in the future. Hitting 12s when the dealer is showing a 6 isn't a common way to generate success. It sometimes works, but it's not likely to *keep* working.

Second, the ends can't justify ill-intentioned means. This book is about creating lasting, long-term, sustainable success, not overnight results. Lots of people can cheat, lie, steal, deceive, or con their way into short-term success. We could point to numerous examples of this in business and in life. But, in the end, lasting success comes from doing things right, ethically, and well. It comes from finding correct principles that stand the test of time. When we only look at results, we can sometimes be blind to situations where results are positive but were achieved the *wrong* way. If you want to be sure your people are learning paradigms and routines that will serve them well for the long haul, you can't get excited about one-hit wonders or freak incidents on the blackjack table. Instead, you find a strategy that is proven to work over time and stick with it.

This often means you can't overcelebrate accidents and coincidences. Sometimes, you'll need to shift focus away from what's happening at present or how great something seems and instead stay true to your guiding principles that you've developed over time and know work for you. You must ask additional questions and do additional research. Just because someone lands a giant sale doesn't mean they're a great salesperson. Just because someone lands 10 giant sales doesn't mean they're a great salesperson, either They might be, but there's much more you'd have to find out about their beliefs, routines, and practices before you could say that definitively. When you want to teach someone how to play their hand, it's critical that you leverage time-tested principles known to work in the grand scheme of things—not just focus on what's working at one specific moment.

PRACTICE 5:
DON'T BE TOO COOL, STAY IN SCHOOL

The worst leaders I've seen are narcissistic and arrogant. They struggle to show humility and struggle to practice many of these V.I.R.T.U.E.S. and behaviors for a myriad of reasons. Some are self-absorbed and have forgotten where they came from. Others are impatient and don't want to share their time in this way. Still others don't feel they should have to. They feel others should just "get it" and "do their jobs" with their heads down. The list goes on, but it's all disgusting and has nothing to do with leadership. Whatever the reasons, most arrogant and overconfident leaders share something in common: they've all stopped learning.

When we're put into positions of leadership, a certain amount of respect and prestige can come with the job. Maybe you're no longer in a cubicle but have your own office. Maybe you had an office but now you have a corner office with a view and twice the space. Maybe it means a lot to you that you have a fancy title on your new business cards. Maybe you now know what everyone around you makes, and before, you didn't. Maybe you're now invited to big important meetings with the board. I don't know what you've been gifted as you've climbed the ranks, but if you were nodding gleefully to everything in this list, there's a chance your title has gone to your head.

The best leaders *never* stop learning. If you want to be an awesome boss, make a point of learning and publicly telling others that you're learning. Share what you're learning about, especially your most recent learnings. Make a point of learning with your team. Never feel that you've become so mighty and great that you must have all the answers. If you really want your team to be open to coaching, teaching, training, and learning, be open to it yourself.

We tend to be creatures of habit and find it easy to get stuck in our ways. Many of us, in our careers and in our lives, settle into a routine and our own way of doing things. As time goes on, we can find ourselves in learning environments far less often. We're no longer in formal education. We might not be going to as many seminars, lectures, classes, or conferences to learn because the assumption is that we *already* know everything. Our lives fill up with other responsibilities: family demands and the schedules of our children, homeownership and its responsibilities, caring for aging parents, community events. We're rewarded for how much we "know" and how much we've "done" or accomplished, and we forget that there's still so much to learn. We forget to make *time* for learning or perhaps choose *not* to make time for it. We don't read as much. We let that natural curiosity and zest we had for learning when we were younger flitter away.

Perhaps a societal expectation implies there's something vulnerable or bad about still "needing" to learn at an older age. Maybe we associate knowledge with strength and thus conclude that learning must be associated with weakness. Whatever the reason, it's not uncommon for people who are more seasoned in life and their careers to stop learning.

"When was the last time you did something for the first time?"
– Darius Rucker

Some of what I'm asking you to do in this book is hard; it's difficult to encourage people to admit their vulnerabilities, be open to your coaching and feedback, engage in dialogue with you about their deepest concerns and worries, get on board and be as excited as you are about the future vision. Thus, we've discussed ways you can show humility to your people, putting them at ease, so they can be comfortable around you. Continuing learning yourself is one way to put others at ease. If you stop learning, as their leader, they'll sense it. They'll know. Then, they won't be as excited as you want them to be to learn. No matter how much you know (or think you know), you don't know it all. There are always more things you can learn.

VIRTUE 6:
Encourage Energy

"It is amazing what you can accomplish
when you do not care who gets the credit."
– Harry S. Truman

ecall a situation where you worked really hard on something, did your best, and gave your all but no one said anything about it. Now, imagine the following:

You make a goal to lose some weight, and this goal is important to you. You work hard at your goal by making radical shifts to your diet, exercise, and sleep patterns. You're a couple of months into these new routines, and it's working! You've lost some noticeable weight, and you're feeling better about yourself than you have in years. It's the holiday season, and you make the decision to travel to see your family for the first time since you've started your new routines. You get excited to show off all the hard work you've been doing. As you drive to the gathering, you even imagine some of the compliments your family will give you, since they'll surely notice your progress. You feel you look great and are excited to bask a little in your success. You're proud of what you've accomplished, and this will be an opportunity to enjoy a moment where others are proud of you too.

But you walk into the family dinner, and no one says a word. You hand off your coat to someone in the foyer and exchange hugs and hellos with everyone. But no one says a word. *OK, maybe no one has noticed yet,* you think, *but surely, they will!* The conversation moves from the foyer to the kitchen, where you're offered a beverage. Twenty or 30 minutes goes by and still, not a word. The group moves to the living room for more conversation. Dinner comes and goes. Finally, hours have passed, it nears time for bed, and still, no one has said a word. You realize that no one is *going* to say anything. How do you feel?

Now, it's fair to point out that not everyone would be bothered by this scenario. Not all humans thrive on the encouragement and acknowledgment of others to feel good. Some get all the validation they need from within themselves, and while that's great, I'd argue it's not common. Many reputable authors, speakers, coaches, and professionals tell us that seeking validation and worth from within can lead to great happiness and helps us depend *less* on external validation from others. I'm all for that. I really am, and as I've practiced manifesting more validation from within myself, instead of needing it from others, I've become a happier person.

However, it's my belief that most people would feel *lousy* both during and after this situation. Most of us want our hard work to be acknowledged and talked about. If this holiday scenario happened to you, it's likely it would affect some of your evening. You might spend time thinking about *why* no one has said anything to you, distracting you from the conversations and interactions with family. You might think, *Gosh, maybe nobody noticed. Maybe it's not as obvious as I think it is.* Or, *Maybe no one cares about me enough to say anything.* Either way, your night is likely to be impacted in a negative way. The excitement you had while picking out a nice outfit, getting ready, and driving to the gathering might be dampened. You might even alter your perception of how well you were really doing on your diet, thinking, *Maybe all this hard work isn't even* worth *it, if nobody is even going to notice or say something.* You might even get back home and take a step back from your new routines or quit them all together.

None of us live in a vacuum. We live in an integrated world where we share much of our lives with others. Many of us cohabitate with others, sharing our living spaces, bathrooms, and even a bed with other people. We share our innermost thoughts, feelings, and emotions with others too. We share joy with others when things are going well, and we share pain and suffering with others when the chips are down or when we experience loss or bad news. This is the way of the world, and we like things this way; it's part of our desire as humans to be social and interdependent.

Think about how many events in life are formal celebrations of progress, accomplishment, and achievement. High schools, colleges, and universities all have formalized graduation programs, right? You're given a diploma and either your department is called or your name is called. Sometimes, you even get to walk across the stage. These public events are as much for the families, friends, and loved ones of the graduates as the graduates themselves! We, as a society, want to bask in the glory of the accomplishments and achievements of those around us. How boring would those ceremonies be if only the graduates were allowed to attend? Instead, whole families put these events on their calendars, clear their schedules, and sometimes travel to see their grandson, daughter, or *whoever* graduate.

Losing weight as the result of several changed behaviors is an important accomplishment in someone's life. It no doubt took hard work, discipline, struggle, sweat, and maybe even a few tears. When the hard work has paid off in the desired results, it can be bittersweet when people don't automatically and excitedly cheer us on and celebrate our accomplishments with us, especially without us having to *ask* them to do so.

Now, let's turn our attention to leadership. Similarly, people want to be recognized and celebrated for all the hard work they're putting into their jobs. Maybe their hard work hasn't quite led to noticeable results yet. Maybe it has. Often, it doesn't matter. Most people want what Gary Chapman has described in his 2011 book, *The 5 Languages of Appreciation in the Workplace*, "words of affirmation." In fact, words of affirmation are largely considered to be the most popular of the languages of appreciation. The other languages of love (for example, gifts, quality time, or acts of service) can also be about recognition, celebration, and acknowledgment of people.

Now, instead of the family dinner where no one acknowledged you had lost weight, imagine that you've been busting your butt for a few months at work. You've been coming in early, pulling some late nights. You've missed happy hour with friends, dinner with family, your kid's sporting event, or Monday night football with the guys—whatever matters to *you*. You've sacrificed for the job, put in the extra hours, and delivered results. Again, nobody says *anything*. Neither your boss nor your peers say anything. How do you feel?

If you're like most, the feeling can be anything from mildly annoying to somewhat painful to downright infuriating. If the adage is true that people don't leave companies, rather, they leave their bosses, then this is an area where you as a leader can't afford to be lackluster. It's so important that you get good at sharing the wheel, giving credit and affirmation away, and acknowledging the success and hard work of others. For some, these words of affirmation are like emotional oxygen that people can't feel complete without. For others, it's not about the words but it *is* about feeling seen, appreciated, heard, and valued, which can be shown in other ways. So don't make the mistake of "going green" and being stingy in the recognition, reward, and acknowledgment department.

However, I've seen too many leaders *try* to make an impact when it comes to acknowledging, praising, rewarding, and recognizing others but end up being ineffective. The road to hell is paved with good intentions, so here's some practices to make sure your efforts and attempts in this space aren't in vain.

PRACTICE 1:
DON'T WAIT UNTIL THE GAME IS OVER TO TALK ABOUT THE SCORE

Where do spectators stand at the Boston Marathon? Since I've never been, I looked it up and found the Boston Athletic Association's answer: "There is ample space every mile from Hopkinton to Boston for fans to gather and cheer on your journey to Boylston Street. Some of the most famous spots are the Wellesley Scream Tunnel just before halfway; Heartbreak Hill in Newton around Boston College; and the final stretch on Boylston Street before the finish."[27]

The tagline above this quote on the BAA's website reads: "Endless Support Along the Way." Endless. Loosely translated, it's without an end.

Can you imagine if the only crowd support marathoners got during a 26.2-mile race was at the *end*? So many runners talk about the crowd support along the way being one of the most important components to keeping their head in the game on race day. As someone who has run 200 half marathons and 11 full marathons, I can attest that spectators not only litter the start line—cheering on their friends and families before the event even *begins*—but continue along the course. At large-scale races, they hold signs, cheer, hand out water and food, ring cowbells, play music, dance, and yell encouraging words until the finish line, when they're literally packed multiple-people deep along the fence where runners run through the finish.

In January 2016, I went to Miami to run my first full marathon and invited my father to come spectate. I was dealing with depression in the wake of what felt like a traumatic breakup, and I had started distance running as a way of recovering and healing. I had only been running regularly for about six months at that time and had done a handful of half marathons in that time, but I wasn't confident in my ability to run a full marathon, especially not without stopping. Yet something pushed me to register. Even so, I was terrified.

My father and his then-girlfriend Margo flew down to Miami to cheer me on, and the night before the race, I had so much anxiety and stress, I couldn't handle my emotions well. I ended up blowing up at them at the dinner table because the food was taking a long time to come out. I was panicking that I hadn't eaten early enough and also wasn't going to get enough sleep. When we got back to the two adjoining hotel rooms we had, I shut my door and went to bed without a word to either of them. Of course, by the time my alarm went off at 4:30 the next morning, I already regretted it and opened the door to their room to see if my dad was up and moving. Before our disagreement, he had promised to walk me to the starting line, and I wanted to make sure he knew I'd still love for him to do that. I was confused when I peered into the dark room and saw Margo sleeping soundly under a pile of blankets, with him nowhere to be found. I even crossed through their room and around a corner, fully expecting to find him in his bathroom. But he was not there. I didn't have time to investigate further.

I was still so nervous and filled with anxiety that my hand was trembling when I closed my hotel door behind me around 5 A.M. and headed down the hallway to the elevator. Never in my life will I forget the emotions that went through me when I found my father sitting on the floor between the elevators waiting for me.

"What are you doing here?" I asked. I had been such a jerk to him the night before, I couldn't believe he'd even want to see me that day, let alone be part of my race day experience. My father looked me right in the eye and responded, "Amy, there was no way I was going to miss this."

In the pitch black of night on that cool January morning, we walked in silence to the starting line. At some point, I muttered an apology, and my father brushed it aside. "It's okay; I understand," he said. "This is a really big deal." And it was. I was 33 then, and I hadn't even run a 5K until I was 32 because I didn't believe I could. Now I was about to run 26.2 miles for the first time. Somehow, my father's words, forgiveness, and presence were enough to get me through the first part of that race.

We hadn't gotten much sleep the previous night, so I understood why my 70-year-old father went back to bed after seeing me run through the start. I wasn't 100% sure if I would see them again during my race, but I was hopeful. About halfway into the marathon, FUD (fear, uncertainty, and doubt) began to set in. *What were you thinking?* my subconscious mind chirped. *You're not a marathon runner! You're not going to be able to do this! This is going to be so hard!* It took everything I had to stay on course. Shortly after the halfway point, my father texted asking where I was. He and Margo were up and wanted to get along the course to see me.

That text changed everything. Immediately, the negative self-talk dissipated, and I felt more excited, empowered, and energetic than I had been feeling in miles. Another text said they were heading to mile 17. I can't even describe the pep that came back into my step and how my mindset immediately changed. My doubt about not being able to finish nearly vanished, and instead, I was filled with enthusiasm and hope. I wanted them to see me run by. I wanted to make them proud. I wanted to make myself proud.

I'll remember mile 17 for the rest of my life. They were there: smiling, cheering, taking pictures. That was the first moment I knew I had to finish that race. I decided then and there that quitting was not an option—not when I had two spectators present, who had flown across the country to watch me run my first-ever full marathon.

I was shocked when a few miles later, they updated me again. They had found a way to mile 22 and would see me there! By then, dropping out wasn't on my mind anymore, but walking for a mile or two was. Hearing they were waiting for me at mile 22 completely erased any possibility of that from my mind. I became determined to make it to mile 22 without having had to walk yet. Again, I wanted to make my audience proud, and somehow knowing they were waiting for me added importance and vigor to this race. Mile 22 was just as uplifting as mile 17. My dad looked like he had found a cup of coffee. Or maybe he was just getting more into it. This time, as I came up to them, he was waving his arms in the air happily and beaming with pride. I could almost see the pride bursting out of him, and somehow, whatever pain I had started feeling all over my body disappeared.

That year, the Miami Marathon course took a right turn onto the Rickenbacker Causeway right after mile 22. Runners run down the causeway about a mile and then turn around to run another mile right back up it, popping back out at mile 24. When I headed back up the causeway and saw that the entry and exit point for this two-mile stretch was nearly identical, a part of me wondered if perhaps I would get to see them once more. I wondered if they would have known to wait for me. But no text had come, and I had no expectations.

Suddenly, as I was struggling back up the causeway, I spotted them! Margo was wearing a bright pink jacket that day, so she was easy to see. I pulled off to the side of the runners a bit and waved to her, my arm outstretched over my head as far as I could reach. Within seconds, she saw me, and it was obvious. She jumped up in the air, several feet, and started tugging on my dad's jacket, pointing and shouting. Then, I saw my father's reaction. He also jumped and waved, with more energy and gusto than I had ever seen. I will never, ever forget that moment, in that race, for the rest of my life. They encouraged my energy. They encouraged my heart. They encouraged me.

It was the moment at which I knew I was going to finish that race without walking for even a second. I was determined and felt I owed it to them. It was the moment at which I knew I was going to get over the ex-boy-friend, who until then I couldn't imagine life without. It was the moment I realized that we can *all* do anything we want in life. Anything at all. We just need to set our minds to it and then do the work.

Also in that moment, I truly identified myself as a marathon runner. Until then, I'd figured that even if I could finish, this would be my only full. I had only wanted to do this one time. That moment was one of the most memorable in my entire running career; it was a key to me falling in love with running. I knew I'd be back for more marathons. More of these moments.

Why was that moment so powerful? Because my heart was encouraged. I was supported, loved, valued, cherished, and appreciated—not at the end of the game, when it was all said and done, but in the *middle* of the game, when I was still playing. I was weary, tired, breaking down, unsure of myself and my limits, but the motivation, support, and encouragement I found in my supporters that day was enough to carry me over the finish line.

What should you take from this? If we wait until the runners are at the finish line to cheer, the runners may never make it there. Think about sports. How strange would it be if you couldn't shout, scream, clap, or cheer your team on until they had won the game? What if you weren't allowed to celebrate after each touchdown, goal, or three-pointer? You just had to sit quietly and observe until the game was over. I'd argue that not only would far less people be interested in attending sporting events, but this would also dramatically affect the players and their level of play. When the players know their fans are out there, supporting them, it *matters*. Think back to the example I described before with the family dinner. After that situation, an individual might be so hurt and disappointed that her hard work wasn't acknowledged that she regresses—or even gives up.

We know these lessons hold true with children. We encourage children so much when they are young and learning how to walk. We applaud babies first for rolling over, then cheer them on when they start to sit up on their own. We are just as excited when they start to crawl (minus the part about having to babyproof the house!), and we go nuts when they take those first few steps on their own. Finally, they learn to walk, and we're ecstatic. Those first few steps are pretty inevitable for most children, but we cheer our kids on like their lives depend on it.

But what about our adult counterparts? So many individuals want that same kind of celebration and recognition for trying new and difficult things at work. Some folks are deathly afraid of public speaking and nervous to even try it in front of a group. Others might be afraid to make cold calls. In the medical industry, maybe it's that first consultation with a patient alone or that first surgery. The reality is that adults need encouragement, especially when they're doing something for the first time, as much as children do. While most children inevitably learn to walk, we believe that us encouraging them by clapping, smiling, nodding, and giving other verbal and nonverbal signs of praise makes it more likely to happen and sooner. So, why don't we do this with adults?

The reality is we don't tend to encourage each other as adults nearly as much. In some cases, we actually do the opposite. Because of that, people may never reach their full potential. They may never learn to "walk"—or even stand on their own, like a baby would—because they don't get that encouragement along the way. I can't express how important it is to find small wins—those little victories along the way as you're making progress toward the bigger goal. Wars are won through a series of small battles. How do we stay motivated to win the small battles? We acknowledge each one along the way.

> **"Faith is taking the first step even when**
> **you don't see the whole staircase."**
> **– Martin Luther King Jr.**

One of the most important things to remember when we're leading other people is how hard change can be and why that is. When we ask someone to change their behavior and do something differently so they achieve different (and often, better) results, we're asking a lot of them. We're asking them to grow and evolve—for their benefit, sure, but for our benefit too. We know the changes they can make will benefit us, as their leader; the goals we've set for and with them; the stakeholders they serve—whether those be clients, customers, patients, or students—and the organization, company, or business as a whole. We're asking them to be uncomfortable and have faith that whatever we're asking them to do will ultimately pay off. The reality is that even though we, as their leader, might be able to see the value and results that changed behaviors will have, the people we're asking to change may not be able see that yet. We're asking them to have faith, which means they have to take the first step before they can see the whole staircase. For many, that can be a daunting proposition.

The biggest thing we're asking others to do, when we ask them to make a change, is to dismantle old habits and replace them with new ones. Habits can be a great thing. Many of them were formed with the help of our subconscious minds and are designed to help us. They serve to protect us and keep us out of harm's way. However, habits can also be a dangerous thing. Because our subconscious minds don't want us to hurt, the subconscious can misread situations and conclude that if we *feel* pain, hurt, or discomfort, that must be a bad sign, a sign of danger looming on the horizon. So, our subconscious minds play tricks on us. This part of our brain tends to choose the path of least resistance. Doing something we've done a thousand times is obviously more comfortable and less scary than doing something new, and so our subconscious tends to fight us every step of the way when we're looking to change our behavior. It taunts us with worrisome questions and statements like the following (the "we" refers to our subconscious mind, our conscious mind, and our bodies):

- Isn't that going to be hard?
- What if we fail?
- What if others laugh at us?
- What if we get judged for that?
- Isn't that going to be hard?
- What if we're bad at that?
- It's probably not worth it.
- It probably wouldn't lead to any better results than we're currently having.
- Wouldn't it be easier to just stay the same?
- Yeah, let's stay the same for now. We can deal with that tomorrow.

When people are working hard to improve both lead and lag measures—a concept best described in *The 4 Disciplines of Execution* and referenced earlier—they're going to have to make some changes in what they say, what they do, and eventually who they *are*. Because of the subconscious mind's desire to pull away from what's new and different, the pull toward what was familiar and already learned; how difficult it is to break habits; fear and doubt; and because you're asking people to take a leap of faith and trust in *you* and in the process, it's critical that you recognize people who are making changes *as* they go along.

Let's say you have a goal for someone to do 10 of something. The person you're coaching is doing two of that thing. After much coaching and involvement from you, they move that number to four. It can be tempting to not recognize them. While it's true they've doubled their production, they're still only at 40% of where they need to be! On a scale of 1 to 10, four isn't that great of a number. The temptation exists to say, "I'll recognize them when they hit the goal, or when they're very close. If I recognize them too soon, they'll get complacent and think they're done. They may even back off."

This thinking is inherently flawed and violates the principal of classical conditioning that we learned from Pavlov's dogs—research that's been around since 1902. Most of us remember the general situation where food appeared, bells rang, and dogs salivated, and maybe you remember that at some point in the experiment, the food no longer needed to appear for the dogs to salivate; just the ringing of the bell was enough.

Most of us can also probably relate to some situation in which we were praised for good work. I'm not sure if elementary schools still do anything on paper anymore, or if we're so digital that all children are handed tablets upon their first day of kindergarten, but maybe some of us remember getting gold stars for good behavior growing up. I distinctly remember getting a "gumball" (a circular sticker in a variety of colors) for each book I read in the third grade, which I could put on the "gumball machine" (a giant drawing of a gumball machine on posterboard) after I had demonstrated I understood the contents of the book I had finished reading. The person with the most gumballs "won" (I use this word intentionally, although my parents likely disagreed) the honor of taking home the entire "gumball machine" (the giant posterboard with the colored stickers on it). In hindsight, this was a great way for our teacher to get rid of the posterboard each semester without throwing it in the trash—just get the most ambitious and nutso student to carry it away. It probably won't surprise you that each semester, that student was me. I was so proud of myself for collecting all those gumballs and winning something, I didn't even mind doing the reading.

The beauty of the gold stars for good work or colorful "gumball" stickers was that you didn't have to wait a long time to see them. In most classrooms where these tools existed, teachers were tapping into a desire that most of us have—to know and understand where we are and to feel *good* about the progress we're making. Ten-yard markers exist on football fields, mile markers exist on marathon courses, and scoreboards hang at every sporting event you attend. Why? We want to know where we are at. We desire and crave feedback. We don't want to wait until the end of the game to know the score.

"Momentum is a cruel mistress. She can turn on a dime with the smallest mistake; she is ever searching for the weak place in your armor, that one tiny thing that you forgot to prepare for." – "Rise & Shine!"[28]

In the example where the goal is 10 and you have a person who has moved from 2 to 4, it's important to acknowledge that progress. They've doubled where they were, moving in the right direction. Without the right reinforcement or recognition, momentum *will* turn on a dime, far more often. Also recall Newton's First Law of Motion, which states:

A body at rest will remain at rest unless an outside force acts on it, and a body in motion at a constant velocity will remain in motion in a straight line unless acted upon by an outside force. …Outside forces are sometimes called net forces or unbalanced forces.[29]

When someone is making progress toward a goal, they're "in motion." Previously, they might have been at rest. Moving forward might mean they've had to turn in a different direction—maybe even the opposite direction! Or perhaps they've simply picked up the pace of what they were previously doing. Any of these scenarios mean that serious work is being done. When we don't acknowledge progress toward that goal and how hard it can be to break old habits and establish new ones, we do our people a major disservice. Not bothering to acknowledge progress doesn't have a neutral effect or positive effect but, rather, a *negative* effect. It can be damaging to not acknowledge progress and the start of success, even when you still want more from people.

Your people come to work and choose to report to you for a reason. They either like you, respect you, or they really, really need a paycheck. But in this age of information and connection, most people can find another job that will also pay them. They come to work for *you*, not because they don't have any other options and they're desperate, but because they value you and believe in you to lead them. Even when the game isn't over, the war isn't won, and the finish line hasn't been crossed, your people want to know that *you* know they're on the right track and you appreciate their efforts and their progress. If you don't recognize that person who is at 40% of what you want them to produce, when they used to be at 20%, you'll often find that they never get to 100%. Just as we recognize a baby's first steps, it's crucial we recognize the steps toward progress our people are making because it means they're overcoming something hefty inside them.

A WORD ON THE LAW OF ATTRACTION

For those of you who haven't heard of the Law of Attraction, I'll share Wikipedia's definition: "Law of Attraction is a pseudoscience based on the belief that positive or negative thoughts bring positive or negative experiences into a person's life."[30]

I was first introduced to the concepts surrounding the Law of Attraction in a most unusual place—my car mechanic's dingy waiting area. The place is like a dive bar. The overhead lights make a weird buzzing sound, the soda and snack machine is perpetually empty, and the whole place smells kind of foul, but the guy does fantastic work. It was late fall 2015, and I was telling anyone who would listen that I was "going through a breakup." I had blurted this out to another woman sitting beside me in the waiting room, and her advice was simple. "You should watch *The Secret*," she flatly said.

"The what?" I asked.

"The Secret," she responded, in the same flat tone. "On Netflix. You do have Netflix, don't you?"

"No, but I think a friend is signed in on my TV," I flippantly answered, sure I was never going to watch any program recommended to me by a stranger in my mechanic's lobby.

As if she could read my mind, she added, "It's a documentary." And then came probably one of the better sales pitches I've ever heard in a car shop: "It'll change your life."

"Okay, well, if it'll change my life," I said, somewhat sarcastically, "maybe I'll check it out."

She stared me down without blinking. "It will," she said. "Watch it."

I can't count how many times strangers have offered me advice without uncovering my needs, so my first inclination was to ignore this recommendation. But to be fair, this woman had figured out my needs without me telling her. I did need to change my life. And something about that woman on that particular day stuck with me. Somehow, a couple days later, I found myself searching for the documentary on Netflix, and sure enough, there it was. Bonus: it was free! Oddly enough, she was partially right: The concepts didn't change my life overnight, but they did become part of my life transformation, and since then, I've been more open to the endless list of book, movie, show, and other recommendations that strangers give me.

The concepts didn't take hold immediately, but one day through random conversation, I found myself asking my boss at the time if he'd ever heard of the concepts espoused in the show. That day, my boss gave me his definition for the Law of Attraction, which always stuck with me. I've heard him say it numerous times since then, and it's much simpler than Wikipedia's definition:

"What you think about grows." – Donnie Peaks

Many books and frameworks ultimately say, usually in far more words, exactly what Donnie was saying. What we think about grows. Our thoughts, beliefs, and what we allow to fill our minds often manifest itself in our physical word and lives. Henry Ford taught us that, "Whether you think you can, or you think you can't, either way, you're right." Stephen Covey taught us about our circle of influence and our circle of concern, arguing that as we focus on one, the other one shrinks. The bottom line is that if we think we're capable, talented, and qualified, we become *more* so. If we think we're not those things, we become less of them. If we go into an assignment, test, or game planning to lose or fail, our mere thought of that makes it far more likely that's what *will* happen. If we go into these things planning to win or be successful, we're far more likely to win or be successful.

By no means am I arguing that only thinking good thoughts and being positive will lead to success. I am arguing that positive thoughts and starting your days with an attitude of gratitude for what's going well, the progress you've made, and how you plan to make more progress will set you on course to do even better.

If Donnie is right, and what we think about grows, then I'd like to add that what we *talk* about also grows. When we see the players in our games making the right moves to become more successful, we bring about more of those behaviors by talking about them. As we've discussed, the best conversations a leader can have with their team are a dialogue, not a monologue. So, showing appreciation and encouragement doesn't have to be a one-way street. Instead of just making statements about what seems to be working, you can inspire more of the behaviors you want by asking questions. This might look like the following:

- So, it seems like you're really on the right track! Great start! What's working for you so far?
- Wow, I really like what I'm seeing lately! What led to this?
- It seems like we're making great progress. What have you been doing differently? Keep that up!
- I'm so impressed with how far we've been coming along lately. How have you been doing it?

What you're showing your folks is that:
1. You care about them.
2. You notice and know what's going on with them.
3. You're aware of how hard they're working and the effort they're exerting.
4. You're happy with the progress they're making.
5. You want it to continue.
6. If it does continue, more positive praise and better conversations will follow.

These discussions are positive for most people, so not having them (the absence of something) can be negative. People hope for praise. They look forward to it. When it doesn't come from us, their leader, and they were expecting it, we're falling short of their expectations. That's a negative feeling, and again, this can easily lead to us *not* getting more of what we want. By acknowledging how far someone has come and celebrating the small wins along the way, we show our people that we're thinking about success and them winning. As Donnie's quote implies, that is often what leads to more success and winning to grow.

Recognizing and appreciating people is a form of showing them that you're measuring their work. When we don't show interest in our people—by paying close attention to what they do and say and recognizing progress when it starts to occur, continues occurring, and eventually leads to a job well done—people assume that we're not really observing or noticing who they are and what they're doing. They think we're not noticing their excellence or measuring their painstaking work. What happens when this occurs? Sometimes, the works stops being done.

If you want to see results, encourage energy by showing appreciation, recognition, and interest in how it's going every step of the way.

BE PATIENT: ROME WASN'T BUILT IN A DAY

Before we get into more specific practices of how we can more effectively encourage the energy, excitement, and enthusiasm of others, I want to offer up a word of caution. We must be *patient* as we go through this process. Rome wasn't built in a day, and your organization's great results won't be built in a day either. Nor will your talented employees build themselves from trainee to expert overnight. In today's fast-food, fast-feedback culture, we expect immediate gratification. Advertising campaigns are constantly trying to sell us on the hack, and our society buys it. People are constantly looking for the quick fix. Commercials tell us how we can lose weight in days or weeks—weight that we've spent years putting on. Fast-food joints have made things even faster by creating apps where you order on your mobile device, and it's already waiting on the counter for you when you walk in. We want and expect everything "in a hurry" these days.

Problem is, leadership doesn't happen "in a hurry." Truly sustainable results and success do not happen "in a hurry" either. Sustainable results and success are enacted over time. This means we often must encourage effort and behavior even before results are showing. This doesn't mean it's a good idea to be patient forever and recognize effort and behaviors in the absence of results that never come. It means we must be aware of what lead measures are going to drive lag measures, and when we see the right lead measures being enacted—even if the lag measure hasn't moved to where we want it *yet*—it's important we still acknowledge the work and effort being exerted.

If you've ever tried to lose weight, you've learned what it's like to be patient when the results aren't where you want them to be. Sometimes, you'll do all the right things for days or weeks and nothing changes. You drink water, cut out sweets, eat healthier foods, exercise, but the scale remains the same for longer than you'd like. I've even been doing everything right from an effort and behavioral perspective, but the number on the scale goes *up* for a while! It's one of the most frustrating experiences—feeling like we're doing all the right things, especially when those things are hard, and nothing is happening.

Be patient and stay the course. Often, when the wheel is almost about to move, we give up. We throw in the towel since "it's not working!" Be careful here. Progress takes time, and if you get impatient or antsy early, you'll expel negative energy onto yourself and others. That could absolutely take you backward. Don't get discouraged when you don't have everything you want up front. The larger the organization or ship you're trying to move, the longer it will take. Think about how long it takes to turn a cruise ship around compared to a sailboat. If you're dealing with an organization of thousands of people, you have a lot to overcome. There are multiple layers of hierarchy, and some folks will test you—consciously or subconsciously—to see if what you're asking of them or challenging them to do is real. They're waiting for the trailblazers or pioneers who embraced the change from the beginning to go out and stub their toe or trip. They want someone else to explore the terrain. Not everyone does this consciously; most folks hold back out of fear, anxiety, skepticism, or disbelief without even knowing what they're doing. So, be patient—but not too patient. If you expect results overnight, you'll feel frustrated when you don't get them. If results are coming but you always want more of them, and quicker, you won't be in a place to show your people how much you value and appreciate them because you'll only be challenging them to go faster and further. Allow yourself those moments to celebrate the small wins with your team. They need it, and if you take some time to do it, you'll get much more success in the future.

PRACTICE 2:
KNOW YOUR PEOPLE

When David and I were 15 months into dating—long enough to know each other fairly well but new enough we hadn't learned *everything* about each other—I tried to surprise him for his 36th birthday. We were doing long-distance at the time, and he flew from Atlanta to see me in Southern California. I was so busy putting the finishing touches on my big display, I asked him to take an Uber from the airport and meet me at my apartment. I've always been obsessive about finding patterns in numbers—a tactic I've used my entire life to remember large numbers or make quick calculations—so I couldn't unglue myself from this idea of 6 x 6 = 36. I decided to set up six stations around my six-room apartment. At each one would be a balloon, a card, a present, and we'd drink a sip of wine at each stop. I had spent the day getting six balloons, six gifts, and six cards so that David could go on a tour of the apartment as he explored the stations. I got a big bottle of wine and several balls of gourmet cheese, which I was really excited about. I rarely allow myself to eat cheese, so this felt like the perfect special occasion to indulge in more cheese than anyone should.

David hated it. As we went through the stations, he refused to take off his jacket, and while it was January, my apartment was warm, so I couldn't figure that out. He only had one sip of wine and didn't want any of the cheese. As I excitedly dragged him from room to room, I eventually noticed that he seemed less and less interested in what was going on. Of course, that impacted my excitement. Eventually, my confusion over his reaction to what I had put a day's worth of time into got to me, and I felt sad and withdrawn. We rushed through the final two stations and went to dinner at a nearby restaurant. When we sat down at the table, David took off his jacket, and I saw for the first time that he was wearing a dress shirt and tie.

"OMG, I love that dress shirt! You look great!" I exclaimed. "Why are you wearing a tie?"

"Well, I know how much you like dressing up," he responded. "And I thought we'd be going out for a nice dinner right away when I arrived."

Over dinner, I learned a few things about David. First, he hates cheese that isn't on a pizza, sandwich, or burger. I'd seen David eat cheese on all those things, so I figured, *Who doesn't love straight cheese in a big ball?* David, that's who.

I also learned that he hadn't eaten in hours, avoiding snacks on the plane, because he wanted to make sure he was hungry for a nice dinner, which he had assumed we'd go have right away. So, me dragging him through the house on a six-station tour before dinner wasn't his idea of a good time. Instead, his stomach was growling. Since the shirt and tie were supposed to be a surprise for the restaurant, he spent most of the tour around the apartment uncomfortable, as he was still wearing his jacket. I had also given David a bunch of gifts, which in hindsight, had been more about me than him. In the end, I really had no idea what to get him (especially six times) and had deferred to things I would want as gifts, not that he really wanted.

In the end, the best birthday gift I could've gotten him was to pick him up at the airport instead of making him Uber. I later learned that David's top "love language" is acts of service, not gifts. He also enjoys saving money, when possible. What started out as me trying to make a grand gesture to shower David with love, appreciation, and encouragement backfired. It led to David feeling disconnected from me, and when those emotions showed, it led to me also feeling unappreciated for all the hard work I had put into the surprise. What I had hoped would be a lovely birthday ended up being a lackluster night for both of us. From my perspective, I had tried hard to delight him with a unique gift experience. In the end, the only gifts David felt like he got were a service charge from Uber and an empty stomach. I clearly didn't understand him yet.

I can't tell you how many times I've seen this happen in business. I've attended lunches designed to surprise someone where only meat dishes were ordered and the guest of honor was a vegetarian or vegan. We took someone away from their planned lunch and forced them into an environment where they couldn't eat, but everyone ate around them. Plus, the event absorbed their lunch hour. Sounds more like a punishment than a reward.

I've seen people get called up on stage to speak and share how they achieved some accomplishment, only to learn later that they are deathly afraid of public speaking and don't like that kind of recognition. I've seen holiday gift exchanges be organized with no consideration for several folks on a team who can't practice or engage in rituals like that because of their religion. No one dug into this prior to the planning, so nobody knew those individuals wouldn't even attend. I can't count the number of times someone has given me a gift in the form of sweets when I don't eat those things.

Perhaps the most memorable recognition event I've ever attended was a quarterly pinnacle recognition event when I was a branch manager. Those of us being recognized for top-level quarterly performance were pulled out of our branches for an entire day for a surprise event. Instead of driving five miles to my office, I had to drive all the way into downtown L.A. during rush hour at the crack of dawn—much earlier than my normal start time. We were bused to the Getty Museum on what turned out to be one of the hottest days of the year. We hadn't been told to wear comfortable walking shoes (actually, attire hadn't been discussed at all), so I sweat all day in a full suit and heels as we explored the property grounds and repeatedly found ourselves outside.

After a day at the museum, we were bused across town to Fogo de Chão. I'm not a meat lover and was also on a diet at the time, so I sat for hours and picked away at a salad while others went through multiple rounds of beef, pork, chicken, lamb, and multiple other things I didn't even recognize. If it was pinkish or brown and dripping, it came by our table no less than a couple dozen times. Most of my counterparts at the event got drunk, which felt wholly inappropriate to me, and by the time our loud, rowdy bus rolled back into the parking structure where we parked in downtown L.A., it was nearly 9 at night. I didn't get home until 10, and after a 14-hour day, I had no energy to work out, let alone do anything else.

At this time, my branch was short-staffed. We were open on Saturdays, and my staff was all hourly, so everyone took a day off for working Saturday, but nobody could take that day off since I needed them to cover me. This pushed me into giving people their day off on days that weren't ideal like Monday and Friday (when we were most busy). I lost a day of work during a time when we were hectic as hell, trying to work through multiple loan deals and investment proposals. I also lost a night of focus on my studies (I was a part-time MBA student at the time). While I could have tried harder to make the most of the day, I couldn't help but view that day as a punishment instead of a reward. It certainly didn't give me any motivation to try harder in the following quarter to make the Pinnacle Group again. Getting up early and home late to negatively impact my branch staff, miss a day of work and study, skip a workout, cheat on my diet, roast in the hot sun, and get a blister hardly felt inspirational.

That event occurred over a decade ago, and I still remember it like it was yesterday. It was probably one of the most disengaging days of my career. I know now that I could have worked tirelessly to network better with my peers and find opportunities to use the day to develop and grow my skills in some way, but I was young, and I wasn't ready to look at the world that way. The bottom line is that most of your employees aren't going to naturally do this either, and it's your responsibility to get to know them so you can host the right events that motivate them in the right way—not be a wash or even demotivate them like this long day in the sun that ended at a meat house did for me. It's your job to get to know your team so you can deliver things that feel like rewards instead of like punishment, just like I've learned to do with David over the years. Last year, on his birthday, I gave him a $500 gift certificate for the airport where he pays for tows to fly his glider, took him skiing, and paid for our ski and boot rentals. Things have changed.

It's easy to say, "It's the thought that counts," and that's true. Looking back on David's 36th birthday, it would have been nice if David had recognized how much effort I had put into the evening and how everything I had done was an attempt to show him how much I cared for him and wanted to celebrate him. But when we're trying to celebrate someone—and encourage them and their energy—it's our job, not theirs, to get the moment right. Recognition has a greater impact if it comes in the form of something they would like. When we find out how people *want* to be recognized (and the ways in which people like to be recognized vary greatly), something magical happens. The people we're recognizing actually feel recognized. They feel valued and appreciated because we've communicated to them in their language of appreciation.

HOW DO YOU LIKE TO BE RECOGNIZED?

I've seen a lot of managers whip out a form when they have a new hire that says, "How do you like to be recognized?" but then forget where they put the form and never look at it again. Don't do that. If you're going to ask people what they like in the recognition department, then it's critical that you *deliver* on it. Asking someone what they want or what they'd like and then doing nothing about it will only serve as a withdrawal in your emotional bank account with them—not a deposit.[31]

Although there are many ways to recognize people, let's discuss five common ways.

PUBLIC RECOGNITION

A memorable moment in my life was when I was recognized as one of the company's MVPs in front of over 1,000 people. On stage, my boss read a long list of my accomplishments that year and how those had transformed the organization. It was such a happy day for me. My only regret was that no one ever caught it on video so I could watch it over and over. As a major "Words of Affirmation" person (my primary love language both at home and at work), I still consider this a highlight in my career. Since this is how I like to be recognized, I find myself recognizing other people a lot this way, which can be hugely dangerous, especially for those who are shy or don't like to be in the limelight. Sometimes it seems like leaders completely ignore the wishes of others and recognize folks publicly who have said they're not big fans of it because "it's just what we do!" Don't assume that doing something repeatedly will help someone "get used to it" or "learn to like it." Some people, no matter how experienced, will never grow into liking this, and that should be heard and understood.

PRIVATE RECOGNITION

I haven't met a lot of people who don't enjoy being recognized privately. Whether it's via email, phone call, a handwritten note, or stopping by their office to say something, people tend to enjoy being told they did a good job. As with every other idea in this book, specificity matters. When we tell someone that we appreciate that particular thing they did or said or point out what their specific contribution led to, people tend to feel that their work is acknowledged and seen. Someone might enjoy hearing words of praise but don't want to have all eyes on them in a big group setting. You doing it in a one-on-one meeting or some other time when it's just you and them can go a long way.

MONEY (OR THE CASH EQUIVALENT)

People love bonuses, raises, cash, money, or gift cards. A word of caution: If you're going with gift cards, it's equally important that you figure out where people shop. I can't tell you how many worthless Starbucks gift cards I've been handed over my career. The only exciting thing about those for me is that I can throw them in my wallet and give them to virtually anyone else, since I'm about the only person I know who isn't fascinated by Starbucks. Sorry, Starbucks, I don't drink coffee, but you've done well with the general public.

PTO/FLEX TIME/TIME AWAY

Say hello to your folks who love spending time with their families. Years ago, when I was in regional leadership, my peers and I hosted a recognition day for a group of branch managers. We did it on a day of a scheduled meeting that had been on their calendars for months, so they already expected to be at their meeting until 6 P.M.

We took them to the Santa Monica Pier to celebrate them. This time, I was part of the team running the show, and I had learned from the Fogo de Chão day years earlier, so we told them to dress accordingly based on weather predictions and to wear comfortable shoes. They got to come into work an hour late, and we did some team-building activities and played some games at our headquarters facility so we could bond. Then we moved the party to Santa Monica in the middle of the day when there was no traffic. The group arrived, we gave them some spending money, and let them decide how *they* wanted to spend their day—either riding the rides, playing the games, or doing some shopping. We asked that they come back and meet us for lunch, and we picked a restaurant with options for everyone. We did our recognition ceremony there, and then turned them lose at two in the afternoon.

I was worried that the day hadn't been long or impactful enough, but something interesting happened later that night. We got a chain of "reply all" emails that flowed in all evening between us and the group, with gratitude and thanks for the five hours back that day—counting the hour they saved in the morning and the four hours at the end of the day. Folks wrote us that they had gotten home early and cleaned the whole house. Others had run errands they had planned to do on the weekends and now felt ahead. Others had surprised their family by volunteering to pick up the kids at school when they weren't the ones to usually do that. Still others replied to us from the mall, talking about how they had chosen to go shopping and enjoy themselves after work. My favorite one came from the branch manager who had the courage to say he had gone home and was lounging on the couch, scrolling on the internet, and enjoying doing absolutely nothing before his family came home.

The one thing all their emails and texts had in common was that they were doing something they wanted to do with time unexpectedly given to them. In planning sessions for this day, I had expressed fears about ending the day too early and also allowing the group to split up in the middle of the day. My fears were that these decisions wouldn't allow enough time for the group to bond as a whole team. My peers had disagreed with me, and I had agreed to experiment with their ideas. I had been dead wrong. As the emails poured in, with them all responding to one another, I watched them grow closer. They grew closer to one another as they each shared what they had done with the time back, but some of them also grew closer to their families, as they invested that time into doing something with or for their family. I even watched them grow closer to us, as the many thanks for time back were so abundant and sincere. I could basically feel their love for us grow in that moment.

The following quarter, when it came time to recognize the group again, we took it one step further. We brought them to headquarters for a few hours, did the team-building activities and bonding, handed out the certificates, and then turned them lose at 11 A.M. The feedback that time was even more resounding.

I've seen this work really well. When folks who value personal time or what can be that illusive work-life balance (although I'd argue it doesn't have to be that way; many models and frameworks are available to find an incredible amount of balance in our lives) are recognized and rewarded in the form of being able to do MORE of what they love, it's a special thing. Telling people in advance that they have an opportunity to win a few hours of free flex time or PTO—or even a day or two, depending on what the task is—can be very motivating for people who have strong values and ties to personal time and family. Delivering that time back as a surprise can be equally as effective, as they won't forget how you made them feel and the impact it had on their life.

DEVELOPMENT AND OPPORTUNITIES FOR GROWTH

For many, recognition is a dish best served with a promotion, raise, title change, or new opportunity. What better way to let someone know they've done a good job than to put them in a more challenging role with better pay and give them more responsibility, right? Well, yes and no. In a moment, I'll share with you the story of Joel.

Now, let's talk about when it's a YES. It's true that most employees are hungry for growth and learning. Most of us go through life with a desire to evolve (either subconsciously or consciously). Most of us find it rewarding or fulfilling to be challenged periodically. In fact, in multiple surveys, studies have repeatedly found that developmental opportunities for growth and advancement rank high for individuals when it comes to thinking about their job satisfaction. Giving a top-performing employee who has done well more freedom or opportunities to learn, grow, and ultimately better themselves can be a great way to show that you notice what's been going on, and even better, you care and are proud of them. When employees see others around them being rewarded with new opportunities to learn and develop, which eventually results in some of those folks taking on new or expanded roles, that motivates others to work harder to get those same opportunities.

IT'S NOT ABOUT YOU, IT'S ABOUT THEM: THE STORY OF JOEL

I've described several examples of different kinds of recognition. It's most important that you find some way to do it. But what about when we assume we *know* what our employees want? Pigeonholing others into our own paradigms is never a good idea, but sometimes, as leaders, we do it. Often, we supervise people in jobs or roles that *we* once had. We work our way up then oversee other people who do those same jobs we did before advancing. It can be incredibly tempting to assume that our people view their jobs and futures like *we* did when we were in their shoes. Don't fall into this dangerous trap.

In my first year managing my own bank branch, I led Joel, who was consistently inconsistent. Sometimes, he'd execute flawlessly without a word from me and blow out his numbers. He was engaged and self-motivated. Other times, he was lethargic and he'd ride the bottom of the sales reports. I struggled to figure this out. At first, I assumed it was a capability issue. But that didn't make any sense. When Joel *was* engaged, he was sharp, smart, and thought well on his feet in unpredictable situations. Before I had arrived, Joel had been promoted twice and given more hours. Obviously, previous management had seen great things in him.

Next, I evaluated his people skills. That didn't seem to be a problem either. Joel was well-liked by the other employees at the branch as well as our customers. During the months where he'd perform well, his interpersonal skills were strong.

I then wondered if the problem was me. I hadn't spent much time with him. What if he felt that I didn't want to invest in him or wasn't gunning for his next promotion? When I was progressing through the ranks, I craved time with my managers. I wanted to learn from them and get continual feedback. I decided I hadn't done enough to recognize Joel during the times he was doing well, and that's why he would slip back. I hatched a plan to reward Joel by giving him more of my time to help him move forward.

This branch was situated inside a grocery store and couldn't have been more than 400 square feet, making it difficult to find a place (or the time) to make outbound sales calls, return calls, or process loans. The branch consisted of three teller stations and only one office our entire staff shared for private conversations with customers or each other. The vault room was tiny but housed a desk with a computer, a phone, and a stool. The branch was so small that we had to make constant adaptations; we'd open checking accounts at the teller line and fill out paperwork for new accounts on top of stacked beer cases out in the aisles. (That's right; didn't I mention this branch was smack dab in the beer and liquor section?)

Our "break room" and restroom were that of the larger grocery store—upstairs. Those conditions were squalid: not clean or well-kept. As time progressed, I learned how much all my employees hated spending time up there. Most of my employees preferred to eat their lunches in their laps perched on the edge of the vault. Others would eat their lunch in their cars. A few lived close and would rush home on their lunch break. Our customer base was primarily college students and, in general, had little money on deposit, no loans on file, no credit, and lived paycheck to paycheck. I had a staff that mirrored those demographics.

I look back now with mild amusement on this whole situation. I was 24, single, and freshly moved to California, trying to figure it all out. I had little clue that I should be doing everything I'm writing about in this book. This was a challenging time in my career, and yet I look back now with an understanding that these challenges became some of my biggest advantages later in my career. This environment taught me how to be nimble and flexible.

I didn't know much about leadership, but I did know that I should have one-on-ones with my employees. I began regular one-on-ones with Joel, which I held in the dingy upstairs break room, so we could have some privacy. I never asked Joel's opinion on where we should meet. Often, the overhead fluorescent lights would either be out or flickering. It was a creepy setting. Nonetheless, I decided this was the perfect setting to address my observations with Joel. Under the low lighting, I shared how I'd noticed his performance was inconsistent and how much I wanted to help with that. "What do you think the problem is?" I asked him directly.

"I don't know," Joel responded.

Outbound calling was a big part of Joel's day. I reflected on my earlier days when I was in Joel's role and recalled that making cold calls had initially been uncomfortable for me. I also remembered how much I craved attention from my managers and was always wanting advancement opportunities.

"You know, a lot of people need help on the phones," I offered up. "It's so easy to be nervous or rush. One of the things that really helped me when I was in your role was when my manager sat with me and helped me. How about I start spending more time with you? I'd love to help you advance from a banker to a senior banker."

"Okay," Joel flatly said.

The new leader I was, I sprang into action and made it my personal mission to help Joel. Instead of asking more questions to get a better sense for who Joel was and what was really going on, I concluded that outbound calling was the problem and more time together the solution. I committed to spending three hours a week with Joel alone, observing calls and providing feedback so he could deliver more consistent results, which then would put me in a position to promote him.

This was another fallacy on my part. I assumed that Joel *wanted* to progress in the organization. I assumed these things without ever *asking* Joel what he wanted. I also viewed my offer to help as nothing but a positive thing. I mean, how could anyone *not* like personal time with the boss? I also believed that time together would inevitably lead Joel to do better, which of course, would be another reward for him. It would likely lead to better monthly incentives and more cash in his pocket.

We started right away, and an immediate problem arose. When we spent time in the only office, we'd constantly get interrupted by others who needed the office to meet with customers. What did I do? The only thing I thought I *could* do—I booted my assistant manager, Regina, from the vault room, which she had essentially made her office. I uprooted her into a standing position behind the three tellers so that Joel and I could make these outbound calls in her teeny room. She was my only employee not in her 20s, but rather was in her 50s, and I didn't even consider her—or her comfort— when I made that decision. Another failing on my part. Joel's and my calling efforts also meant those who wanted to eat their lunch in that room, on the ledge of the vault, were also exiled. I made these decisions without regard for them either.

This process went on for several weeks. We'd close the door so Joel's calls wouldn't distract other employees. Joel made calls, and I'd sit behind him, looking over his shoulder so I could nudge him and point to varying things I noticed about the customer's profile, such as a high balance, multiple credit card payments going out, an upcoming birthday, or someone not being signed up yet for online banking.

How wrong I was. Not only did Joel's performance not improve, but it got worse. Joel went from being an inconsistent performer to a consistently *bad* performer. I had figured it would only be a matter of time before Joel's performance improved, so I was stunned. Joel was getting the biggest gift I had to offer—the value of my individualized attention, private time, and all my great insight. How could he not be getting better?

Even though this happened roughly 15 years ago, I'll never forget the conversation I had with Joel when I sat him down to talk about this. Joel looked me right in the eye and said, "Amy, sitting in a hot, musty room with you breathing over my shoulder and grading me as I make calls isn't exactly my idea of recognition. It doesn't feel like a reward; it feels like a punishment. You spending all this time with me and no one else makes me feel like you don't trust me. I know how to make calls."

I was stunned. In life, we tend to grade each *other* on results but grade *ourselves* on our intentions. This was a classic case of that. I had fallen prey to believing that my intentions—not my results—were what mattered. My intentions were to invest in Joel, to help develop and grow him, and to show him I cared. Instead, he felt I was there to watch over him: to judge, to assess, and to punish. Like my day at the Getty Museum, what was intended to be a form of recognition ended up being the opposite.

This was hard to hear. I told Joel I'd think about what he said, and I'll admit, I drove home somewhat irritated. I thought, *So you want me to trust you, but you aren't performing consistently. You haven't really earned that trust. We can't leave it this way.* But I also felt, in my heart, that Joel's opinion did matter, and I didn't want to force someone into something they didn't want to do. *Leadership is more than this,* I thought. *You just haven't figured out the answer yet.*

It took me a few days to finish licking my wounds from Joel's feedback, but when I did, I realized I had never bothered to ask Joel an important question. While I had assumed he wanted to move up in the organization, I had never asked him if he wanted those things. I had simply *assumed* he did, because in my twisted mind at that time, "who *doesn't* want to move up in their organization, progress, and make more money?" After all, *I* had always wanted those things.

A week after our initial conversation, I sat down with Joel and asked him a question: "What do you want to do next?" After a minute of thought, Joel looked me square in the eye and said, "You know what? That's a great question. No one has ever asked me that before. I don't know," he said.

"You don't want to advance into a senior personal banker?" I asked.

"I just don't know," he answered, "But…I don't think so."

For the first time in my professional career, I found the strength and courage to listen. That afternoon, Joel and I got into a great conversation, and I learned new information about him.

Joel shared that he was still finishing his college degree and was studying graphic design. He had joined the company a few years earlier as a part-time teller. The job was supposed to be a side gig. But Joel did so well, the organization had asked him to take on more hours. He did. He continued to do well and was asked to take on a promotion and move into a sales role. He did. He was then asked to go full-time. He did. What he was *not* ever asked was what *he* wanted. He wasn't asked about how school was going or if going full-time would work well with his other life plans. He wasn't asked about how he was feeling about his job, his education, or his life.

That day, I learned some sad information. The full-time hours and promotions meant that Joel had been putting school on the back burner. He was only taking one or two classes a semester, and what had once been the most important pursuit in his life—graphic design—was now in the back seat because a job that was intended to make extra cash was now consuming all his time. Joel didn't have an aptitude problem. It wasn't that he wasn't personable. It was that this job had taken him away from his real passion in life. The job was getting in the way of what mattered to him most—finishing his college degree. It also dawned on me that *someone* should have asked these questions in the past, and I should have asked these questions when I met him. So much time had been lost. I made a commitment to change.

Over the next month, Joel and I had more conversations, and we decided to take him back to part-time hours so he could pick up more classes in college. While I initially did this for Joel because it felt like the right thing to do, to my surprise, it ended up helping all of us more than I could have ever expected. I was able to hire another part-time person to fill the other half of Joel's hours, and that extra flexibility allowed us to move Joel's schedule around so that when the new semester started, he was able to take a morning class—a class he had been wanting to take but hadn't thought possible because he "had to work" in the mornings. The extra body also afforded me more flexibility to cover peak hours on days like Friday and Monday where I could bring both the extra person and Joel in when I really needed folks the *most*. This ended up being a win-win solution for everyone.

A few months later, I observed another odd phenomenon. Joel was doing *much* better than ever before. His results had improved and were consistent. Joel was producing nearly as much as a part-time employee as he had been when he was a full-time employee, and his results weren't wavering. Our relationship was changing too. Joel began to loop me in when it came to challenges he faced with clients. We talked often and worked out solutions together. I could hardly believe it.

As time went by, Joel was no longer quiet or curt with me but friendly and energetic. It was because I had started to practice several of the principles in this book. I'd asked Joel about his vision for his career and himself. I'd *involved* him in some decision-making. I'd engaged him in dialogue as part of *talking terrifically*. I'd figured out how to reward him in ways that mattered to him. I only wished I had asked more questions of him sooner. Things were going great.

Then, one day, Joel came to one of his regularly scheduled one-on-ones with a sad demeanor. I recognized something was off and immediately asked about it. Joel told me he had something he wanted to talk to me about, but it could wait until we were done going through reports. "Heck, no," I replied, pushing aside the papers I'd laid out between us. I'd learned that employee concerns always come first.

Joel paused, looking visibly anxious. "Okay," he finally said. "It's time to pick classes for next semester. There's this one class I really want to take." Joel paused then started slowly, "I think I've finally figured out the answer to your question. I think I know what I want to do next. It's not so much graphic design I want to do but motion graphics. You know, for animation? Like, animated films? Well, there's this computer skills/programming class I think could really help me get there."

"That still sounds great!" I offered up, confused.

"Yeah, but the class is on Wednesdays and Fridays…in the afternoons. I can't *not* work on Fridays. It's our busiest day."

"When do you have to register for the class by?" I asked.

"By the end of the week," Joel answered, staring at the table.

"Yeah…that's tough," I said, pausing. Joel's head sunk.

I thought for a moment about how much had changed in the past few months. Suddenly, like a ton of bricks, I realized I had learned even more from him. An epiphany came crashing down on me: As much as I had learned about valuing my people as unique individuals and asking better questions to get to know them, I still hadn't entirely gotten it.

Joel had answered the question I had asked him a few months earlier: *What do you want to do next?* Joel hadn't known, but he had committed to thinking about it. Through dialogue and trust, we had made alterations that allowed him to focus more on his education. With the extra flexibility, space, and time away from work, Joel had figured out the answer to my question. He had found his passion, his direction, his meaning, and his WHY. It just didn't have anything to do with the bank.

I realized then that what I'd *meant* when I asked Joel the question was *not* "What do you want to do next?" but "What do you want to do next at the *bank*?" For me, there was no need to specify "at the bank" because what else would I be asking about? We worked together—at the bank. I had mistakenly thought I could only help him advance *within* the bank.

But I had it wrong; Joel had it right. The way he had interpreted the question was far superior to the way I had meant it. I realized what had *actually* led to the increase in Joel's performance, the better relationship, and even the current conversation was that Joel had felt whole. He had felt valued, appreciated, and truly heard and seen. Someone had asked him about his wants and desires, and he had perceived that I truly cared about those. Because he had become a better person in his personal life, he had also become a better person at work. It almost didn't make sense to me. We had cut Joel's hours, altered his schedule, and ceased what I thought was a genius coaching plan. We had stopped talking about him getting an upcoming promotion. It had been counterintuitive to me, but suddenly, it became self-evident. My world changed, once again, as I realized that true empathy and care is one of the most important skills of a leader. I felt Joel's heart beating through his chest. I knew what I needed to do.

"What if we could find a way to make it work?" I asked.

"What? How?" Joel asked.

"I don't know," I answered slowly. "But maybe we could figure it out. Together."

For one of the first times in my leadership career, I felt someone look at me with love and respect. And figure it out, we did. Joel registered for the class *before* we figured it out since he was up against a deadline, and I wasn't smart or fast enough to figure out a solution by then. But I was determined to find a solution. I trusted us to do that.

In 1519, during the Spanish conquest of Mexico, the Spanish commander, Hernán Cortés, burned the ships he and his men arrived on so that they would have to conquer or die. Only success or death. When Joel registered for the class before we had a solution, we essentially had "burned the ships."

I couldn't back out of the commitment I'd made. Joel and I discussed multiple possible solutions together, which brought us even closer. It also forced us to practice problem-solving skills and teamwork. As we brainstormed, we decided that our best bet was to initiate a transfer between our branch and a neighboring branch, which could have involved Joel transferring. The solution ended up coming from Joel himself. It wasn't uncommon for the bankers in the region to know each other, and Joel identified the exact person we ended up trading to our branch in exchange for one of our other employees to their branch.

This was incredibly beneficial for me too. Discussing an interoffice trade meant that I had to develop my negotiation skills and build a relationship with a peer of mine who I didn't know very well. She and I hammered out a solution and became closer because of that. We also developed a friendship that started with this negotiation and lasted until I left the company.

The solution itself ended up being perfect. We gave away a teller who wanted to be closer to home and learn to work with business owners—a client type our branch didn't have many of. In exchange, we were handed a cross-functional employee who could work on either side of the branch, just like Joel. This individual could do teller transactions but also work the desk, which meant he could cover for Joel on Friday afternoons when he'd need to leave. This afforded me, once again, more flexibility. I could hardly believe that what started as me trying to figure out how to better motivate an inconsistent employee had led to so much *good*. I had a bigger staff. I had a friendship with a peer. I had gotten the chance to cultivate and develop my problem-solving, negotiation, and leadership skills. Everyone was happy, including the transferred employees, but especially Joel. Joel's loyalty to both me and the organization went through the roof.

I moved on from that office to manage other branches and eventually left the company. Sadly, I lost touch with Joel. He stayed with the organization a few years longer. I can't tell you how humbling it was to hear from others later that he had graduated college and fulfilled his dream by finding work in film, doing exactly what he told me he wanted to do in a dark, dingy break room: motion graphics and animation.

This experience taught me so many valuable lessons, but the biggest was this: get to know your people. Get to know who they *are*, what they *want*, and what makes them *tick*. You should be able to answer these questions for each of them, not because you fill in the blanks with all the things *you* wanted when you were coming up through the ranks, but because you've asked them what *they* want, given them the space and time to really think about it, and created a safe environment for them to tell you. You can't just *tell* someone, "I care about you and your development"; you have to *show* them. I had also learned a lifelong lesson around recognizing and rewarding success. It starts with really knowing your people and what they want—not just out of their job, but out of *life*. And it's our job as leaders to help people become better human beings, not just better employees.

No matter how hard we work at this, it requires near constant focus. This story of Joel was in 2007. The "reward" day at the Getty, which felt more like a punishment than a prize, took place in 2010. On that day, I was able to feel firsthand how difficult it can be to not be recognized in ways that are meaningful to *you*. Yet I sometimes still struggle with this concept. Even though more than a decade has passed since I first started thinking about these concepts, I still find myself needing reminders from time to time.

Back in 2017, I was out visiting branches for the credit union I was working for and had gotten especially excited about a young man who was doing a great job for us as a teller. His referral and sales numbers were through the roof, and management was saying great things about him. In a few branch visits to his location, I had ensured that he was observed while I was on site so that I could sit in on his coaching with his leadership team and see what was on his action plans. Without ever really bothering to get to know him or ask him, I had concluded he would love my involvement. Just like Joel.

One day, I showed up at his branch location and found him on the teller line, where I eagerly said, "Hey, I hear we're going to be doing some coaching and role-playing with you today! I'm so excited about how much FUN this is going to be!"

Chad turned to me, looked me dead in the eye, and without missing a beat, said, "Well, Amy, I guess you and I have different definitions of what fun is!"

We laughed it off, and I felt comfortable that I had a good relationship with this guy. But nonetheless, that experience affected me. Instead of ignoring it, I drove home wondering if perhaps Chad felt that we had been spending too much time with him and not enough with the other tellers. Perhaps he felt targeted—that he was the chosen one to be called into the office and given coaching too often. Perhaps he didn't view the "help" as very helpful at all. Driving home from that day, I asked myself some tough questions: *How well did I really know this guy? Did we really get along as well as I thought? What if spending time together was only fun for me but no one else?*

We often have distorted images of ourselves. We think we know how much people like us, but sometimes, we're wrong. We think we know how close we are to someone, but sometimes, we're wrong. So, we need to ask. We need to consider the possibility that, sometimes, we're simply wrong. Other people's perceptions of us hardly mirror our own accurately. They can often be wildly different, and sometimes years can pass without us even *knowing* it. Don't let this happen to you. Create a safe environment where your people can talk to you—and then ask. Get people like Joel to say that sitting in the back room together feels more like punishment than prize. Get people like Chad to tell you that they're not having any fun. Then, once you know that people can be honest with you, even when it's tough, go out and seek some critical, honest feedback. You might learn that others feel you're creating a culture that's all about you and not about them. That's not motivating—it's the opposite.

PRACTICE 3:
BE SPECIFIC

Leaders who don't bother to recognize people won't get great results. However, leaders who aren't specific when they recognize people won't get great results either. Over the years, I've witnessed many leaders who seem to know recognition is important and try to do it. They'll even use a mix of styles, taking special care to recognize people in front of others as well as recognize people privately or even say, "Hey, you've been doing a great job lately. Why don't you get out of here early today?"

Although recognizing people makes them feel good, recognizing others isn't *all* altruistic. We recognize people for a job well done because we want to see our people do that same job *again*. When we see behaviors we don't like and want to stop, we talk to our people. So, it only makes sense that when we see behaviors we *do* like and want it to continue, we should talk to our people. But how can an employee continue, or enhance, something they know little about? This goes back to earlier segments of this book, but when we recognize something we've heard or seen, we have to be *specific* in what we say.

Here's some examples of recognition that sound okay on the surface and may make someone feel good for a moment:

- Great job today.

- Good work last week.
- Fantastic job with that project.
- Your presentation was good today.
- You've been doing well lately.
- Seems like things are really coming together for you.
- I'm really impressed with your work lately.
- Jake said you were doing a good job, and I wanted to pass that along.
- You've been so consistent lately.

Would these examples drive more behavior worth recognizing? Do they turn your people into superstars? Are they guaranteed, or even highly likely, to produce better behavior in the future? No.

When we verbally praise or recognize, it's critical we say two important things:

1.   Specifically, and objectively, what we observed (I call this the WHAT);
2.   The impact it had, why it matters, and to whom (I call this the SO WHAT).

When we recognize, we want to cite as many details as we can. These might include the following:

- **Who:** Who was involved in the act or action, who was affected, and who was benefited by the recognition
- **What:** What specifically happened, what specifically was said, what specifically was done. This is an objective account of what transpired, so quotes are a great tool.
- **When:** When this happened and when you observed it
- **Where:** Where this happened and where it took place
- **Why:** Why does this matter? Why was this a big deal?

Here's some examples of what this might look or sound like:

- Sean, I observed you leading that project meeting on the new software tool yesterday afternoon and wanted to say that I *loved* it when you said to the group, "I really want to see what additional questions you all have. Please, share. What's on your mind is really important to me." After you said that, Peter and Lucas both chimed in; they hadn't until then. You got so much more feedback after you did that; it really worked. Please, do that again; it seemed to be a turning point in the meeting.

- Sally, thanks for letting me sit in on your coaching with Tom on Monday morning. I thought you did a great job by sitting next to him on the same side of the table instead of being across from him. I was blown away when you pulled out the scoreboard with all his current performance and put it between you. I loved how you said, "Tom, walk me through this. What are you most proud of?" You really put him in the driver's seat and showed him that he has a real part in his own performance. We've been talking about getting our employees to take more ownership, and asking him to walk *you* through his current results did exactly that. Keep up the great work. Please do that again!

- Mark, thanks for speaking up many times in yesterday's all-hands conference. I counted and noticed you contributed eight times over the course of the day. My favorite contribution was when you responded to the keynote speaker and built onto her point by saying, "That's one way to look at it, and I like that, but one struggle I have with that is the scheduling and time management piece. I want to understand better. How do we do this when there's numerous other priorities in the way?" You weren't afraid to push back and enter a real concern into the discussion, but you were also respectful. That's what gave other people the permission to ask more questions later; everyone was so much more comfortable after you did that.

Now, you might be wondering, *Who has time for this? Certainly not me! I have so much to do! There's no way I can afford to write things down, this specifically, and then go back and tell people.*

Yes, there is. Yes, you can. When evaluating how much time we do or don't have for something, we tend to make a cardinal sin of assuming everything else is going to remain the same. In other words, we tend to think about what a change in our behavior is going to cost us in the short term without really doing an equal evaluation of what it's going to *yield* us in the future.

Sure, taking the time to verbally recognize people or do so in writing, especially in this way, takes *time*. It means you'll have to pay closer attention to what people are saying and how they're saying it. It means you'll have to pay closer attention to what people are doing and how they're doing it.

First, this may not be a bad thing. Most bosses seem to overlook or even ignore some of the key behaviors of their people, and if you don't observe it, there's no way you can coach to it. So, forcing yourself to pay closer attention to the way your folks interact with others, approach their own work, keep their commitments, use language, and think can help *you* dramatically. You'll become a more effective coach, and your people will start to perform at a higher level because they'll get the message that you really take the time to observe and notice them and what they do *matters*. This will obviously help *them*, but anytime you help those you're leading to be stronger, you automatically help yourself.

If you coach this way, you'll get dramatically better results. Most of the reason we both coach *and* recognize is that we want to shape the behavior of the people around us. When we recognize in a way that calls people's specific attention to *exactly* what they said, how they sounded, what they did, and how that was perceived by others, you connect (for them) the IMPACT their words and actions had on *others* as well as the impact their work or being on time or thinking outside the box had on *results*. When that impact is understood, people change, and not just incrementally, but exponentially. The rate of change and fervor behind it can almost feel magical, and yet, it's not at all. It's quite predictable.

Hyrum Smith teaches in his book, *What Matters Most*, that all humans have four basic needs: to live/survive, to love and be loved, to feel important or significant, and to experience variety. When we recognize people with precision, for exactly what they've done, we help people strongly experience the middle two needs of this model. We show the people around us love because we've paid attention to what they did and said, and we cared enough to observe it and give them feedback. We also teach people that they matter and that they're important. Perhaps getting specific recognition like this in today's workplace is so rare that we also help them experience variety!

If you want people around you to repeat their behavior, we have to connect their minds and memories specifically back to exactly what they did and said. When we do this, we allow people to relive their past moments, and then we attach to those memories a positive experience. Who doesn't like getting praised and feeling like their work mattered and they made a difference? Virtually no one that I've met.

We often jump over dollars to get to dimes. We approach time and life with a scarcity mindset—that there's only so much to go around, and if one piece of the pie is taken, that's less for everyone remaining. I've seen nothing but positive effects come from switching to an abundance mindset, which means we believe there is more than enough for everyone. When we switch the script and recognize that a worthwhile investment of our time can give us time back in the future, we achieve greatness. I guarantee you that the time you spend recognizing people in specific, unique, and personalized ways will drive their performance to much stronger levels far beyond what you see in them today. When that happens, you'll have better results, better revenues, and more empowered and engaged people who won't need you as much. That will give you plenty of time back to live the other 6 V.I.R.T.U.E.S. of great leaders.

PRACTICE 4:
THINK OF RECOGNITION AS A TRAFFIC LIGHT

When it comes to coaching, we're giving feedback on three main areas: (1) things we want our folks to *start* doing, (2) things we want them to *stop* doing, and (3) things we want to see them *continue* doing. This coaching model is like a stoplight. Items you want folks to start doing are your *green* items—a go, or a sign to start. If you're at a red light and the light turns green, you change your behavior. You start to roll forward and move, which you weren't doing before.

Yellow items are those things you want your team to continue doing. When a light turns yellow, most of us continue as we were. I'll be the first to admit I've sped up many times when I see a yellow light. But the driver's education books I've read all state that a yellow light means to proceed and do nothing different. You move forward, as you were, but with caution. You continue your behavior of movement.

Red means stop. When we see a red light, once again, we must change our behavior and stop the movement we had. We bring our movement to a close. This is the third thing we coach people on—what to cease doing. Great coaches are always coaching to the traffic light: things that we want to start, stop, and continue.

Recognition is the same, and I'm not sure everyone gets that. Which part of the three-pronged traffic light do you see getting recognized the most? For me, it's the *yellow* part of the light, the behaviors someone is already doing that we want to continue. The last section mainly talked about this yellow/continue part of the traffic light. I shared statements like, "Betsey, what you did in there today was great (remember to be *specific*). I'd love to see you *do that again*." Hopefully, Betsey does.

But how do we "recognize" behaviors we want to see people start or stop? This is an important question to answer because starting a new behavior and especially stopping an existing behavior are much harder things to do then continuing a behavior. Thus, the red and green parts of the light are where we need to recognize others the most.

When we see people trying something new for the first time (or one of the first times), it's so important that we recognize how hard people are trying and the level of effort that went into starting that behavior. When someone has been doing something that we've asked them to stop and they do stop (even for the first time or one of the first times), we should recognize that too.

Perhaps someone has stopped coming into meetings late and started showing up on time. That should be recognized. Perhaps someone has started speaking up more in meetings and stopped being silent. That should be recognized. Perhaps someone has stopped interrupting others as much and has started to practice active listening. That should be recognized.

When people are making changes to their behavior, it's one of the most critical times to recognize them. They're likely out of their comfort zones and feeling awkward. Behavioral change is hard, and we need all the encouragement and reassurance we can get. So, when we see changes to behavior, think of that car accelerating its speed from a stop or slowing down to a halt after moving. We should recognize those things. That's where the person is expending the most amount of energy.

What about things that have yet to start (or stop)? How do you recognize that? The art of doing this is a hybrid of coaching and recognition. You might say something like, "Eileen, you are so good in how you participate in team meetings with your direct reports. You listen to them carefully, ask clarifying questions, wait until they're done, and seek constant feedback. They clearly love it and love you for it. I would *love* to see you start doing the same thing with your peers. I think it would have an incredible impact and help you grow your leadership skills or progress your career. What do you think about that?"

In this case, you've seen the behavior you want to observe more of, in some small or isolated way. Using *that* can help you have a conversation about how you'd like to see that behavior in other ways, with other people, in other settings, or much more consistently.

What if the behavior hasn't started at all in any capacity? No problem. You can still choose to recognize the person in your ask for this behavior to start. In this case, you might say, "Carlos, I've been thinking a lot about how we can grow your skills and help you contribute more. There's a real need for us to send morning reports with some data and analytics to the team. I think you would be terrific at this because you have such an eye for detail. Would you mind starting that routine so others can benefit from your knowledge?"

Here you're helping someone feel both loved and important by expressing *why* you want *them*, in particular, to start the behavior. You're still talking about the impact that it would have on others or the organization on a whole if they change their behavior. They haven't done anything yet, but you're already foreshadowing that if they do, more recognition will follow. The belief that "more will follow" is something that you can prove to people by recognizing them again and again when they do execute on what you've asked.

Remember Virtue 3 on Routine Regimen? Making a consistent pattern of recognizing others and doing so often is critical to your mission. People crave recognition and feedback, so when they know you can be counted on to provide it, especially in situations where they're willing to change their behavior, you become an accelerant to change. You're that extra reason to do it, that gasoline on the fire in their heart that sets them ablaze, because you'll feed those flames in their heart if they deliver.

What about the red light? What about those behaviors that you want to see end? How do you "recognize" someone to stop something? Again, show them what's at stake (recognition) if they stop doing something. You might say, "Gene, you know how much I care about you, and I really liked what you said the other day about how you want to grow and progress. I really think you have what it takes to be a superstar around here, and I know you deserve my true and honest feedback to get there. I've been thinking a lot about what you need to do to make that happen, and I realized that coming in late peri-odically and missing deadlines here and there is holding you back. I think it's preventing senior leadership from seeing you for the mature and talented professional you are. I'd like for that to stop so we can advance you. What are your thoughts?"

In this situation, you've affirmed how much you care about this person, you've reminded them how bright their future is, and you've described how the effects of their behavior could be harmful to them and that bright future. You've ultimately asked someone to stop their behavior, but as you've done it, you've chosen to recognize their potential and greatness and recognize, once again, how much they matter.

We rarely do these things when we're asking people to start some-thing new or end something old. In fact, when we ask people to change their behavior, it never feels like recognition—it often feels like critical coaching. Most people walk away from conversations when they're being asked to start or stop something feeling less about themselves than when they walked into the conversation. They often feel that they've been told there's a problem, they're not good enough, and what they've done is wrong. These feelings often lead to guilt or, worse, shame. When we feel guilt or shame, it's hard for us to change our behavior, and so we often don't. This often leads to even worse conversations because then we've asked someone to change their behavior and they haven't. Conversations then can be tough or even disciplinary.

This is such a shame because, if we're good leaders, then we're giving feedback because we care about the individual and we want to help them succeed. That's not a bad thing at all; it's a great thing! I've had multiple bosses who never really cared about me as a person, and I felt it. We all can probably relate to that. When someone takes the time to acknowledge our efforts and how hard change is—but also tells us how much they believe in us and how much the change would help us—the conversation feels totally different, and we're much more likely to do something about it.

In 2012, I was a top-performing distract manager by all accounts. My then boss, Lynn Lu, demonstrated these concepts so well when she became the only person who's ever written me up. She placed me on disciplinary action for an isolated event where I failed to use sound judgment. Initially, I felt hurt when she slid the document across the table and handed me the pen. I remarked I had already learned my lesson, and the incident would never happen again. I felt hurt that things had come to this. This felt unnecessary, and I also felt pain since I had been performing so well. I wanted to continue to feel like a top-performer.

Lynn looked me straight in the eye and said, "Amy, I absolutely know how well you're doing. You're one of my best. And I already know this will never happen again. That's *why* I'm having you sign this. To *ensure* it. It's not because I don't care about you. Rather, it's because I *do* care about you, and I want you to continue to grow and be here."

I'll never forget that moment. I walked away, and instead of feeling hurt, I felt valued. Although Lynn had written me up, I felt more motivated and inspired to do better than ever. I had realized how high the stakes were, and I was all in. I wanted to play, and I felt that I had a boss who was in my corner. Often, leaders won't hold their people accountable, especially in writing, because they worry they'll damage the relationship. Lynn taught me that *real* care isn't always polite or nice—it's honest. At times, it hurts. Real care addresses real issues and helps people challenge themselves to do better. It's been a long time since I signed that piece of paper, but since that day, was I never afraid to tell someone the truth about how they were really doing. Instead, I always connected it to what great hopes or dreams I had for them and their role.

Here's the final step. When people start or stop behavior on a more permanent basis, it's imperative for us to comment on *that* too. You might say something like, "I see what you've done here. You haven't been late a single day in over a month. I know that was a big change, and I really appreciate it. Thank you for making that change," or "I see you're sending out those reports now every Monday. Everyone is loving it, especially me. I look at them every week. It's making a huge difference. I know that was hard to do, but it doesn't go unnoticed."

When we say things like that, we acknowledge that change is tough for most, and we respect and appreciate the work that went into *making* that change. Do that, and you'll see people be able to pivot and change the speed they're driving much more easily. The genius of that is that, over time, you help your people adapt. They recognize that changing their behavior doesn't have to be painful, scary, or difficult. When they know there's a rainbow on the other side of the storm, they often learn to adapt faster so they can get to it quicker, and now you've not only helped people feel great about making change, but you've changed how they *approach* change. You've made them more agile and, thus, stronger employees and human beings. What does that make you? A great boss.

PRACTICE 5:
GET OUTSIDE YOUR HOUSE

"Recognize your people" is a mantra that many leadership books and classes teach. Most of us know that we should recognize our people—that is, the people who roll up to us either directly or indirectly, those who are "in our charge," as Simon Sinek likes to say. The advice often ends there.

This message is wholly incomplete. Why on earth would we only recognize our "own" people? Don't other people need recognition too? Why do we recognize at all? We said earlier that it's because we want people to feel special, loved, valued, and important. So why wouldn't we want everyone around us to feel that way? This includes our peers, our boss, our clients, and—my gosh—everyone in our personal lives.

When was the last time you recognized your boss, telling them they were doing a great job? Or used the traffic light approach to ask your boss to start, stop, or continue something that felt important to you? What about your peers? In so many organizations, we view our peers as our competitors. They're fighting for the same recognition, rewards, promotions, praise, and spoils we are, right? And there's only so much of that to go around? This ties back to the scarcity mindset. The best thing we can do, especially when we're in leadership, is to lift other people up. No, that does not only mean your *own* people. That means *other* people, as in *all* other people.

When you take the time to use the recognition approaches described here with everyone around you—including peers, your boss, your direct and indirect reports, and even other employees or members of the organization that aren't affiliated with you, as well as your clients, vendors, and the janitor who cleans your halls and empties your trash, or the maintenance men working on the building, or the gardener outside working on the landscaping—something powerful happens. You infuse positivity and positive reinforcement into the whole organization and share those feelings of being loved and mattering with *everyone*. Organizations with happy employees, happy vendors, and happy clients succeed. Heard of the expression, "Pay it forward"? That's what happy people do.

I can't help but share my favorite quote from the 2001 movie *Legally Blonde*. Reese Witherspoon, as Elle Woods, explains, "Exercise gives you endorphins. Endorphins make you happy. *Happy people just don't shoot their husbands. They just don't.*" In case you haven't seen the movie, spoiler alert: Elle turned out to be right. There's something sensationally powerful about this: Happy people don't behave badly. They just *don't*.

There is nothing to be lost and everything to be gained by you recognizing everyone around you that you see doing great work. When you can help others feel valued, important, noticed, appreciated, and loved, you will help infuse happiness into them. Happy people do great things and affect others as they do it. When people are recognized and noticed for their hard work consistently, they are likely, after some time, to make the connection that recognition feels good to them. When they make that connection, they are likely to then pass it on or pay it forward to others in the form of recognition. The organization you're a part of is more likely to be successful and win, which in turns, feels good to *everyone*.

In most organizations, things aren't done in vacuums or silos, although it sometimes seems that way. We can tend to be somewhat territorial as humans, and we identify first with "our" team, or "our" group, or "our" department. This makes sense, since you spend the most time with those in your clan or your division versus others, but it's one of the most deadly and dangerous things that can happen in an organization. It makes you protective of everything from your people, your talent, your ideas, your time, to your words. Cue the scarcity mindset again. I've seen managers who are quick to recognize and celebrate their own people but slow to recognize the talent and contributions of those on other teams. When something is going wrong or a project is behind, they're quick to defend their own team but slow to defend another team. We often don't even notice that these things are happening, but these behaviors reap havoc on organizations. Marketing and sales don't get along. Human Resources is the enemy, and it's not a good sign if they drop into your meeting unexpectedly. Accounting holds the purse strings. "So-and-so" is known to nix every good idea. "Watch out for this person." "Be careful about what you say in front of that person." Blah, blah, blah.

During one of my stints as a district manager, I visited one of my branches and found the branch manager and a personal banker, Vincent, talking together in the lobby. I went over to say hello and asked how their days were going. The branch manager shared some "good news" with me, which was that he had just finished talking with a customer whom the personal banker had just helped. "This customer wanted to meet with me so he could tell me what a great job Vincent had done," he said excitedly.

"Well, that's great! What was the situation?" I asked, eager to get the specifics so I could use my words to recognize Vincent properly and in a lasting way that Vincent would remember.

As the branch manager described the backstory, I was immediately dismayed. Apparently, the customer had a terrible experience at another location in the company multiple times. He had spent several weeks trying to resolve the same problem and had been promised follow-up calls and resolution by this other branch during those weeks. Finally, in despair, he drove several miles out of his way to come to this branch to resolve it. When he met Vincent, who was able to solve his problem, he was so thankful and floored that he wanted to see the manager to talk about what a great employee Vincent was.

"He said that he's going to start driving the extra 30 minutes to come see us," added the branch manager. "I think I'm going to submit this as a success story."

I was stunned and could hardly believe what I was hearing. I composed myself and took a moment to recognize Vincent on how well he had handled the customer's situation and shared how happy I was that the customer had found resolution with someone he felt he could trust. Then, I focused on my questions.

"Did we find out who the other person was?" I asked. "Did we get a name?"

"Well, no, not really. But the great news is that this branch isn't even in our market," Vincent said, sharing which branch it was. "It's not one of yours," he reassured me.

I was anything but reassured. I turned to the branch manager. "Are you or Vincent going to call and provide feedback and coaching to the branch manager over there?" I asked. "So that branch and that individual can improve?"

My branch manager looked surprised. "Well…no, I wasn't going to do that," he finally answered.

"Why not?" I asked.

"Well…it's not in our market. And everything is fine now," he added. "The customer is going to start coming here from now on."

"Everything is *not* fine now," I replied. "We've now got a customer who thinks he can only come to this location, which is 30 minutes out of his way. We talk about being convenient for our customers, and we've got someone who has literally inconvenienced himself as he passes other branches so he can come here to do his banking. This customer also thinks that only some of our locations are acceptable and others aren't. The customer doesn't know that this branch is out of our market, and the customer doesn't care whose market that branch is in. We haven't delivered a consistent brand promise to this customer. That's the opposite of our strategy."

What concerned me most about this story, outside of the lousy and inconsistent experience a customer of this bank was receiving, was the mindset of my people. I had a branch manager and a personal banker who both believed that anything that happened outside our four walls (as a district) was not our problem. They were thinking about their team first instead of the organization—or even the customer. They viewed something as a success because it happened on their tiny and private island—forgetting that this situation was an opportunity for us (as a company) to learn and grow. What should've become a chance to build a better partnership with this other branch in this other district and provide some coaching, feedback, and guidance so we could grow the whole organization stronger was instead viewed as a celebratory moment. We had totally missed the mark, and I was dismayed.

I'll never forget when Jason Sasena, a senior vice president over mortgage banking, once explained it to me: "I hate the word partner. We always talk about other lines of business as partners. Our mortgage partners, our small business banking partners, our financial advisors are partners to the branch."

I was surprised; I had thought "partner" was a good word. But Jason clarified and expanded my understanding of true partnership in an instant. "We're not partners," Jason continued. "That implies there's a separation between us. We all get a paycheck from the same *one* company. We're literally all on the same *one* team." That moment was profoundly shaping in my mind. He was right. The word *partner* implied we weren't on the same team but, rather, two distinct teams in need of partnering together. In the same branch, no one ever referred to their coworkers or colleagues as partners. It was simply another associate, another colleague, another team member.

We face these challenges every day. We think of our own house first—the people closest to us. We forget that our peers and fellow teammates in other departments, divisions, and groups are after (or should be after) the same common goal as we are. We forget that we're all trying to achieve the same one company vision and mission. We forget that we use the same core values to get there. Sure, we may play different roles, but we're all part of one group.

I've learned that organizations do best when people align *first* with the organization, then with their team, and then with themselves, as an individual. When we think this way, we see different behaviors, and those lead to different results. We don't see a personal banker celebrate because they personally did well with a customer, even when another employee botched the situation for weeks or another office messed up. We see people who are eager to help each other, give feedback, provide coaching, and only really celebrate success when the success is shared by all.

If you're leading a team of individuals and only spend time within your four walls, that's a bad thing. If your company has Core Value Awards or other recognition processes like submissions for an Employee of the Quarter or Year, and you can only ever think about recognizing your *own* people, that's a bad thing. If you truly don't know what other people in the organization are doing, and you have no idea what you'd recognize your peers in another line of business or office for, that's a bad thing. It either means you're not spending enough time with them to truly collaborate or you're not paying close enough attention to them when you *are* spending time with them.

When you do this in public ways, others overhear you, and you truly lead by example. In my most recent role of a COO, I built a relationship with the external maintenance man who does work on our building. He worked exceptionally hard and did so much great work for our organization. These types of people tend not to be noticed by most executives or leaders in the world. It's like we take them for granted or forget they exist. This means that we forget how things get done around us. We forget where the fresh water and snacks in the break room originate from, or how building improvements or beautification get done, which means that we don't really think it matters. When I first started recognizing this person shortly after joining the organization, he was somewhat quiet and standoffish around me, and it made me wonder if I should bother recognizing him at all or if I was making him uncomfortable.

In full transparency, a range of thoughts went through my head when he wasn't initially responsive. I thought, *Okay, this person probably doesn't have a college degree. He's here in ripped blue jeans, covered in paint, and spends his life fixing and repairing things. He doesn't care if I talk to him; he's just here to collect a paycheck and probably doesn't have much to say.*

I quickly realized how assumptive and judgmental that was. How much education he has doesn't matter. I knew nothing about this person, but he was a human being like everyone else who spent time in the building. Plus, it's in my nature to use words, so I continued. After a few months, he slowly warmed up to me. After a few months with the organization, I asked him to come drill some holes into my wall because I wanted to hang up some art in my office. After I was done showing him what pieces I wanted to put where, and he was wrapping up measuring where the holes would go, I confided in him and got a wonderful life lesson back in exchange.

"You know," I said to him, "I feel a little awkward or embarrassed putting up all these pictures in my office. Nobody else really has anything like this in their offices. You've worked here a long time. Do you think this is okay?"

He smiled at me and said, "I think it's great you're doing this. You're right—a lot of people around here don't really put much in their offices. I've always wondered why. I bet a lot of people want to make their offices more colorful and decorated, just like you, but are afraid. People are often afraid. You doing it, in the role you're in, will probably show other people that it's okay to do it and give them permission to do it too. I think you should."

I smiled, nodded, and gave him the green light to start hammering away, but inside, I was changed. Only a month before this, I had the thought (no matter how briefly it lasted) that this gentleman wasn't fully aware of everything going on and didn't have much to say or offer. How wrong I'd been. After continued recognition on my part, he had opened up and given me a concise summary of so many elements of great leadership. Articulately and eloquently, he had shared thoughts on how people are often ruled by fear and hold back who they truly are. He had described to me the importance of people feeling safe and secure to be themselves in their work environment. He had reminded me of how important it was to trust oneself and believe in one's own desires and beliefs. He had shared perspective about the importance of leading by example and how our behavior can influence others around us. He had aptly described so much of great leadership. He had done all that in under a minute.

As I continued to recognize this man's efforts, I noticed other people start to do it too. A few times in meetings, leaders would even comment on how fabulous he was and how complete his work was. They were the same people I noticed often recognizing other groups or departments instead of their own group or department. Recognition goes a long way, and we never know what we'll learn in exchange or how we'll grow from recognizing others. We never know what other people will teach *us*.

If you don't know whom outside your own team to recognize, spend more time with people. Go and watch people in action. We talked earlier about how important it is to be out in the field, observing your team behave and act so you can be specific and tailored with how you coach and recognize them. It's important you can do this with peers as well. When you ask to stop by and see a peer in action—whether it's them leading a meeting or you shadowing them in their natural habitat—you show *interest* in them as a person. When you conclude these sessions with great feedback and share what you learned from them, you lead by example where recognition and acknowledgment are part of the environment. People want to return the favor, and you'll find that every positive sentence you utter to a peer or other employee in the organization that you don't normally interact with comes back to serve you.

Outside of the reasons I've talked about (it takes time, we don't see many examples of this, we're often hardwired to be competitive with other groups, we don't spend enough time with people outside our own clan to know what their accomplishments are), I've never understood why more people don't do this. We need other teams to help us win. We can't do it all on our own. So why do we primarily recognize only our own teams and people? If you're having experiences where you're working with other teams and it's clunky, or they're not meeting expectations, what usually happens is your team all complains to one another. You'll naturally blame the other team and think first about how others aren't meeting expectations. This is failing in building relationships. If you want other groups or other teams to do well, you need to recognize what they are doing well or find a way to give them feedback about what you'd like to see in a caring and kind way. They are people too, and they're probably doing the best they can. The fact that they have another job or role in the organization means they do something different than you. That means you don't know as much about what they're going through as they do, and perhaps it's harder than you think. Giving those folks some love will help improve their behavior and help them be better peers to you, which will help make your job easier.

In the story I shared about Vincent, as great as it was that he delighted this customer, the interaction didn't start off great. In fact, the interaction started with the customer coming in annoyed and irate, sharing a sob story about how bad things had been. Vincent had to listen to the backstory and apologize for the mess. While he was happy to have turned things around, it never should have come to that. Had the member been able to get the right service universally—from anyone in that organization—Vincent would've had more time to make outbound calls that day, meet other customers (who never got called), and make new connections, which might've led to something much greater. We lose so much time because we don't gain efficiencies that come from trusting one another. Such trust comes from having a fully built relationship, which comes from showing appreciation and love—often through acknowledgment and recognition. Stop wasting valuable time and recognize everyone—not just members of your own team.

The final piece in the puzzle is to recognize your boss. Sometimes we think that feedback with our bosses can only roll in one direction—down. But think about this: Have you ever been recognized by your own team? Has a direct report of yours ever commented to you that they think you're doing a stellar job? How did that make you feel?

If you're like me, you probably wanted to do more, try harder, and show up in an even bigger way for your team. It takes self-awareness, humility, courage, respect, and love for people to recognize their boss. If you've had this experience—good. It's time you pay it forward to your boss (assuming they deserve recognition). If you don't really have anything to recognize your boss for, then you can roll with the traffic light model of recognition and ask your boss to start or stop something because you want to have a better relationship with them or be a better performer for them, and you think a change in their behavior would help you do that. Whenever we connect a reward, prize, or something someone wants to a behavior that we want to see start, stop, or change, people tend to get more excited about making that change.

I'm assuming your boss isn't a robot or a machine, so just like you and your team, they need recognition too.

Don't just stay inside your home and recognize your own family. Get outside, walk down the block or street, and see what your neighbors are up to. Think about the garbagemen who take away your trash or sweep your streets. Find ways to recognize everyone in the whole community. The bonus is that focusing on what people are doing well helps us feel more positive and grateful inside, which leads to us feeling happier. If nothing else, at least now you won't shoot your husband (or spouse). You just won't.

VIRTUE 7:
Showcase Swimming

"What you do speaks so loudly,
that I cannot hear what you say."
– Ralph Waldo Emerson

This final chapter is all about leading by example, walking the talk, and being able to model much of what you ask of other people. You might be thinking, *Understood. What more is there to say? Why is that a whole virtue?* Not so fast. It's not that *simple*, nor is it that *easy*.

This is an important concept, and the most common way I see this concept get twisted is when people think it means that *you* should do, or be willing to do, *anything* you'd ask your people to do. Guy Kawasaki, American marketing specialist, author, and Silicon Valley venture capitalist, said it best: "Don't ask people to do something you wouldn't." Numerous other quotes and sayings that mirror this concept are so popular, they're almost cliché, but they're still valuable.

However, I want to be clear: that's *not* what this Virtue is about. The best leadership I've had over the years always practiced this Virtue of showcasing swimming, but many of them did *not* jump in and do my job alongside me, nor did I expect them to. While it's true that they *could* have, what's important is that they *didn't*. They chose not to because their job was *not* to do the things they asked others to do. It was to enable and help others do those things much more effectively. To do so, they had to showcase swimming. We're going to explore the differences between that and bosses rolling up their sleeves and getting in the trenches with their team.

Let's take my last role, for example. A lot of things that I couldn't have done and shouldn't have done myself, I did ask others to do. As COO, I oversaw our Facilities group. They lifted heavy boxes and did other manual labor that not only did I have no business doing, but I literally couldn't physically do. There are professional basketball coaches in the NBA who don't have the ability to dunk a basketball as well as their top players (or at all), but that doesn't mean that they can't and shouldn't effectively coach those players and that team. In my COO role, I also oversaw our call center; they do numerous transactions on members' accounts that I have never been trained to do. I didn't know how to open an account, take a loan application, or submit a fraud claim. I've never done those specific things for our members—at least, not at that organization, using its programs. I'd imagine that not every airline CEO has the training or license to fly its aircrafts, and most executives of retail stores wouldn't know how to ring someone up for a purchase if they stopped by one of their locations.

Does any of this make us poor leaders? No, absolutely not. It means we hold a different role than the people who roll up to us, and we're there to do different things. Many leaders have done the things they ask their people to do in the past. But for other leaders, especially those in senior or executive roles, they'll supervise people who do a job they've never done.

Showcasing behaviors for your teams isn't about doing every last thing that you ask them to do, but it's about embodying the key behaviors that you're asking of them. If you ask your employees to show up on time, you should do so as well. If you ask your employees to be honest and straightforward, even when it's difficult and they're afraid of the outcome, you should do that as well. If you ask your employees to keep their commitments, you should also be prepared to keep yours. If you ask your employees to feel tremendous passion for the customer or the client, you should share that same passion and express it just as loudly. If you ask your employees to do their best, give their all, and work hard, you should also do your best, give your all, and work hard.

In other words, showcasing swimming is not about being able to do every task or function you'd ask your people to do, but it *is* about being able to demonstrate every single Virtue in this book. If you're leading other leaders and you buy into the V.I.R.T.U.E.S. in this book, then it's critical that you don't just teach this framework to the leaders around you, but that you practice all of them yourself:

- If you want others to have vision and share that vision with others, you should as well.
- If you want others to involve their teams in all that they do, you should also involve others.
- If you expect others to have routines and live by them, you should have routines and live by them.
- If you expect others to talk, train, and communicate well, you should do the same.
- If you expect others to focus on understanding and learning, you should also do that.
- If you expect others to encourage energy by rewarding and recognizing success, you should too.
- If you expect others to walk the talk and showcase leadership, you should also do that.

You can't just talk about how others need coaching and development or sit in your ivory tower and discuss "problems" or "issues" that arise. You need to become actively involved in ensuring that you've provided coaching and development to others, providing them the tools and resources to solve problems. Otherwise, you're part of the problem.

Senior vice presidents wouldn't be effective if they went and did every task or function that they ask of their managers, and managers wouldn't be effective if they did every task or function that their individual staff members do. But if you expect your staff members to challenge themselves and their thinking, stretch themselves to take on more challenging tasks, to get back up and brush themselves off after they fail, to identify a solution each time they have a problem, and to feel gratitude for what's going well, you have to be willing to do those things yourself. If anything, you have to toe (and tow!) the line and lead the way for others.

When we ask people to do something then turn around and don't do those same things ourselves, especially when they're the kind of things on the aforementioned list, we literally lose the ability to lead others. We shoot our credibility in the foot and run on the mantra of "Do as I say, not as I do." Nobody likes to work for that kind of leader.

Here's a list of DON'Ts that I'd file under Showcase Swimming for your team:

- Don't complain about the company or its leadership. Instead, propose solutions.
- Don't talk poorly about others. Instead, show loyalty[32] to others and take accountability.
- Don't procrastinate, miss deadlines, or break any kind of promise. Instead, keep all commitments.[33]
- Don't be late. Instead, be punctual or early.
- Don't dress unprofessionally. Instead, hold yourself to an even higher standard than others.
- Don't interrupt others. Instead, listen first.[34]
- Don't lose your temper or lose control. Instead, create a safe space for people to openly share.
- Don't forget to follow through. Instead, own the outcome and adhere to the Oz Principle.[35]

These may seem obvious, but I've watched leadership do these things many times then wonder why others around them *also* do these things. What? I can't think of anything more egotistical or arrogant. We, as leaders, get frustrated when our people do the same things people have seen us do. If your company or group has a vision, a mission, or core values, you must be *especially* stellar at showcasing them, assuming you want your team to practice them too. If your company has a core value around teamwork and respect, you better be prepared to live that every single day. If your company has a core value of integrity or transparency, you better be prepared to live that every day yourself. If your company or team has a core value around innovation and growth, you better be prepared to live that every day. Leaders who deviate from living the overarching vision, mission, and core values of the company earn a special place in the land of hypocrisy and double standards. A lack of showcasing these things is especially hard to recover from. It's one of the ultimate withdrawals that can happen in the emotional bank account of your relationships with your team.[36]

We've all probably had that manager or boss or teacher who talked about how important it was to do something and then turned around and did the opposite. Invariably, we lose respect for these people, and what they say loses meaning. This doesn't always happen consciously. Instead, for most of us, it's a subconscious response, but one we somehow remember.

While getting my MBA in 2008, I saw this lesson in action. We attended class in the evenings, and during our first year of instruction, we took two classes at a time. Our program was divided into two "cores," and we'd take our classes in adjacent but separate rooms. In the middle of each evening, there would be a short break when the two professors teaching us that semester would switch rooms while we stayed put. By the end of the night, both groups had been taught both topics by both professors.

During spring semester, my first class each night was taught by an especially vocal and passionate professor named Carl. As he began class one evening, he pulled down a dry erase whiteboard to use it, only to find that it was covered in writing from a professor who had taught earlier that day. To add insult to injury, he couldn't find any spray to go with the paper towels, so someone had to leave the room to go grab him some so he could effectively erase the whole board. Carl had the tendency to become impatient whenever there was any delay in the advancement of learning, and as he waited for the student to come back with the erase spray, he had a hard time containing his irritation. Carl loudly complained, "This is the classic sign of a *terrible* professor. They don't clean up after themselves. There's a rule in academia: You always erase your board." When the board was finally erased, he spent a majority of class drawing and writing all over it, and after the formal lecture was over and we moved into Q&A, Carl rolled that board up into its place.

At the break, he and the professor switched classrooms as usual, and early in our class with the second instructor, she, too, pulled down the whiteboard to use it. Sure enough, clear as day, was Carl's writing *all* over it. In fact, the whiteboard was even more marked up than when Carl had found it some two hours prior. The entire room burst into laughter.

Fourteen years later, I still remember this moment. We were all in stitches. "He didn't erase the board!" many of us howled. I also remember the sheer confusion on our second professor's face. She hadn't been there for our Carl's earlier rant, so nothing was amusing to her. To us, it was everything.

Carl had made such a stink over the failure to erase the board. Then he had turned around and done the same thing only an hour later. One thing that stands out to me was how immediately funny everyone thought it was. The room that night was filled with much ethic, racial, religious, gender, and age diversity, but we all cackled away. The concept of hypocrisy or double standards is *universal*. As Larry the Cable Guy would say, "That's funny. I don't care who you are."

But there was also a sad reality to it. Many of us, including myself, viewed that professor, until this moment, as a leader: someone I could trust to do the right thing; someone who knew a lot of things. I had placed an expectation on him to lead by example and show me the way. Sure, he was only there to teach us in a particular subject, but I had viewed professors as pseudo experts on life too. My mother was an educator for 36 years and taught me from a young age that we should always respect those who educate and teach us.

That day, what I observed was not leadership but stupidity. Carl had made such a show out of being irritated by someone else's behavior but engaged in the same behavior immediately afterward. I might not have been able to put it into words then, but it was the ultimate betrayal of accountability. For years now, my definition of accountability is that "We do what we say." When people do the opposite, it becomes difficult to trust them. Without trust, we have nothing.

Leadership is hard work. Some say, "you're always on stage," and that's true. Others aspire to be you or be like you. They, too, want to know and understand how they can rise up the ranks, make more money, have the corner office—which many believe comes with respect and a feeling that you've made it. They watch you so they can learn and absorb from you and figure out how to mirror your behaviors so they can end up like you. It's a compliment of the highest order, but "with great power comes great responsibility,"[37] and sadly, some are not ready for that responsibility. For those who aren't, they really shouldn't be in leadership.

Now, let's explore some key behaviors you can do to showcase swimming.

PRACTICE 1:
SIGNAL YOUR BEHAVIOR

"People don't buy what you do. They buy why you do it."
– Simon Sinek

From my perspective, this quote was the foundation for Simon Sinek's book *Start with Why*, where Sinek used common-day examples like Apple to explain a theory that people don't buy what others—a company, a boss, a friend, a spouse—*do*, but rather, *why* they do it. My belief is that people also don't *care* about what you do as much as they care about *why* you do it.

Stephen M. R. Covey, author of *The Speed of Trust*, talks often about how important it is to both declare our intent and signal behavior. He explains that signaling our behavior when we're on the thruway and wanting to make a lane change isn't about us—it's about others. We're telling others what we plan to do, and then, they know to look for it. When we keep our commitments, or act in accordance with promises we previously made about our behavior, everything makes sense to our audience. In fact, when we declare our intent and signal our behavior, people around us tend to focus on what we do even more; because they were previously told what to expect, they're now waiting and watching for it.[38]

When we set expectations with others about *what* we plan to do and *why* we plan to do it, we facilitate the learning process for others. When we don't say, in advance, what we plan to do and why we're doing it, people may not have the learning we want them to have when they see us act. They might not have any learning at all. They might assume our actions are by chance. They might not recognize any kind of patterns in our behavior. They might not recognize that our reasons for what we do align with the V.I.R.T.U.E.S. in this book. They might not even connect the dots and recognize that by declaring our intent, signaling our behavior, and then following through, we've effectively held ourselves accountable to doing what we say and kept our commitments—concepts from both *The Oz Principle* and *The Speed of Trust*. When this happens, people miss some of the most important parts of what you're doing—the *why*. Declaring your intent and signaling your behaviors are surefire ways to help people understand your *why*, which, as Sinek says, is the aspect of your behavior that people buy into.

Take the V.I.R.T.U.E.S. outlined in this book. When you set expectations by declaring your intent and by signaling your behavior, you leverage an opportunity to show people that your actions are because of the following reasons:

- To better communicate an established vision, mission, or core values—or to act in accordance with those things
- To involve others around you to empower and engage them
- To uphold consistent routines and habits
- To better coach, develop, teach, train, and grow others
- To ensure there's learning and understanding taking place
- To encourage, recognize, and reward others, showing them they're valued and appreciated
- To model behaviors, lead by example, and showcase swimming

In practice, signaling your behavior might sound like the following:
- Tomorrow, I'm going to drop by the new hire training orientation because I want them to know how much I care about them and their success. I also want them to feel comfortable reaching out to me anytime.
- I'd like these reports turned in by Monday end of day because once they're submitted to me, I'm going to review them, give you each

feedback, and return them to you by Thursday. That way, you've got another few days before they're due to my boss the following Tuesday.

- In this presentation, I'm going to speak for about 35 minutes on the results of our data and our recommendations. At that time, we'll move into Q&A for the remaining 25 minutes. I ask you to hold your questions until the end because I really want to be sure we get through all the slides, and I also think there's some answers to early questions that will come later in the presentation.

- On Friday, I'd like to come sit in on your team meeting. I want to reward and recognize the staff for how well they did with this recent project, but I also want to observe and gather insight for *you* on how you lead your meeting. Please don't be nervous; this is all about me ensuring I'm developing you toward the goal we put on your development plan earlier this year about being a more effective leader.

- I'm going to work on this at home over the weekend, and I'll be sure to have it back to you by Monday morning.

- I want this communication to come from me because I know this conversation is going to be tough, and I want to lead by example for you guys in having a difficult discussion.

When we tell people what we're going to do and why we're going to do it, we allow people to really get to know us. They're able to clearly identify what's important to us as we share the methods to our madness with others. People begin to understand that we're not just flying blind or shooting from the hip, but that we have reasons for what we do. They recognize that our behaviors and actions aren't accidents but clearly thought out and always with an end in mind.[39] By doing this, you help create connections for people. They recognize that you don't act haphazardly but with purpose, and then they are often influenced to follow suit. When we act with deliberate intention, we tend to create much more success. Modeling the way for your team on this by openly sharing your *why* for almost everything helps them do the same.

PRACTICE 2:
TELL YOUR WORST STORIES

Once you're learned, embraced, and begun to practice the true essence of leadership, you'll find that the best things that happen to you often don't come from above but from below. For many true leaders, the accolades, acknowledgment, and awards received from superiors are nice, but they don't mean as much as the results and success you see your team having. True leaders don't do it for the applause from the grandstands; they do it because they want to make a difference in the lives of others around them. They're determined to help other people become better, stronger, more capable. They're determined to help other people win. They're determined to help other people get the accolades, acknowledgment, and awards. When that's happening, they know their job is getting done.

When you're in leadership, one of the best things that can happen is to find yourself surrounded by a truly engaged team, full of people who are wanting to learn, grow, and improve. If you're a great leader, then you also realize that people are malleable. You know that nobody is perfect, and instead, people are in constant states of evolution, change, and flux. You recognize that it's part of *your* job to help this evolution process occur, and you're constantly seeking out new information and ways to ensure that happens.

This whole book has been about that—how to inspire, engage, and empower other people—but I still have another way for you to do that. If you want them at their *best*, you'll need to let them see you at your *worst*. Why? Because growth is hard. When people are trying to become stronger and more capable, they need to exist in a safe environment. They need to be able to stub their toe, struggle, suffer, fall, fail, and make mistakes. They need to be able to do all of that and then start again. The problem is, most of that doesn't feel good to average human beings, and at most organizations, management does one of two things: "you either condemn or condone" (as discussed in Virtue 1). Most leaders either make things worse or they make things better. Rarely do people or environments stay the same under leadership.

A common misconception many people have is that those above them are infallible. It's easy for employees to look at a boss or a boss's boss or the

CEO and make assumptions that those people didn't have to struggle, work for it, or go through as much pain as *they* do.

I've sat in hundreds of coaching conversations with staff-level employees who were being coached by managers who reported to me. Often, I'd chime in and offer words of advice or a perspective that I gained when I was working in their same role, years before. Often, I'd hear the same thing: "But, Amy, that's easy for *you* to say!" Or, "But, Amy, I could *never* say or do it like that—I'm not *you*." In almost every case, as we talked more, I would dig into what those statements meant and would find the same thing (over and over). Many of these individuals believed that it had been easy for me when I was doing their jobs. That I had somehow, magically, started my professional life with the skills I have today. That I had never struggled, never failed, never erred.

This, of course, is complete ridiculousness. Over the years, I've shared a thousand stories of my failings and hardships—and trust me, there are many. I didn't share these stories only with my direct reports or other people in management. I'd share them with my indirect reports too. I'd share them with people who were multiple levels below me. I'd share them with my peers. I'd basically share these stories with anyone who wanted to listen. Why? Because I wanted to showcase two important things: (1) we all struggle, and that's okay; and (2) humility.

SHOWCASE STRUGGLE

The first is universally true. We *all* struggle. We *all* fail. We *all* make mistakes. Anyone who says they haven't or doesn't is either flat-out lying (to others or to themselves) or is too arrogant, naive, or oblivious to know. In other words, they don't *think* they've ever failed, and that, in itself, is a colossal failing.[40]

Remember the Leader's Pledge from the beginning of this book? Well, to accomplish that pledge, you must also make an agreement with yourself that:
1. People can change and are changing all the time;
2. It's your job to help them with that; and
3. You need to constantly be thinking about *how* you can help them with that.

It's important to understand that employees believing that you, as the leader, are infallible and don't fail or struggle is entirely damaging to this whole process. The more they believe that *you* can do something easily, the more they're likely to believe that *they can't*. It can be counterintuitive. It feels good when people admire and respect us for how awesome we are. But the reality is that we shouldn't want people to put us on a pedestal and revere how capable we are. We want to inspire courage in others. We want them to put *themselves* on a pedestal. We want them to know how capable *they* are. We want to push, test, and stretch our people, and they'll do that more often and better if they aren't afraid to fail.

"It has been said that after meeting with the great British Prime Minister William Ewart Gladstone, you left feeling he was the smartest person in the world, but after meeting with his rival Benjamin Disraeli, you left thinking you were the smartest person." – Bono

You'll have no idea how much it'll mean to your people, and how much more they'll trust and respect you, if you can help them understand that you absolutely *have* been where they've been. That you *have* walked a mile in their shoes. You, too, started a job for the first time and had that slightly awkward first day when you didn't know anyone or anything, including where the restroom was located. That you, too, remember how challenging or stressful a new role or new assignment was. That you, too, made a bad sales call, where someone hung up on you and you didn't close the deal. That you, too, once had a lapse in judgment, said the wrong thing on a conference call, or turned something in late. That you, too, made a mistake that cost the company money and had to admit it to your boss. That you, too, have been anxious, nervous, worried, scared about flubbing a presentation. That you, too, didn't always know how you'd fare on a performance review. That you, too, once were written up or fired.

We all learn from our mistakes, and most of us learn more from our mistakes than the things we do right. If all we talk about is the things we've done right, we never allow other people to have the realization that we are just like them. That once upon a time, we didn't know everything either and we had to work to figure it out.

The beauty of showing people that you, too, have arrived home from work crying once or twice, burned a bridge with someone who was supposed to be an ally, or totally dropped the ball on something is that you allow people to recover and heal from their own wounds, and even feel less wounded in the first place, if and when these things happen to *them*. Instead of leading people in ways where they feel they need to put on a show around you, you lead people in ways where they feel they can be themselves around you. When people feel that way, great things happen. People are comfortable trying things that may not work out because they know that if they fail, it's not the end of their career. After all, you admitted your failures to them and somehow it all worked out for you, right?

There are huge benefits to developing a team around you that isn't worried about how failure "looks" or isn't worried about failing. There are endless examples of innovators and inventors that literally "failed" thousands of times before they found the right way. Colonel Sanders is rumored to have knocked on over 1,000 doors before his recipe for Kentucky Fried Chicken was picked up; without his persistence in the face of so much rejection, KFC as we know it would never exist. Thomas Edison is another revered hero in our history; without his tenacity and healthy relationship with mistakes and failure, we might not ever have discovered the light bulb.[41]

"I have not failed. I've just found 10,000 ways that won't work."
– Thomas Edison

I could always tell which of my offices and locations had a leadership problem with this dimension by what people did before they interacted with me. If you catch people in corners adjusting their name tag so it's perfectly aligned on their blazer, smoothing their hair, or rehearsing lines before they meet with you (like it's a play with an audience), you've got a problem. When people nervously twitch when they talk to you, and you get the sense that there's certain "things that shouldn't be said" when you're around, you've got a problem. What you've created, or *someone* has created, is a belief that leaders are *different* from everyone else and there's a divide between them and you. That belief will kill your strategy and your team's ability to achieve break-through results. This is one of the key reasons showcasing swimming is so important: you're demonstrating for people that there's not some major separation between you, the leader, and everybody else.

When people think you're looking for perfectionism, they can't do their best work. What you want people to believe and know is that all you're asking of them is their best *effort*. You want them to understand not how powerful *you* are, but how powerful *they* are. You want them to try new things. Maybe you'll never get them to a point where they're not afraid to fail, but at least when they are afraid to fail, they act anyway (which is the definition of courage).

Effort is an important piece of the equation because it's something we can *control*. We often can't control our environment. We don't get to control weather, traffic, other people, the past, and how much training or coaching we've had previously. But we can *always* control how we show up and how we set intention. When we teach people that trying new things and practicing a new skill is going to be hard but *worth* it—and any failures or mistakes along the way are the breeding ground for learning, which only makes us stronger— we give people permission to fail. However, we don't *give* them permission to fail only by saying, "Hey, it's okay to fail." We give them permission by telling them our worst war stories about how we failed too.

"Success is not final, failure is not fatal: it is the courage to continue that counts." – Winston Churchill

In 2005, while working at the branch that did a great job of involving everyone in everything, I learned how to truly embrace rejection and failure, thanks to Trish's brilliant leadership. New in my sales role, I was struggling to find candidates for residential loans and home equities, which was a major focus at that time. No matter how hard I tried, I felt that everyone I talked to about these products said "No." That was a bad feeling. Shortly after sharing my woes with Trish, she launched an experimental campaign that transformed my thinking around failure. She organized a competition for all of us to see not how many Yeses we could get the upcoming month, but rather, how many Nos we could get.

At first, I thought I had misunderstood the terms of the assignment. "You must mean how many yeses we can get," I said more than once. "No," Trish explained. "The winner of the competition will have gotten the most Nos."

Gosh, I thought, *even I can do this!*

Each of us were given a jar, and we'd all write down a piece of information about each customer we'd asked so Trish could do a bit of inspection to ensure these conversations were happening. We established some ground rules for the competition, and shortly after, we were off to the races.

In only a month, I was forever changed because of this experience. Trish's competition ended up having two huge impacts on me. First, Trish permanently changed how I felt about rejection and failure. Prior to the competition, every single "No" I received from a pitch would sting like a dagger in my heart. For me, it had always stunk. But now, I felt good about the Nos I'd get. *Welp, I didn't get the sale, but at least I get to put another person in this handy-dandy NO jar*, I'd reason as I scribbled down the information about the conversation I'd had before plunking the slip of paper into the jar. As time went on, hearing "No" became somewhat exciting. I knew I was one step closer to winning the competition. I've always been competitive, and Trish knew that. Now, instead of feeling like I was losing when I heard that dirty word, I felt like I was winning.

Second, as time went on, I noticed something else. I started asking almost everybody to talk with me about their borrowing picture. I'd never make a recommendation or ask someone to consider a product that wasn't right for them, but I needed to get as many Nos as possible to win, so I needed to take more "at bats." To find these chances, I needed to have more conversations. Because I felt that I was so bad at these conversations, I had previously been avoiding them. Now, I had a reason to have these discussions—I wanted to win the competition—so I talked about these topics all day long. As I did so, a few things happened. Since sales is a numbers game, the more people I asked, the more Nos I got, but the more Yeses I got too. Because I was simply asking more people, I was finding a handful of people who did want to move forward. As the weeks rolled by, I noticed that I had a record number of pending applications in my pipeline. As several of those applications closed, I also hit goals around funded volume. My goal to get a record number of Nos had the effect of garnering me a record number of Yeses as well. Genuis.

This wasn't the only side effect of this competition. As I increased the number of "at bats" I took, I noticed I was getting better at talking about these products. Because I wasn't shying away from it, and rather diving in headfirst, I was getting far more practice in having these conversations. As I practiced more, I became more proficient. As I became more proficient, I started getting different results. More people started saying "Yes" to me, not just because I was asking more people, but because I was getting more proficient with my ask.

I ended up winning that competition and taking home a portable DVD player (a hot item in 2005). But winning the competition was far from the biggest win. I had already won so many other things: greater proficiency and confidence in having a conversation that was previously tough; better results in both applications and closed deals than I'd ever have before; and perhaps most importantly, a newfound mindset that asking is always better than not asking, hearing "No" isn't the end of the world, and the courage to get back up and try again (and again) is what matters most in life. In effect, Trish's creative competition had taught us the following:

> **"That knowing is better than wondering, that waking is better than sleeping, and even the biggest failure, even the worst most intractable mistake, beat the hell out of never trying."**
> **– Meredith Grey, title character of *Grey's Anatomy***

When I started the Management Development Program at M&T Bank in 2004, one of the first people I remember speaking to our class of 54 recent college graduates was a young man named Michael Sheets, who had only competed the program a year or two ahead of us. Michael was already successful and rising the ranks within HR at M&T, and we were about a week into our program. I thought Michael walked on water. He seemed to be incredibly well connected in the company; he knew everyone. He also seemed to be a one-man show, capable of doing anything (or so I thought). He had been in touch with us during our recruitment days and through our hiring process. Once employed, Michael had been coordinating our flights and hotel arrangements and had handed me my first-ever shiny corporate card. I had seen him shaking hands with the company's CEO in a hallway earlier that week. By the time he was on stage, speaking to our entire group, I had gained a tremendous amount of respect for him. I thought he could do no wrong. It was only later that I learned Michael likely had a lot of help in orchestrating everything for our group and making it look effortless.

Michael's speech was surprisingly short, and he made good on a promise he made early on to take questions and establish dialogue with us (declaring his intent and signaling his behavior immediately made him more credible to me). When someone asked him for some advice as a first-year management trainee, Michael wasted no time being the first leader in an organization I'd heard publicly admit something that I only later realized was sheer gold. He said:

"I was always so afraid of messing this up." – Michael Sheets

He went on to explain how risk-adverse he had been in his early days for fear of making the wrong decision. He worried that one mistake could impact his career or, worse, cost him his job. Michael talked about how much he regretted this kind of thinking. He then encouraged us to be brave enough to take chances, to speak up when we didn't know something, and to try new things—even knowing that some of those ideas might not work out.

It was a small thing, but Michael's biggest piece of advice was basically: fail fast, fail often, and fail forward. The only reason he was able to share such wisdom and advice was because he had done the *opposite* when he was in our shoes—and lived to regret it. The best part was that he wasn't ashamed to talk about it publicly. Rather, he openly embraced it. It wasn't just advice for a first-year management trainee—it turned out to be great life advice.

Today, when leaders tell me how nervous they are to conduct a termination, I tell them about the first time I had to terminate someone. I was so nervous that the document was shaking in my hand. When leaders tell me how hard making sales calls is for them, I tell them about all the people who readily dismissed me and hung up on me when I was starting out. I tell people about all the poor decisions I made over the years and how I got fired from Burger King when I was a college freshman for giving my friend Steve a few free sandwiches. (Hey, they were the ones that were about to be thrown out!) For me, I learned so many lessons in each of those moments, even the one from Burger King. I talk about how proud I was for being honest when the manager asked me if I had given away the free food. "Of course," I had answered without hesitation. "We were about to throw it away." I still remember the look of shock on his face as he let me go. He seemed surprised that I had been truthful. That day, I questioned myself and wondered if I had done the right thing by telling the truth. I later decided that I absolutely had done the right thing. Being fired from that job was a key moment in defining my most important personal values for my life; turns out, integrity was at the top of the list.

If your people don't know these stories, and they're under the false impression that you waltzed out of the womb and into your current role, they'll never become the best possible version of themselves because they'll be too busy spending their days in awe and admiration of you to recognize that they can end up being just as successful.

Give your people permission to fail. Show them it's okay to struggle by showing them your battle scars and wounds. Help them understand that you didn't start your career in the role you're in now.

GIVE HUMILITY A HOME

The second reason we tell people about the times we screwed up is so we can showcase a little (but important) thing called humility. You'll see excellent leaders do this in different ways. Some of them use self-deprecating humor, which I'm not a huge fan of, but I have seen it work moderately well for a few leaders who have really worked at it. The way I see humility best shown is when leaders are willing to acknowledge their weaknesses, opportunities, and struggles publicly and often proactively—that is, they'll do it without being asked. Not as a joke. For real.

If you really want to embrace this concept, then you can go all out and ask your people for feedback any time they see you struggling with something you've told them is a weakness for you. Talk about showcasing! We expect our people to be coachable and to openly take our critical feedback. When we're willing to take it, in return, and from people who roll up to us, we exercise true humility. The skill showcased here is that it's okay to be coached; it's okay to confront and talk about these failures, struggles, and shortcomings; and that you're (once again) just like everybody else in that you have those too. Everyone around you knows that you also have a boss. Most people will assume that you, too, are getting coaching and feedback. They might even imagine that you, at times, have to take tough feedback—the same kind they receive from you. But when you are willing to take coaching from them, you actually showcase yourself being coached; that's not something all bosses are willing to let their people see. When you do, however, your team learns to trust and respect you even more. Doing this also has a secondary benefit: you get feedback from some of the people who know you best. Your boss's feedback is going to have some natural limitations; your boss probably isn't around you all the time. Your team is going to see things that your boss can't or won't. So, opening yourself up to get feedback from this additional source gives you an incredible advantage over those who won't do this. You get to learn a lot more about yourself. You develop more self-awareness. When you're open to doing those things, you're going to be in a better position to win and succeed.

"Humility is not thinking less of yourself. It's thinking of yourself less."
– Rick Warren

In general, humble people are more successful than people who are filled with pride or ego. No one I have ever known likes arrogance in a person. When we admit our mistakes and talk about our struggles, we show others what that behavior looks like, and then those people, in turn, follow in our footsteps. This is especially important if you're leading other leaders. When someone is feeling weak and vulnerable, it's difficult for them to seek help and talk it through with another person, especially a boss. But if they know that their boss is a humble person who doesn't need to be in the limelight, but instead never misses a chance to build others up, they'll be more likely to go there for help. The more you can instill attributes of humility in others, the better. Teams comprised of largely humble people can establish momentum and traction that others can't. When people can openly admit their mistakes or say that they don't know something, the speed of learning, curiosity, and trust accelerates rapidly.

"We love to see vulnerability in others. We hate to see it in ourselves."
– Joseph Whitaker, chief executive officer

I've known Joseph for over eight years—six of which I spent working for him. It's the longest I've worked for anyone. I can also attest that I've never met another leader as influential, rare, and unique as Joseph. The reason I stayed with him so long is I worried I'd never meet another leader like him again. I desperately wanted the mentorship he provided.

Joseph is right. We *love* seeing other people being vulnerable. That's a great reason why telling your previous horror stories is a great idea; it requires you to showcase vulnerability, and if people love it, then give the crowd what it wants. The other benefit is that our teams are likely to imitate and emulate everything we do. If we can agree that humble people are more likely to be successful, then why *wouldn't* you exude humility in front of others? It means other people are more likely to act humble too and, thus, be more successful. People may love seeing *you* be vulnerable and humble, but *they* may not like to do it as much. If you are able to showcase being vulnerable for them, they'll be more likely to embrace it on their own. They'll see it's okay to be vulnerable, and they'll see what it looks like to do it. You've laid the foundation for them to do it, and at some point, they won't hate it as much because they'll realize that showcasing vulnerability isn't an act of weakness; it's an act of strength and courage.

You'll also teach them what it looks like to accept criticism well and to critique oneself—in a healthy and accepting way. If you teach others humility by showing it to them, your people are likely to show it when you're not around, which will help *them* build relationships with others. If people like seeing humility, then the patients, guests, clients, customers, partners, and other employees of the people you've taught humility to will like it, and more connections will be made, more things will get sold, more rave reviews will get filed, and more repeat business will be done.

When you share the tough stuff, other people around you share the tough stuff too. Soon, everyone will know it's okay to share the tough stuff, and people will be more likely to offer up tough criticism of each other as well in an honest way because they won't be so worried of someone blowing up at them for it, rejecting it, and storming off in a huff—leaving the relationship permanently severed. Helping everyone around you be humble not only assists in how they react to tough feedback, it also means they'll be better receivers of feedback. People who receive feedback well are more likely to get it. There becomes a culture of acceptance for the tough stuff. So not only are you putting your people in a position to be more accepting of *your* tough feedback, but you're also putting them in a position to be more accepting of the tough feedback that they might get from *anyone* or *anywhere*. This might include their friends, family members, or spouse. This might include at home, at church, or at their soccer club. This can only be a good thing. Knowledge is power. If you've improved the *ability* or *desire* of your people to get tough feedback, then you've also improved the *likelihood* that they'll get it. This means you now have a team of people who is getting more development and coaching than you could ever provide alone, and your team has the mentality to handle it. Bravo.

PRACTICE 3:
GET IN THE POOL

I've met a raft of leaders who are well poised to showcase swimming. They've set a clear vision, care about their people, facilitate some meetings, deliver some coaching, recognize and reward success, and they really do want to go beyond the talk and walk the walk. They're periodically around, and when they are, they demonstrate what *it* (whatever *it* is) looks like. They lead by example. The problem is, they're not around enough to really be effective.

We don't only demonstrate whatever it is that we're asking of people so that others can't complain about us. Or so that others feel their leader is credible and is "doing it too." A more important reason we want to showcase our skills is so people can *learn* from us. Talking about doing something is an incredibly weak substitute for actually doing it. It's really *no* substitute at all. Many of us learn by *seeing* and by *doing*, not by hearing. Role-playing is a step better but still not enough. Involving our people in the ways we discussed in Virtue 2 is a good start. Observing and coaching our people in all the ways discussed in Virtue 3 is a great start. But if we're not around enough to lead by example and let folks learn from *us*, we're sorely failing our teams.

You must get in the pool. If you want your team to have big breakthroughs in understanding, then you must get in the pool, get wet, and swim some laps. Sometimes, you'll want to show them what it looks like. Sometimes, you'll want to put yourself in difficult situations like you'd ask them to be in. It's not always that you'll *do* exactly what you're asking them to do, because we already outlined you might not have the precise skills they have, but you do need to be around enough to comment about and help with what they're going through. You might be the one asking the tough questions.

If you're coaching a swim team, you wouldn't just bark orders from the side of the pool. You'd get in the pool at some point and swim laps with the team. From your view *in* the water, you'll likely notice things that you wouldn't or couldn't from your vantage point outside the water.

One of the biggest failings of leaders is they allow their teams to *tell* them what's going on with everything around them then take that opinion at face value. The problem with this is that most of us are not very self-aware as individuals. We don't always have the ability to effectively and accurately self-assess *ourselves*. In the movie of our life, we're the main character, and we tend to assess ourselves through rose-colored glasses. We use our own paradigms and own perspectives to read and judge the situations around us and how we behave in those situations. We tend not to think things are our fault, and we tend to overrate our skill sets. If you're relying on your people to tell you about the problems they're facing, and you're then spending time talking about how to solve those problems with your teams *without* going out and seeing things for yourself, I can assure you that at least some of the time, your solutions are coming up short.

"We judge ourselves by our intentions and others by their behavior."
– Stephen M. R. Covey

In many situations, direct reports of mine detail their stories of woe. They're quick to tell me all about the problems they're facing with a peer, another work group, a project that is falling behind task. They want guidance and help. When I was younger, I would readily try to solve all their problems. I learned early that I needed to ask questions about what was going on—what had or hadn't been said or done by all parties involved—to make a full assessment. So, I'd make my assessment and deliver the thoughtful advice that my employee was looking for based on my experience. Easy! Or so I thought. Over time, I realized that one of two things usually ended up happening in these situations.

First, the person would come back after some amount of time with the same problem. It would seem we were living the déjà vu experience of Bill Murray in the movie *Groundhog Day*, where he finds himself destined to live the same day over and over until he has enough meaningful learning to change his mindset (and himself) so that life starts to look different. At least, that's my assessment of the movie. In short, history tends to repeat itself in predictable ways until we do something different to change our circumstances. My employees would come back and tell me that they'd tried what I suggested, and it didn't work. Maybe things had gotten better but only slightly. Or maybe things did get better for a short while, and then my employee was right back in the situation again. What I'd often learn later is that the individual I'd been helping hadn't accurately assessed the situation and what the real problem was. Because of that, the solutions weren't right-sized, and so they'd go back trying to hammer in a nail with a screwdriver. Because there was no change in the *actual* areas that needed help, the overall results didn't change either.

"Insanity is doing the same thing over and over again and expecting different results." – Attributed to Albert Einstein

In other instances, the person I'd been coaching wouldn't come back to detail any more woe, but one of the following things would happen:

- I'd get a general sense that things hadn't improved. Sometimes, the person would feel like things *had* gotten better, but I'd find out through another involved party that things actually were not better.
- Things might have felt better to both people on the surface, but that was only in the short term; the group still hadn't gotten the breakthrough results they had hoped for.
- I'd sense that my employee was too embarrassed to come back and discuss the issue again for fear of looking incapable of improving, fixing, or solving it, so they would just drop it.
- The employee would decide that pursuing the problem was too time-consuming, too awkward, or too cumbersome, and they would just stop pursuing the goal. Then, they'd set their sights on other things worth fixing.

Whether you want to help people who are experiencing the same problems repeatedly or you want to know what kinds of problems people are having, you have to get involved at some point, especially since most people don't know what they don't know. Over the years, I've had many employees tell me that they're frustrated by a strained relationship with another individual and that the problem is primarily the other individual's fault. When I dig into it more, I find out it's really my employee who is causing the rift in the relationship, but they're not even aware of it.

Go out and observe the things your people are going through. Whatever your people do, if you want to lead by example in helping them be their best, you must watch them. You must get involved with them. You must get in the pool and see how they swim. When I stopped accepting everything people would tell me about what was going on in their work and their relationships at face value and, instead, went to see it for myself, everything changed. In general, the déjà vu stopped.

I've had employees tell me that they just can't work with another person and how their meetings with the other person never go anywhere. When I've asked permission to stop by to observe the group, I've observed the complaining employee making all sorts of silly mistakes that break down trust and impede progress—interrupting others, never showing any compassion or care for others, even doing something so egregious as call others by the wrong name. I've had direct reports tell me that one of their employees is argumentative and giving them a lot of lip. When I've asked permission to join one of their meetings or coaching sessions, I've been blown away by how the leader might be doing some of these same behaviors—rudely cutting their employee off, acting confrontational, not allowing any margin for mistakes. I've had employees tell me that a cross-functional committee they've been asked to lead is disengaged and unprepared for their meetings, only to sit in and watch that same leader run a highly disorganized meeting that has no agenda or structure. Only after you've gotten in the pool to watch how your team is swimming laps can you have the confidence to say, "I think it's actually *you*. I think there's something more you can do here. I think *you're* causing some of this, and you didn't even know it."

This might sound daunting and scary. Perhaps you fear that your employees won't want you to do this (who wants their boss or leader to come *watch* them do something?). Sure, folks are often resistant to these kinds of ideas up front. But I guarantee that if you add real value for your team, by using the other V.I.R.T.U.E.S. in this book to get involved, drop in, observe, and then detail what you saw and what you'd do about it, your employees will come around. They'll especially come around if you end up being right and what you advise them to do pays off in the end. It's important that you reaffirm your individuals too, reminding them that you're there to help them because that's how much you care about them. It's also important that you couple those statements with some recognition of what you saw that's working well. If you do these things, your people will get far more excited to have you jump in and swim laps with them. It shows you care and that you're not above what they do, but it will also allow them to get the true feedback they need. If you can help someone, through this process, also develop more self-awareness that they can use in the future, that's a bonus.

PRACTICE 4:
OFFER HELP, BUT DON'T FORCE HELP

In the previous section, notice that I used the words "asked permission." This can be an important part of showcasing swimming. The whole reason we do much of what we do in leadership is to help others. When we're offering to help someone, it's important that person wants your help. If you found out that your friend was moving next weekend, you wouldn't just go over to her house and start packing boxes or dismantling furniture. Why not? Because you'd first want to be sure that she needed that kind of help. For all you know, she has movers who are going to do those things for her or a different plan entirely.

When it comes to swimming laps in the pool, it's important that there's agreement about what your help looks like. Otherwise, you can quickly become too overbearing. When you swim laps with your team, you're offering to visit your people, watch them in action, collect observations, and share those observations. Many times, you might offer your analysis and ask people to think about things as they explore their own solutions. Other times, you might make full-blown recommendations or perhaps a direct ask for a specific action you'd like someone to take. This will go most smoothly when people want you to do this. If they don't, nothing you do will be effective.

The most common mistakes to make when you're showcasing swimming is that you get *too* involved. Maybe you overstay your welcome and spend too much time with your team. Maybe you get involved too frequently. Maybe you do too much talking and controlling when you're there. Perhaps you are overbearing. If your team feels any of these things, you can bet that the time with you is not benefiting anyone. Your team should be happy to see you and welcome your presence. If they aren't happy and don't welcome you, it's likely you're not living all the V.I.R.T.U.E.S. in this book.

When we overstep healthy boundaries and get too involved, it usually comes from a place of good intentions. We want to see our people be successful, and we're eager to lead by example, model the way, and showcase the exact behaviors we want others around us to learn. We think we're helping—and to some degree, we are. People can really benefit from seeing their boss do something that they'll have to do later. But when we get so involved that we strip our people of their power to act or shut down any creative, innovative processes, we do a disservice not only to those around us but also to ourselves. I've done this numerous times in my career, especially when entering new roles. I've been so eager to see development, progress, and change, I get incredibly involved. I also wanted to know people. I invited myself to numerous meetings, coaching sessions, one-on-ones, and recognition lunches. Before I knew it, some of my direct reports felt I was doing their job for them. Without realizing it, I had stunted their growth. I hadn't asked how much help they wanted or needed but instead assumed it must be a lot. I started showing up—all the time—without pausing to find out if others around me wanted to do it on their own.

Setting boundaries is an important part of this process. Examples of what you might say to do so include:

- Donna, I would really love to see you coach so I could give you some feedback to help you improve your skills. Would you mind if sat in on a future one-on-one you're conducting with one of your employees? This would also help me get to know them better. I'd be a fly on the wall—just there to observe.
- Ray, I know how badly you've been wanting that promotion, and I really want to give you feedback to help you get there. Would you mind if I went out in the field with you this Tuesday for a couple of hours? We could then have lunch together and part ways.

- John, thank you so much for sharing your concerns with me about Lisa and how your relationship is going. I've been there before and have a lot of thoughts for you, but I also know you've said that you want to deal with it. How do you want to move forward?
- Luke, I'd really like to see improvement in the areas we talked about today, but I also know you're still implementing lots of your own ideas. How about you continue to experiment with your ideas for another month, and if we don't see improvement by then, we can test some of my ideas?
- Leticia, I really appreciate you getting me involved in this situation you're having. Where do you want to go from here? I have a lot of suggestions, but I want to first know how much help and support you want or need.

When we set boundaries this way, we still allow people to chart their own course. We let them know we're there for them, have suggestions and ideas for them, and want to get more involved. But it's also important that people get to have some autonomy in their day. When we lead others using all the V.I.R.T.U.E.S. in this book, others around us become more capable and stronger. They can handle tough situations and make hard decisions. Sometimes they'll simply need the space and time to do that or a sounding board.

If you've allowed your people to self-solve on their own a few times and they're still not figuring things out, you can absolutely ask permission to get more involved and shift into statements that share you want to get more involved and why.

PRACTICE 5:
SAY YOU'RE SORRY

I'll end this Virtue on showcasing behaviors with something that may sound obvious but often isn't. Sometimes leaders make mistakes. They have a lapse in judgment. They make a poor decision. They lose control of a situation. They say something they don't mean. They overreact. They misestimate. They fall behind. They forget to show care and compassion for others. This happens. We're all human.

Over the last several years, David and I have been fortunate enough to travel a good deal, and on our journeys, we often meet other couples. I delight in asking couples, especially those who have been together for several decades, what the secret is to making a healthy marriage work. Over the years, we've probably heard nearly 100 answers. Our favorite came from Phil, a man from the U.K. whom we met on a Mediterranean cruise in 2018. His one piece of advice to us was, and I quote, "No cold bum treatment." In other words, never go to bed angry and face away from each other. Remembering Phil's advice, we often chuckle at the way he phrased that. But Phil was onto something that has showed up in countless other answers. Many people have told us how important it is to admit when you're wrong and say you're sorry.

I don't care how great of a leader you are; at times, you're going to screw up. You aren't so mighty and infallible that you won't err. It's not reasonable to expect perfection out of yourself—or anyone. When you err, it's important for you to say you're sorry. If you've made a mistake that has wronged a group, it can be especially impactful to acknowledge it publicly and in front of the entire group. For whatever reason, certain leaders really struggle with this.

When we apologize to someone, we showcase a lot of things. Once again, we show others that we're humble. We show others that our egos don't stand in the way of doing the right thing. But we also showcase compassion. We show others we care about righting wrongs[42], the fourth behavior in Stephen M. R. Covey's book *The Speed of Trust*. In the aforenoted endnote, you'll find a video that Scott Miller, a 25-year associate of FranklinCovey, published on this topic. In 80 short seconds, he covers much ground on how important it is for leaders to right wrongs and choose to apologize to others, but one of my favorite points is how important it is for us to be specific when we apologize. This is nothing new. As we discussed in the coaching section of Virtue 3 and the recognition section of Virtue 6, specificity is extremely important when we're trying to understand others and also be understood. So, when you apologize, it's critical that you are specific about what you're apologizing for. We don't just say, "I was a real jerk the other day—whoops!" or "I think I made you feel bad last week. I didn't mean to." Instead, we offer up a meaningful apology that tends to have the following components:

- We outline the time and place we think the infraction occurred.
- We offer up a reason or explanation for it.
- We explain the impact or consequences we believe this had.

- We make a commitment to do better in the future.
- We ask for forgiveness.

This might sound something like the following:

> "Jan, I really want to apologize to you today. Three days ago, you were trying to grab my attention after the group meeting, and I feel that I totally brushed you off. The reason was that I was running late for a board meeting, and I was also feeling nervous because I didn't have all my slides ready to go. I imagine this might have made you feel insignificant or like I didn't care about your situation. I'm going to work hard to ensure if this ever happens again, I'll tell you why I'm in such a hurry. I never meant to hurt you, and so I really hope you can forgive me."

When we do this, we show others that it's important to us to take responsibility and be accountable for things that didn't go well, instead of blaming others or hoping others might forget our mistake. The beauty of being in leadership is that there's less things you *must* do—out of obligation or duty—and more things that you *choose* to do—out of love or passion. If a leader makes a mistake, it's not always likely that the leader will choose to apologize. Sometimes, this is because no one would even know if the leader made a mistake. This is what makes it so special when leaders *do* choose to apologize. They might not have been caught for their error or found out. So, when leaders proactively choose to call attention to their blunders simply because it's the right thing to do and because they care about the people around them who may have been affected, it's a unique thing.

In some cases, you might be apologizing for hurting someone's feelings. Acknowledging that you did something that hurt someone else can be prickly. When you choose to step up and apologize for the sake of bettering the relationship and righting things—so there can be future growth—you do something great. You prioritize the feelings of others over your own, and you show people that you recognize there is more than one way to look at things. You recognize that something that wasn't a big deal to you might have been huge to them. You show others that you're not only focused on yourself and your own feelings, but also the feelings of others.

When others make mistakes, we often expect them to apologize and own those mistakes. We'd never be proud of someone on our team who refuses to admit wrongdoing or consider how they might have unintentionally come across to another. Great leaders don't tolerate this behavior, and this *is* a case where we wouldn't ask someone to do something that we are unwilling to do. If we want others to apologize, recognize fault, show care and compassion, and right wrongs, we have to be willing to do those things ourselves.

The list of mistakes I've made in leadership is long, but here's some ones that stand out. I've:

- Failed to keep a commitment or promise I've made
- Said something that had unintentional consequences
- Steered a group down an incorrect path
- Shut down someone else's idea too soon, without listening enough
- Interrupted people and cut them off
- Forgotten to acknowledge someone when busy or while in a rush
- Deviated from an agenda or plan of what would happen
- Gotten too involved and overtaken situations that others should have handled
- Seen things only from my perspective instead of the group's perspective
- Gotten angry and said something I didn't truly mean
- Not considered where my team was at and what they could handle

When I've publicly apologized for these things, the results were always incredible. People have stated that they felt tremendously better knowing I'm aware of how I came across. It inspires them to become more self-aware too. People have stated how happy and grateful they are to have a leader who went home and considered them and their feelings. People have stated how rare they feel it is for a leader to admit fault and how much they appreciate I'm leading by example on it. Whatever the reason, people like to know they're working for someone who is willing to share in mistakes. It sends the message that you're truly on their team and the relationships you have with them matter. You're not just using them as means to an end, but you genuinely care about *them*. When we do this, we give people the permission to act the same way, and they will.

CONCLUSION

When I was about 13, my maternal grandmother flew from Tulsa, Oklahoma, to visit us for Christmas in Buffalo, New York. That year, when we arrived at Midnight Mass, our church was already so crowded that we couldn't find four seats together. We did, however, manage to find two sets of two seats in pews across from each other in the third row. My grandmother and mother sat together on the right end of one pew, and my father and I sat on the left end of another, directly across from them. Back then, it was commonplace for couples and families to hold hands during a set of several prayers that came before Communion. Strangers didn't usually hold hands with one another, but those who knew each other did.

My grandma and I were on the ones on the ends of our respective pews that night, and when it came time for those prayers, I took my father's hand per usual. I noticed my grandmother taking my mother's hand across the way. Since the tradition was that families hold hands together, I instinctively decided to make that happen. Still holding my father's hand, I stepped out into the aisle about halfway, stretching out my father's and my arm. I nodded at my grandmother, who saw what I was trying to do, and she stepped out into the aisle too and met me there. She and I joined hands, and our family of four was connected.

I didn't think anything of this until a few minutes later, when I happened to glance over my shoulder, I did a double take. Literally every single person on the ends of their respective pews had come out into the aisles and joined hands. This continued for all 14 rows behind us. It dawned on me that these people behind us probably didn't know that my grandmother and I knew each other. They only saw a young girl step out and reach for an elderly woman's hand. Everyone behind us had followed the lead. It didn't matter that we were holding hands because we were family, and most (if not all) of them were likely strangers. They all chose to jump in and do it anyway. After these prayers, Communion began. Everyone feeds in from the front, and so I was one of the first to be back in my pew. Once back, we'd always kneel for the remainder of Communion. That night, as I knelt, it was hard not to make eye contact with everyone walking by. Everyone from our whole row was nothing but smiles, and almost everyone gave me a special wink or nod. I realized later that this was the first time a group of people had allowed me to lead them. The irony was I hadn't even intended to.

That moment was an incredibly powerful one. In the prologue of this book, I said that the first moment I realized leadership mattered was the day the regional executives came to visit us at the bank, and Debbie the teller got ignored (along with the rest of us). However, this moment that came years before then was where the first subconscious roots for this framework began. In that moment, I subconsciously practiced so many V.I.R.T.U.E.S. I showcased swimming. I modeled the way and led by example without intending to. What was an honest moment of love for my grandmother was likely seen by others as an act of vulnerability or courage. Others saw me take a chance on befriending an older lady, and they found both the desire and strength to do the same. I involved others. Because I involved her in an act, and the row or two behind me also did, everyone suddenly felt inspired to act. The experience showed me that "anyone can play." I was barely a teenager, but others bonded together because of what I did. I encouraged energy. I like to think that everyone felt the Christmas spirit a little more intensely after those minutes of togetherness and closeness. Because of this, people felt inspired to act in ways they normally didn't. They changed their behavior. They seemed to like it. I felt joy inside that I couldn't explain, but I know now it's because practicing these V.I.R.T.U.E.S. simply feels *good*.

Anyone can do what I did on that snowy Christmas Eve. These V.I.R.T.U.E.S. work in any setting, including a place of worship. But they work in families too, at home. I've witnessed them work in academic settings. They certainly work in business. These V.I.R.T.U.E.S. work best when they're used together. While I saw great results from using only a few of them unintentionally as a young girl, I can assure you that they work best when you intentionally employ all of them. When you use them, you'll notice that they align and empower people.

People spend a majority of their lives at work. Everyone has talents, and most of your teammates are probably more capable than you know. When you use these 7 V.I.R.T.U.E.S. consistently, here's what happens: Because you've set vision, your people are clear and aligned about where you're headed. Because you've involved them, they are engaged, excited, and empowered. Because you've showed them the importance of routines, they are structured, organized, focused, and disciplined. Because you've talked terrifically and created a safe space for them, they speak their minds, ask questions, and are educated. Because you've understood how learning works, they are curious, feel comfortable with making mistakes for the sake of learning and growth, and are comfortable leveraging their resources. Because you've encouraged energy, they feel valued and appreciated for a job well done. And because you've showcased swimming, they are proud to have a leader who is vulnerable, humble, transparent, and walks the talk.

Doesn't that sound like a dream? Well, it doesn't have to be. You can start now—today. You can become the best boss they've ever had. You can leave a legacy they'll never forget. You can create an environment where the hours fly by because no one feels like they're at "work," but rather, doing something they love and are constantly fulfilled and challenged by. The 7 V.I.R.T.U.E.S. will help you accomplish all that. What are you waiting for?

ACKNOWLEDGMENTS

There are many people who, together, helped me discover the concepts in this book. I want to recognize them all, in chronological order. Without you, this book wouldn't exist.

RICH GOLD

You were the first person to give me a "real job." The conversation in your kitchen after a night of babysitting started 7 years of employment with one of the best banks I've worked for. It changed the course of my life. Had you not pulled some strings to get a 17-year-old girl a job at a bank, these past 22 years would've looked vastly different. It all started with you. At M&T, I felt your leadership even when I couldn't see it. I could see your people carrying out your vision in the final years I was there, even when you weren't around, and it was the first time I really understood *that's* what leadership is.

JOHN POWELL

You were one of the first people to extend trust to me at M&T. My best friend's mom passed away from ALS during my senior year of college, and I missed her funeral because I was scheduled to fly to D.C. and interview with you. I was too afraid to ask for a reschedule. I look back now and know it would've been okay. I wish I'd had the courage to speak up, but fortunately, you gave me the job and taught me what courage was. You taught us that *real* leaders know when and how to speak up. Since then, I've been able to help many other people be where they need to be—at complicated things like funerals, but at simple things too, like a kid's dance recital. Too often, employees think their lives need to revolve around their job, even though our jobs are only one part of our lives. When we help others have balance, they do a better job at work. You've always accepted people for who they are, and you also valued their families and loved ones as much as you valued *them*. You weren't the only, but you were the first.

You always valued conversation. You showed me that great managers don't engage solely in monologues but rather dialogues. The group dinners at

Clyde's will never be forgotten. Leaving your leadership in 2007 to move to California was an incredibly hard decision for me.

TRISH SCHNEIDER

You were one of the best branch managers I'd ever seen. I only worked for you as a banker, and yet, you gave me so many opportunities to be a leader. You excelled in Virtue 3, but you were also the first person to show me all 7 V.I.R.T.U.E.S. You had that branch spinning like a top, and all of us loved working there. We couldn't wait to get to work and be in one another's presence.

I made my first big mistakes while working for you—misquoting rates and screwing up loan files—and at first, I was afraid to tell you. But anytime that I came to you with a problem, you showed me grace and forgiveness, which allowed me to focus on the learning. You created a safe environment for us to be honest and forthcoming, and you truly believed in training and coaching.

You empowered John to lead me, and I learned what partner relationships look like. For years, I modeled my view of what great branch management looks like after you. I continually thought of you during my many years in branch, district, and regional manager roles. In many instances, people would tell me something couldn't be done, and I would say, "Oh, yes it can, I've seen it," because I had seen it with *you*. You showed me what's possible. You brought out the best in people and walked that line between courage and compassion so beautifully, which challenged me to grow in all the right ways. You made 2005 one of the best professional years of my life.

JOHN GIBSON

When I think of you, I beam. You taught me leadership can come from *anyone*, at *any time*, in *anyplace*. Willingness on all sides is all that's required. The time you invested in me was one of the greatest gifts I've ever been given. You taught me how to actually *use* my securities licenses, profile, and connect. You were the first person who taught me how to be comfortable with being uncomfortable in sales. You helped me have better conversations, and you showed me what integrity looks like. You didn't do anything that wasn't in the best interest of the client.

I loved that you always had me sit in on the appointments I set for you. You'd always start your profiling sessions the same way, explaining how you were about to "ask a bunch of dumb questions," which weren't dumb at all. You always understood the client's transactional strategies, borrowing picture, assets, savings, and more before making a single recommendation. Over the last decade, I've often been asked what I would be doing if I wasn't in leadership, and my answer has always been the same, which essentially is: *Be John Gibson.* I wish every financial consultant was like you: involved, passionate, committed, authentic, and honest. You cared so much about your clients but also about us. I never really felt like you were a partner at that branch; I felt you were a *part* of the branch. You were a great mentor and advisor, and I'll never forget it.

COLLEEN SCHULER

You were the first real peer I had. We filled the same role in that small branch in Riviera Beach, and yet, I had *so* much respect for you. You had so much experience and were wise beyond your years. I learned so much from you. I was constantly eavesdropping on your conversations and overhearing the most wonderful nuggets, which I'd then try to emulate.

I also saw us as competitors for a bit. You were the best banker the region had, and I wanted to do as well as you. Following in your footsteps brought out so much joy in me. Working beside you was the first time in my life that I truly loved my job. I had *liked* jobs before. Some of them, I had liked very much. But I had never *loved* my job until I met you. I went through massive growth and development in 2005, and so much of that was because of you. You brought out the best in me.

Privately, I always looked up to you and wanted to be like you. You were so well-spoken and well-respected. You were admired and loved by all. You remind me of the famous Jimmy Valvano speech in 1993, made a couple of months before he died. Remembering you over the years has made me laugh, think, and cry. It's Jimmy V's definition of a "full day." It's been 17 years since I sat next to you at work, but I remember those full days like they were yesterday. You showed me what successful peers do. It took me a long time, after you, to find the courage and humility to respect peers like I respected you because you set the bar so exceptionally high.

SANDY WALIA

You came into my life at a time when I desperately needed leadership. I had begun to lose faith in what leadership looked and felt like, and you changed that all. When it was announced that you'd be our new leader, our morning calls transformed overnight. We stopped reporting solely on lag measures and results and began to tell the stories of the people behind the numbers. Instead of just counting beans, we connected to the all-important *how* and *why* questions about our employees and customers. It was not only permissible but encouraged to share stories about the people whose lives were truly changed by our work. You handled recognition so well and allowed us to be ourselves, which we desperately needed.

You made yourself present and accessible. Other district managers didn't visit me much. You did. People responded to your leadership. You'd say hello to everyone and took an interest in everyone. No matter what level, they all felt like they could talk to you. I saw that and modeled my behaviors after you when I moved into those roles.

Your direct reporting leadership team became closer because of you. Prior, we were only acquaintances, but we became friends. We confided in each other but also pushed each other in a way that hadn't existed before you. Good leaders do this well, and experiencing it with you at the helm was where I learned to cultivate this too.

After you, I found my way to other organizations that felt more like a fit for my values, but my days working for you were some of the happiest I had during that tough time in my career. You brought hope and meaning into our lives, and you were the brightest light I found in an otherwise dark time. That really stands out to me. Your success today is anything but a surprise.

BARRY SIMMONS

You are the epitome of this entire book. You are one of the sharpest and most intuitive leaders I've worked for. Intelligence isn't a requirement for great leadership. Some outstanding leaders are *not* especially bright. Instead, they have high emotional intelligence and leverage the talented individuals around them. You, however, exude *all* of that.

You were such a surprise to me. I attended that MBA conference to meet with another organization and met you. After only one conversation, Bank of

America became the front-runner in my mind. I was utterly impressed with everything you embodied. You've never disappointed me.

There are so many things that made our time together special, but the biggest thing that stands out is your commitment to routines. Everything we did took place on a schedule and with structure. I was never the same. Whether it be the monthly business line reviews, the branch visits, or our weekly calls, everything was on the calendar in advance. We didn't cancel or reschedule anything. We did what we said. You taught us the value of keeping commitments.

My entire life is that way now. All my routines run on a cadence, at work and at home. I prioritize my big rocks first, which gives me time left over for the unexpected and the urgent. There's also time for relaxation, leisure, and fun. It's the same at work. I don't tolerate people coaching or meeting "when we *need* to." No, we meet because we *choose* to, and we schedule such meetings on a cycle. We do these things, not because we want to stay the same, but because we want to get better. You taught us that. You commanded respect of all. It's easy to see why.

KARLA LEE

Transparency and authenticity are the essence of who you are. Those became traits that I hungrily aspired to develop because of you. I hadn't quite seen anyone do it so profoundly well, and I desperately worked to emulate it during our time together. My months as a market performance manager under your leadership were some of the best of my career. I loved how I could always count on you to give me critical feedback. There was always something more to think about, some angle of the problem I hadn't considered. Before you, I had begun feeling bored and misaligned at work. With you, I felt alive, challenged, and fulfilled. I literally couldn't wait to show up.

You were the first person to take a chance on me and put me in a district/regional role. I felt you wanted my success as much as I did. When I became a consumer market manager with a market of my own, you were never far away. You were at every event and on every business review, and your feedback was some of the best I'd ever heard.

You were the first female executive I saw in leadership who is brilliant, both from an IQ and an EQ perspective. You've always known what, when, and how to say things. You weren't easy on people. You were tough, but people adored you for it. You were fair and consistent, and everyone craved your critical feedback because they knew it was a key to unlock the door to the next level of their development—a door everyone wanted to open. We also knew that your feedback, in addition to being spot-on and intelligently sharp, also came from a place of great care and compassion. I learned so much about true courage from you. I'll never forget you.

LYNN LU

You were my second boss when I became a district manager. I was so happy working with you. Of all the V.I.R.T.U.E.S. in my book, you practiced Virtue 6 better than almost anyone I've ever met. This had a lasting impact. No matter the topic, you always asked the same question: "How will this affect our *people*?" We did nothing without talking about that. Recognition was a part of every meeting. I'd seen recognition done effectively *within* a branch, but I hadn't ever quite figured out how to truly recognize my own people at the regional level until I met you. You showed me how executives could recognize middle management too. I have many certificates acknowledging my own achievements from the time I worked with you. Ten years later, I know exactly where they are. They are still sacred to me. Thank you for making me feel special and like I could do anything.

JOHNNY MONTES

There's no past leader I talk about more than you. We met at a pivotal time. The organization was drastically raising the bar when I arrived in your region, and I had a lot of work to do to meet the new expectations. Early on, I gave you a lot of headaches and performed poorly. For a while, there was no week when I didn't turn something in late, underestimate the importance of something, or screw something up. For the first time in my life in school or work, I constantly felt behind. It was a rude awakening and also the best thing to ever happen to me.

You ran a tight ship—the tightest I had experienced—and you were the first person to teach me the concept of the 20-mile march. I was fascinated by that story and noticed that you lived it every day. Virtue 3 was essentially crafted, created, and founded by you.

Under you, I learned that if a meeting started at 8 A.M., showing up at 7:45 was late. Why? Because we should be there early, to mingle and network and to prepare for the day. Under you, I learned that if something was due on a Friday, we should have it turned in and awaiting approval on Wednesday. Why? Because that's what organized and successful people do. They plan. Under you, I learned that if someone is out of the office, they should set up an away message on their inbox. Why? Because why *wouldn't* they do that? If you don't, what happens when someone tries to get a hold of you while you're away? You might leave someone wondering. Real leaders *never* leave people wondering.

We managed talent aggressively under you, and you challenged me to think longer and harder than ever before about who I had working for me, why, and what they brought to the table. One day, you asked me about the performance of a particular branch manager.

"Well, when he's good, he's *really* good," I responded. "But he's not consistent."

"So, he's bad," you responded.

"No, he totally has the *capability* to do it. He's just doesn't always *use* it," I said.

You then taught me one of the most valuable life lessons I've ever learned. "Inconsistent performance *is* poor performance, Amy. Top performers are, by definition, *consistent*. If he's good and bad, then he's *bad*. Bottom line."

I had never thought about that before. There were so many things I had never thought about before you.

Days out in the field with you scared me, but they were also the days I learned the most. It was because of you that I started having better dialogues with my team. That changed everything, as did your lessons about consistency. I'll remember you for the rest of my life.

DONNIE PEAKS

Your fingerprint is all over this book. You've influenced so much of the material, and it's probably why I've quoted you more than anyone else.

Early in our relationship, you found out that my then-boyfriend might accept a job that was 100 miles from our house. You called me with a brilliant suggestion. You offered to change the regional alignment and reporting relationships so that I would have an office or two that was near his work. My then-boyfriend never took that job, but I never forgot about the care behind your offer. Months later, that same relationship fell apart. I didn't need to tell you—you knew. You quickly observed I wasn't quite myself at work. You wasted no time in expressing concern for me. When I admitted that I was struggling, you encouraged me to take some time off. We had only been working together for six months, but you extended trust and said, "I'm not worried about your results. I'm worried about you." It was one of the first times I truly felt your respect and love for me—not just an employee, but as a human being. That mattered.

When I was going through our leadership academy, we all submitted long research papers about our competitors. I had explored two other organizations in-depth and was excited about my findings. Still an academic at heart, I desperately wanted to earn the equivalent of an "A." One weekend, I spent hours organizing my research, and I wanted your feedback. I shot you a long email with several pages of my work. I was stunned when only 10 minutes later, an email from you landed in my box. *Wow!* I thought. *I can't believe he's already responded!* I eagerly opened it, preparing to digest your suggestions. You had but one piece of feedback for me: "Amy, It's Sunday."

Out of the many things you taught me, that's a favorite. Great leaders respect the personal time and space of others. They also respect their *own* personal time and space. It's been a long time since I sent a business email like that on a Sunday. You've taught me that when we, as leaders, send emails at midnight or on weekends, we sometimes subconsciously and unintentionally send the message that others should do the same. So, tread carefully. Because, as you've said more times than I can count, "It's not what you *said*. It's what they *heard*."

In addition to the numerous quotes from you in this book, I'll add a few more favorites:

1. It's okay to let your people influence *you*. It's okay to change your mind.
2. *Doing* what's right is far more important than *being* right.
1. People sometimes quit on you but don't *tell you* they've quit on you.
2. When you meet someone, always remember three types of names: the names of their kids, their spouses, and their pets.

DANIELLE ORGANISTA

You know I've spent much of my life at war with myself. Learning how to truly love myself and others has been a major challenge and the worthiest one I've ever pursued. Without you, I may not have found the strength and courage to pursue it. Since meeting you, I've changed jobs, bosses, companies, boyfriends, homes, and hobbies. You've seen me through it all. But the most important thing I've changed is my perspective. I remembered how helpless I used to feel, how quick I was to blame everyone or everything around me, how obsessed I was with what others thought, and how little of a relationship I had with myself. I wasn't trained to see myself for who and what I really was, and I rarely, if ever, took the time to slow down and sit with my thoughts quietly. That learning has been transformational.

You've taught me that I am enough and that everything is okay—even when things are going badly, it's okay. You've taught me to slow down and appreciate the journey and where I'm at. You've taught me not to endlessly try to paint over all the cracks in the cup but to love the cup exactly as it is. You've taught me to not seek perfection. You've taught me to stop worrying so much. You've taught me to live in the present moment instead of allowing my brain to live in the past or the future. You've taught me to take things day by day, to trust myself, and to be kind to myself. If not for you, I don't know if I would've ever gotten over the breakup, picked up ski poles, or learned to set boundaries with other people. I still struggle *not* to get on the scale every day, but I'm working on it, and the beauty of what you've taught me is that's okay. Thank you for seven years of advice, counsel, and mentorship.

JOSEPH WHITAKER

In our first meeting, we sat on couches in your office that were directly next to blocks on the wall with the vision, mission, and core values. Those concepts permeated our conversation that day, and I sensed a level of alignment in that room between what was *said* and what was *done*. I loved that. I thought, *I bet if I worked with him, he would change my career.* I didn't realize you'd end up changing my whole life. But that's what's happened.

I look back now and laugh at the abysmal level of self-awareness I had when we sat down for our first mentoring appointment. I told you that my biggest failure was not getting a branch manager role on my first try. Looking back, it's so clear that being unable to recall more failures was, *in and of itself,* a major failing. I lacked humility and awareness. Then, I didn't imagine how much I would come to enjoy failure or, at least, develop a healthy relationship with it.

I've evolved into an entirely different person over the last eight years, and these years of awakening have been some of my favorite years. They've also been the hardest. Even that is such a profound difference. My former fixed-mindset self would have never been able to associate a *favorite* thing with a *tough* or *hard* thing. It's funny what a changed mindset will do.

At some point in 2019, Katia astutely (but somewhat jokingly) made the comment to me that "Wow, ignorance really *is* bliss, huh?" I chuckled then with the understanding of what she meant. In some ways, when we don't truly know ourselves and don't see all our flaws for what they are, we can have the false perception of being free. Life can be easy. We don't have to think much. We can detach ourselves from things—blaming other people for our problems, concluding that it's usually someone else's fault, shrugging off situations that don't go our way, and moving onto the next failure (again, without ever really recognizing it as failure). It's probably what Oliver Wendall Holmes would call "the simplicity on *this* side of complexity," but we both know he wouldn't give a fig for that.

Getting to know myself over the last several years, and seeing parts of my personality that aren't so pretty, certainly hasn't been easy. It's absolutely removed me from the bliss Katia described. Sleepless nights come more often, filled with thoughts about what more I could have done in situations. When we become self-aware, there's a constant gravitational pull back to our circle of control. Before I crossed over, I lived in my circle of concern. I didn't know I had a choice. I'd argue with other people and not give it a second thought. I went about my day and waited for apologies that sometimes came but often didn't. When friendships ended, I didn't always know *why.* Now, when I have disagreements with people, it's usually not 10 minutes before my brain is asking that pesky question: "Are you *sure* you're right? Are you *sure* this isn't partly your fault? Are you *sure* there wasn't *something* you did to cause this? Are you *sure* there's nothing you can do now to improve things? Better be *sure.*" Goodbye, ease. Goodbye, bliss.

On the surface, the ignorant life I was previously living had the illusion of more freedom. But I now know what *real* freedom is. Often, real freedom doesn't come with ease but, rather, a ridiculous amount of hard, grueling work. Contrary to popular belief, it's discipline and consistency that ultimately award us freedom. Often not in the short term, but always in the long term. And although hard to accept, I've learned we buy ourselves freedom when we move things back into our circle of control. Because then, we can do something about it. It may not always be blissful. But the perception of bliss I had *before* was mentally shackling. My new mindset has set me free. I used to associate pain with suffering, but you taught me suffering is a choice. It's optional. I choose joy on this journey.

Learning to accept and love myself as a work in progress is the most rewarding learning I've ever had. My quest for self-improvement is continuous and without a finish line. It's an example of "grateful but never satisfied." I can have patience and compassion for exactly how I currently am. I can also continually strive to do better every day.

When people ask me today if I've had any failures, I ask them how much time they have. I fail often because the things I'm setting out to do now are more challenging, and I'm an imperfect person. However, there is so much joy and fulfillment in doing these things, and this game of life is infinite. Plus, we both know what the "greater danger" is.

I could've written an entire book on your teachings alone. But for now, I want to say that this book of leadership lessons wouldn't *exist* without you. Without your mentorship, I wouldn't have written a personal mission statement. You've altered my life's entire trajectory. I know there's been moments I've been a royal pain as a student. Thank goodness you're such a gifted teacher. The past eight years under your guidance have been a joy. I vow to practice and live the success journey wheel for the rest of my days. I've come too far to ever go back.

Thank you for affecting me so profoundly. You are the source of so much of my inspiration when I feel weak; you're the re-programmer of old programs. Thank you for believing in me—enough to send me to Atlanta for three months in the summer of 2018, which altered our entire relationship; enough to give me a call center to run when I had no experience doing that; enough to put me in a COO role; but most importantly, enough that I found the courage to pursue this dream. I now am more equipped to believe in others and love others in ways I couldn't fathom before you, which is a cornerstone of truly great leadership. It's only fitting the book officially ends here, with gratitude for you, the most influential mentor I've ever had.

Endnotes

1   Brendon Burchard, "What Great Leaders Actually Do," Brendon. com, July 19, 2014, https://www.youtube.com/watch?v=6SOT-BHAcLV4&t=64s.

2   See video in endnote 1.

3   "MindSpring Presents: 'Greatness' by David Marquet," Mind-Spring, October 8, 2013, https://www.youtube.com/watch?v=O-qmdLcyES_Q.

4   "David Marquet," Wikipedia, accessed January 12, 2022, https://en.wikipedia.org/wiki/David_Marquet.

5   "Kick the tires," Wiktionary, last edited November 13, 2020, https://en.wiktionary.org/wiki/kick_the_tires.

6   Published in 2006, *The Speed of Trust* is a book that profoundly impacted my life. Stephen M. R. Covey breaks the concept of trust down into the four cores of credibility (integrity, intent, capabilities, and results) and shares 13 behaviors that high-trust leaders and individuals can practice to build trust both at work and at home, which are broken into 13 behaviors that have to do with character, five that have to do with competence, and three that are both.

7   In Liz Wiseman's book, *Multipliers* (2010), she discusses the five dimensions of a Multiplier, one of which is the Liberator. In that dimension, under a section called "Create Space," Wiseman advises great leaders to shift the ratio between talking and listening and says that "liberators are more than just good listeners. They are ferocious listeners."

8   One of the stories Collins uses to model the elements of thriving through uncertain circumstances is that of **Roald Amundsen** and Robert Falcon Scott through their contrasting journeys in 1910 to be the first to the South Pole. Amundsen and his team trekked between 15 to 20 miles each day no matter the conditions. When Amundsen's team encouraged him to go further on days when weather was ideal, Amundsen would say no, knowing the importance of rest and recuperation for the team and the overall journey.

9   Joseph Luciani, "Why 80 Percent of New Year's Resolutions Fail," *U.S. News & World Report*, December 29, 2015, https://health. usnews.com/health-news/blogs/eat-run/articles/2015-12-29/ why-80-percent-of-new-years-resolutions-fail.

10   Statistics borrowed from "5 Surprising Employee Development Statistics You Should Know," ClearCompany (blog), September 9, 2021, https://blog.clearcompany.com/5-surprising-employ-ee-development-statistics-you-dont-know.

11   In *The Biology of Belief* (2005) by Bruce Lipton, it's estimated that the subconscious part of our brains can process information up to 1 million times faster than our conscious minds. Author Vince Poscente reports that the subconscious mind can process 4 billion bits of information at one time, compared to our conscious minds, which can process only 2,000 bits of information at one time—up to 2 million times faster than our conscious minds. Poscente discusses this in the video "The Ant and the Elephant Concept," ELEPHantPOWER Systems, September 1, 2011, https://www.youtube.com/watch?v=GioPDCLM8Is. Another reference on this is "Understand the Difference Between Conscious & Subconscious Mind," Our Subconscious Mind, accessed January 20, 2022, https://oursubconsciousmind. com/understand-the-difference-between-conscious-subconsci-ous-mind/.

12   In his book, *The 7 Habits of Highly Effective People*, Stephen R. Covey states that valuing differences is one of the key ways to synergize. Synergize is the 6th Habit in Covey's model, and in basic terms, synergy means that the whole is greater than the sum of its parts.

13   In 1981, George T. Doran published work in the November issue of *Management Review* that extended upon John Locke's findings. "There's a S.M.A.R.T. way to write management's goals and objectives." More information can be found at https://www. achieveit.com/resources/blog/everything-you-need-to-know-about-smart-goals/, accessed February 4, 2022.

14   In *The 4 Disciplines of Execution: Achieving your Wildly Important Goals* (2012), Chris McChesney, Sean Covey, and Jim Huling explain how to achieve effective execution using 4 key

disciplines of execution (4DX). These 4 disciplines can help anyone—from frontline workers to senior executives—become more engaged in their work and produce outstanding results.

15 For more information on the third discipline and keeping a compelling scoreboard, see https://franklincoveyme.com/ the-4-disciplines/discipline-3-scoreboard, accessed February 4, 2022.

16 For more information on lag versus lead measures, see https:// www.franklincovey.com.au/discipline-2-act-on-the-lead-measures/, accessed February 4, 2022.

17 For more information on "WIGS," see "What is 4DX? An Introduction to The 4 Disciplines of Execution," Barry Hynd, Finance Cornerstone, accessed February 4, 2022, https://financecornerstone.com/what-is-4dx/. "Focus on the Wildly Important" and "Act on Lead Measures" are the first two disciplines of 4DX, and each Monday, what I'm really preparing and getting on paper during my strategy time are that week's "lead measures," which will directly influence the success of a previously set WIG.

18 One of my favorite videos on this topic is when Stephen R. Covey shows the "big rocks" concept at a 1994 conference. "Big Rocks," FranklinCovey, August 24, 2017, https://www.youtube. com/watch?v=zV3gMTOEWt8.

19 Mark Murphy, "Neuroscience Explains Why You Need to Write Down Your Goals If You Actually Want to Achieve Them," *Forbes*, April 15, 2018, https://www.forbes.com/sites/markmurphy/2018/04/15/neuroscience-explains-why-you-need-to-write-down-your-goals-if-you-actually-want-to-achieve-them/?sh=-60ca1c9b7905.

20 Hear this discussed ever so briefly by James Clear, "Atomic Habits, Never Miss Twice," BigSpeak Speakers Bureau, February 15, 2019, https://www.youtube.com/watch?v=dMwnQO8MUjw.

21 The LCD is "the lowest number you can use in the denominator to create a set of equivalent fractions that all have the same denominator." Definition from Edward Furey, "LCD Calculator – Lowest Common Denominator," CalculatorSoup, accessed November 29, 2020, https://www.calculatorsoup.com/calculators/math/lcd.php.

22   Excerpt from Tim Denning, "How to Think Like Arnold Schwarzenegger – Lessons From His Book," *The Startup*, March 13, 2018, https://medium.com/swlh/how-to-think-like-arnold-schwarzenegger-lessons-from-his-book-f2331ebc1140.

23   "The Peter principle is a concept in management developed by Laurence J. Peter, which observes that people in a hierarchy tend to rise to their 'level of incompetence': employees are promoted based on their success in previous jobs until they reach a level at which they are no longer competent, as skills in one job do not necessarily translate to another. The concept was elucidated in the 1969 book *The Peter Principle* (William Morrow and Company) by Peter and Raymond Hull." Definition quoted from "Peter principle," Wikipedia, accessed December 5, 2020, https://en.wikipedia.org/wiki/Peter_principle.

24   In her book *Multipliers*, Liz Wiseman discusses this concept at length in her section on Challengers, which is one of the 5 dimensions of a Multiplier. *Multipliers* is one of the best leadership books I've ever read, and while I was already working hard to practice behaviors in all 5 dimensions of a Multiplier when I first read the book in 2015, my entire philosophy on leadership evolved to a much greater degree upon reading this work. I've since read the book cover-to-cover an additional three times with three different teams of direct reports who were also in leadership. This book was revered by every member of those teams (over 20 people total) as one of the best leadership books they have ever read.

25   Six Thinking Hats is the proven technique from Edward de Bono. Sometimes referred to as "6 hats" or "the six hats of thinking," these techniques focus on enhancing the structure of thinking so that group decision-making and idea evaluation can be dramatically improved. The Six Thinking Hats use parallel thinking as an alternative to traditional ways of thinking. This way of thinking is often much more productive than adversarial thinking, discussion, or debate. There are six different colored hats that can be put on or taken off to indicate a mode or strand of thinking. Only one hat is worn at any one time by the individual or group (in parallel), allowing more thorough, expansive

thinking, increased creativity, and decision-making. The Yellow Hat is considered the optimist's hat. It asks the group to take a positive view of things and looks for benefits and values.

26 This concept originates from Joseph Smith Jr.

27 "Spectator Information," Boston Athletic Association, accessed April 11, 2021, www.baa.org/races/boston-marathon/watch/spectators.

28 "The Ultimate Motivational Clip – Rise & Shine!" posted by Addicted2SuccessTV, May 16, 2013, video, 2:09, https://www.youtube.com/watch?v=hbkZrOU1Zag.

29 Carol Hodanbosi, "The First and Second Laws of Motion," National Aeronautics and Space Administration, last updated May 13, 2021, https://www.grc.nasa.gov/www/k-12/WindTunnel/Activities/first2nd_lawsf_motion/.

30 "Law of attraction (New Thought)," Wikipedia, accessed April 12, 2021, https://en.wikipedia.org/wiki/Law_of_attraction_(New_Thought).

31 An "emotional bank account" is a term a coined by Stephen R. Covey in his book, *The 7 Habits of Highly Effective People*. Covey argues that similar to an actual bank account, where both deposits and withdrawals can be made, we have figurative "emotional bank accounts" with those around us, including people at work and at home. Things that help foster trust in the relationship are viewed as deposits, and things that hinder it can be considered withdrawals. For more information on the "emotional bank account," look into this topic within the 7 Habits framework or see Carrie Cabral, "Emotional Bank Account – 6 Examples for Stronger Relationships," Shortform, April 3, 2020, https://www.shortform.com/blog/emotional-bank-account-examples-7-habits/.

32 "Show Loyalty" is the fifth behavior of high-trust leaders in the book *The Speed of Trust* by Stephen M. R. Covey. This behavior is summarized on the FranklinCovey website as: "Give credit to others and speak about people as though they are present. The opposite is to take credit or not represent people fairly. The counterfeit is to appear to share credit but then downplay others' contribution when they are away. To exhibit a trustworthy

character, give credit freely, don't badmouth people behind their backs and don't disclose others' private information." Taken from "The 13 Behaviors of High Trust," FranklinCovey, accessed January 31, 2022, https://resources.franklincovey.com/the-speed-of-trust/the-13-behaviors-of-high-trust.

33   "Keep Commitments" is the 12th behavior of high-trust leaders in *The Speed of Trust* by Stephen M. R. Covey. Information about this behavior on the FranklinCovey website is: "It is the quickest way to build trust in any relationship. The opposite is to break commitments and the counterfeit is to make vague, unreliable commitments, or never make them in the first place. Some cultures view commitments differently, and understanding the difference is key to getting dividends and avoiding trust taxes. People tend to see family commitments as more flexible than work commitments, but they are just as important. Make keeping all commitments the symbol of your honor." Taken from "The 13 Behaviors of High Trust," FranklinCovey, accessed January 31, 2022, https://resources.franklincovey.com/the-speed-of-trust/the-13-behaviors-of-high-trust.

34   "Listen First" is the 11th behavior of high-trust leaders in *The Speed of Trust* by Stephen M. R. Covey. This behavior is described on the FranklinCovey website as: "Genuinely understand another person's thoughts and feelings, before trying to diagnose or advise. The opposite and counterfeit are to speak first and listen last, or not at all, and to pretend to listen while waiting for your own chance to speak. Listening teaches you which behaviors create dividends. Use your eyes and your gut to listen as well as your ears, and don't presume you know what matters to others." Taken from "The 13 Behaviors of High Trust," FranklinCovey, accessed January 31, 2022, https://resources.franklincovey.com/the-speed-of-trust/the-13-behaviors-of-high-trust.

35   *The Oz Principle*, first published in 1994, defines "accountability as 'a personal choice to rise above one's circumstances and demonstrate the ownership necessary for achieving desired results to See It, Own It, Solve It, and Do It.' The book is organized around the Steps To Accountability model, which shows how to create both individual and organization accountability

for achieving results. The model is divided in half by a line that 'separates success from failure,' with Above The Line being the area of 'accountability and success' and Below The Line being the area 'self-victimization and failure.'" Quoted from "The Oz Principle (book)," Wikipedia, last edited December 12, 2021, https://en.wikipedia.org/wiki/The_Oz_Principle_(book).

36   See endnote 32.

37   This quote is widely attributed to a character in *Spider-man*, but some credit Voltaire with it.

38   You can find an interview where Stephen M. R. Covey talks about this topic in "3 Steps to Accelerate the Speed of Trust… in 3 Minutes," InsuranceNewsNet, June 29, 2018, https://www.youtube.com/watch?v=IriCJ3z5tVs.

39   "Begin with the End in Mind" is Stephen R. Covey's 2nd habit; more information can be found at https://www.franklincovey.com/habit-2/, accessed February 1, 2022.

40   Two great reads on these topics of how we can handle adversity, struggles, mistakes, and failure come in Ryan Holiday's book, *The Obstacle Is the Way* (2014), and Carol Dweck's book, *Mindset* (2006).

41   Find many relevant points from Ehsan Nazim, "Why you Need to Fail More," Illumination, August 4, 2020, https://medium.com/illumination/why-you-need-to-fail-more-30dbf19055d2.

42   For a great video on how leaders can right wrongs, see this video from an author of several great leadership and business books. Scott Miller, "Right Wrongs," FranklinCovey, accessed February 1, 2022, https://resources.franklincovey.com/mkt-mmtlsv1/right-wrongs-4.

About the Author

Amy Chambers has over 21 years of experience in the financial services industry and has spent 15 of those in leadership. By the time she was 28, she was managing 260 people for a large commercial bank and has held numerous District Manager and Regional Director roles—before ultimately becoming a Chief Operating Officer for a credit union overseeing numerous divisions including Retail, Call Centers, Wealth Management, Facilities, and Operations Support.

During her years as COO, her organization grew at a rate of nearly 20% annually. Throughout her career, she's led over 500 people to success. She's worked with and for every kind of leader imaginable, and in her two decades of observing, studying, coaching, and mentoring others—she's developed a framework of principles that work, every time, to help transform culture, engage people, and deliver results—EVERY TIME.

Amy holds an undergraduate degree from the University of Notre Dame, where she double-majored in Political Science and Philosophy, and an MBA from USC where she concentrated on Marketing and General Management. She's been a part of numerous clubs, organizations, and boards both during her time in school, and after including Director of Communications for multiple Alumni Clubs. She's originally from Buffalo, NY but has lived in numerous states including New York, Indiana, Maryland, and Florida.

After losing her most beloved uncle to ALS in 2015 and also going through a traumatic breakup that same year, Amy made a decision to transform her mindset and put hundreds of hours into studying the principles of mindset, satisfaction, happiness, and fulfillment. She worked to overcome fear, take control of her destiny, and pursue goals she had only dreamt of—but never quite made reality. Today, Amy is an Executive Coach, Career Coach, Life Coach, and Business/Leadership Consultant—helping her clients all transform their lives, as well as a business consultant on leadership, culture, talent, and success.

Amy trained herself from being unable to run a mile without having to walk- into a marathon runner. In the past 7 years, she's ran over 190 half marathons, 11 full marathons, and hundreds of other races, totaling almost over 11,000 miles. She's also become an avid skier—something she was once deathly afraid to do. Amy is a long-time cyclist, rollerblader, tennis player, and photographer. Some of her favorite accomplishments include a gallery opening she hosted for her photography and biking a few 100-mile centuries. In 2020, she bought her dream home, and currently resides in Long Beach, California with her boyfriend of 6 years, David. Outside of leadership, running, and David, her top passion is travel.

www.ingramcontent.com/pod-product-compliance
Lightning Source LLC
Chambersburg PA
CBHW071541210326
41597CB00019B/3081